T0294183

THE GR5 TRAIL – BENELUX AND LORRAINE

About the Author

Carroll Dorgan was born and educated in the United States. Pushed by the absence of jobs for inexperienced history graduates where he happened to be living in 1975 and pulled by his wanderlust, Carroll pursued a teaching career for a decade in international schools in Iran, Belgium, England and France. He then returned to California to qualify as a lawyer, but soon moved back to Europe to practise international law in the Netherlands and France. In all of those places, he explored nearby hiking trails. While living in Liège, he discovered the GR5, which passes near the city on its way from Hoek van Holland to Nice.

Over the years, the GR5 became his favourite trail. Carroll hiked in the Olympics, Cascades, Sierras and Green Mountains in the United States and the Pyrenees and Auvergne in France, but he was always drawn back to the GR5. Upon completing a trek on the GR5 in the Vosges, Jura and Alps in 1989, he dreamt of hiking the entire trail someday. The dream became a plan and then his first adventure after retiring in 2015. Carroll enjoyed that long trek so much – and is so keen to share his enthusiasm for the trail – that he returned to the GR5 to write this guide to the Northern GR5. Carroll lives in France with Mary, his wife and hiking companion.

THE GR5 TRAIL – BENELUX AND LORRAINE

THE NORTH SEA TO THE VOSGES MOUNTAINS

by Carroll Dorgan

JUNIPER HOUSE, MURLEY MOSS,
OXENHOLME ROAD, KENDAL, CUMBRIA LA9 7RL
www.cicerone.co.uk

© Carroll Dorgan 2018
First edition 2018
ISBN: 978 1 85284 959 7
Printed by KHL Printing, Singapore
A catalogue record for this book is available from the British Library.
All photographs are by the author unless otherwise stated.

Route mapping by Lovell Johns www.lovelljohns.com

To Mary, my companion on all of life's trails

Updates to this guide

While every effort is made by our authors to ensure the accuracy of guidebooks
as they go to print, changes can occur during the lifetime of an edition. Any
updates that we know of for this guide will be on the Cicerone website (www.
cicerone.co.uk/959/updates), so please check before planning your trip. We
also advise that you check information about such things as transport, accommodation and shops locally. Even rights of way can be altered over time.

The route maps in this guide are derived from publicly available data, data-
bases and crowd-sourced data. As such they have not been through the detailed
checking procedures that would generally be applied to a published map from
an official mapping agency, although naturally we have reviewed them closely
in the light of local knowledge as part of the preparation of this guide.

We are always grateful for information about any discrepancies between
a guidebook and the facts on the ground, sent by email to updates@cicerone.
co.uk or by post to Cicerone, Juniper House, Murley Moss, Oxenholme Road,
Kendal, LA9 7RL.

Register your book: To sign up to receive free updates, special offers and
GPX files where available, register your book at www.cicerone.co.uk.

Front cover: Vineyards around Machtum on the Moselle River (Stage 35)

CONTENTS

Eben-Emael's church (Stage 20)

Symbols used on 1:100K stage maps

～	route
- - -	alternative route
Ⓢ	start point
Ⓕ	finish point
❯	direction of route
	woodland/forest
	urban areas
	international border
▬■▬	station/railway
▲	peak
▲	youth hostel
Å	campground
■	building
♏ ♁ †	church or chapel/monastery/cross
♜	castle
)(	pass
•	other feature
·	water feature
✳	viewpoint

Relief
in metres

1000–1200	
800–1000	
600–800	
400–600	
200–400	
0–200	

Addional features on section overview maps

⊕	airport
●	stage

SCALE: 1:100,000

0 kilometres 1 2
0 miles 1

Contour lines are drawn at 50m intervals and highlighted at 200m intervals.

GPX files

GPX files for all stages can be downloaded free at www.cicerone.co.uk/959/GPX.

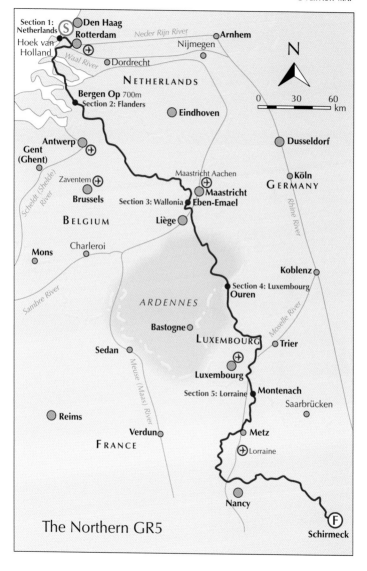

Section 1: Netherlands

Den Haag
S
Rotterdam
Neder Rijn River
Arnhem
Hoek van Holland
Nijmegen
Waal River
Dordrecht
NETHERLANDS
N
Bergen Op 700m
Section 2: Flanders
0   30   60
km
Eindhoven
Dusseldorf
Antwerp
Gent (Ghent)
Maastricht Aachen
Zaventem
Köln
Scheldt (Schelde) River
Maastricht
GERMANY
Section 3: Wallonia **Eben-Emael**
Brussels
BELGIUM
Liège
Rhine River
Mons
Charleroi
Koblenz
Sambre River
ARDENNES
Section 4: Luxembourg
Ouren
Moselle River
Bastogne
LUXEMBOURG
Trier
Sedan
Meuse (Maas) River
Luxembourg
Section 5: Lorraine **Montenach**
Saarbrücken
Reims
Lorraine
Verdun
Metz
FRANCE
Nancy
F
The Northern GR5
Schirmeck

9

ROUTE SUMMARY TABLE

Note that the stage distances in this table are the distances you will need to walk to reach accommodation (or centres of accommodation) if you stage the route in this way, and therefore vary slightly from the distances in the route planner in Appendix A, which are all between points on the GR5.

Stage	Start	Distance (km)	Time	Page
1 The Netherlands				
Stage 1	Hoek van Holland	18.5	4hr 15min	38
Stage 2	Maasland	12.8	3hr 30min	43
Stage 3	Brielle	18.0	4hr 15min	49
Stage 4	Rockanje	13.2	3hr	52
Stage 5	Goedereede	18.5	4hr	56
Stage 6	Herkingen	24.0	5hr 15min	59
Stage 7	Nieuw-Vossemeer	18.7	4hr 30min	64
	Section Total	**123.7**	**28hr 45min**	
2 Flanders				
Stage 8	Bergen op Zoom	27.0	6hr	72
Stage 9	Kalmthout	22.8	5hr	79
Stage 10	Brecht	13.5	3hr	83
Stage 11	Zoersel	21.5	5hr	87
Stage 12	Herentals	16.5	3hr 45min	92
Stage 13	Westerlo	24.0	5hr 15min	96
Stage 14	Scherpenheuvel	10.0	2hr 15min	101
Stage 15	Diest	15.5	3hr 30min	105
Stage 16	Lummen	18.5	4hr 15min	110
Stage 17	Stokrooie	16.0	3hr 45min	114
Stage 18	Bokrijk Provincial Domain	20.6	4hr 45min	118
Stage 19	Zutendaal	30.0	7hr 30min	123
Stage 20	Maastricht	13.0	3hr 15min	130
	Section Total	**248.9**	**57hr 15min**	
3 Wallonia				
Stage 21	Eben-Emael	19.0	4hr 30min	138
Stage 22	Visé	24.5	6hr 30min	142

Stage	Start	Distance (km)	Time	Page
Stage 23	Soumagne	15.5	4hr 30min	147
Stage 24	Banneux	17.0	5hr	151
Stage 25	Spa	16.0	5hr	155
Stage 26	Stavelot	25.0	6hr 30min	160
Stage 27	Commanster	26.0	6hr	166
	Section Total	**143.0**	**37hr**	
4 Luxembourg				
Stage 28	Ouren	20.0	6hr	176
Stage 29	Obereisenbach	23.0	7hr	180
Stage 30	Vianden	14.0	4hr	186
Stage 31	Bleesbréck	16.5	4hr 30min	189
Stage 32	Beaufort	16.8	5hr	194
Stage 33	Echternach	26.4	7hr 30min	200
Stage 34	Wasserbillig	14.0	3hr 30min	205
Stage 35	Grevenmacher	26.0	6hr 30min	209
Stage 36	Remich	27.3	6hr 30min	215
	Section Total	**184.0**	**50hr 30min**	
5 Lorraine				
Stage 37	Montenach	30.0	7hr 30min	224
Stage 38	Saint-Hubert	24.6	6hr	229
Stage 39	Metz	24.2	6hr 30min	235
Stage 40	Gorze	15.6	4hr 15min	241
Stage 41	Pagny-sur-Moselle	19.5	5hr	244
Stage 42	Montauville	33.2	8hr 30min	249
Stage 43	Liverdun	32.0	7hr	254
Stage 44	Bioncourt	21.0	4hr 45min	259
Stage 45	Vic-sur-Seille	23.7	5hr	263
Stage 46	Tarquimpol	22.8	5hr	268
Stage 47	Gondrexange	22.4	5hr	272
Stage 48	Abreschviller	21.8	6hr 30min	276
Stage 49	Col du Donon	8.3	2hr 15min	281
	Section Total	**299.1**	**73hr 15min**	
	Route Total	**998.7**	**247hr 15min**	

Rock face in the Petite Suisse Luxembourgeoise (Stage 32)

INTRODUCTION

A signpost at the starting point of the GR5 in Hoek van Holland points to Nice

When you step off the ferry at Hoek van Holland – or alight from the metro at the station next to the terminal – you will see a tall signpost with arms pointing in different directions. There, marked with the standard white-and-red blaze that will be your lodestar in the coming days, weeks or longer, is your sign: GR5 Hoek van Holland – Nice 2289. Fear not – those are merely kilometres, not miles! The thought that the trail indicated by this sign close to the blustery North Sea goes all the way to Nice, on the sunny Mediterranean, is both thrilling and daunting. So you touch the signpost for good luck (or take a selfie) and set off, but you may make a short detour to the nearby beach to dip your toe in the North Sea before starting this trek. If you're attracted to symbolic gestures – or just want a unique souvenir of the adventure – you might even collect a small sample of North Sea water to carry south.

You're hiking on the fabled GR5 (Grande Randonnée 5 or Grote Routepad 5), a long-distance trail that passes through the Netherlands, Belgium, Luxembourg and several regions of eastern France (Lorraine, the Vosges, the Jura and the Alps), plus small segments of Swiss territory around Lac Léman (Lake Geneva), to Nice. Some people trek the entire GR5 in one outing, which may take three to four months. Many others hike sections

13

of the GR5 that interest them, sometimes completing the entire trail over the course of several years. Hiking through, say, the Ardennes, you may meet people who got together last year to walk across the Netherlands and who are planning a walk in Luxembourg next year. Some people simply walk on interesting trails that happen to be part of the GR5, such as the path in Voornes Duin that approaches the bird sanctuary around Breede Water in Holland or the trail across the forested ridges of the Côte de Moselle south of Metz.

This guide has been written for everyone who walks on the GR5 in the Netherlands, Belgium, Luxembourg and Lorraine – the 'Northern GR5'. The guide will launch through-hikers from Hoek van Holland and accompany them to Schirmeck in the northern Vosges Mountains, where it passes the baton to Cicerone's guide: *The GR5 Trail – Vosges*

and Jura, in turn followed by *The GR5 Trail – The French Alps: Geneva to the Mediterranean*. Those planning a shorter walk on the Northern GR5 can select a section in this guide that looks most interesting and is best suited to the season and time available (or see Appendix B for some shorter suggestions). There are also many options, outlined in the route descriptions, for travelling to and from points along the Northern GR5 using public transport.

WHAT IT'S LIKE TO HIKE THE NORTHERN GR5

Walking on the Northern GR5 is relatively easy and ideal for those who don't want to hike up and down steep mountains – or not just yet. In fact walking the length of the route, about 990km from Hoek van Holland to Schirmeck, would be excellent fitness training for

Countryside southwest of Maastricht (Stage 20)

the mountains of the Vosges, the Jura and the Alps.

There are many different ways to enjoy the Northern GR5. Some trekkers stride forward at a sustained rhythm, with their sights set perhaps on the Mediterranean Sea. Others meander, taking time to admire the view here and to visit a museum there. Some trekkers consider it important to walk the entire trail, while others do not hesitate to catch a train or bus to avoid a section of the trail that does not interest them. You can spend nights in comfortable hotels and B&Bs, supplemented by the occasional youth hostel and gîte d'étape. Or you can camp (discreetly) near the trail with a tent and sleeping bag. Similarly, you can choose to eat and drink very well or subsist on cheap, high-calorie fuel. And, of course, nothing prevents you from mixing these approaches. A fine dinner and night in a good hotel can be a well-earned reward after several days of opening tins and roughing it.

This northern European expedition is also much more than a walk through nature – it's a cultural experience. You will cross the Delta region of the Netherlands, through two regions of Belgium (Flanders and Wallonia) that comprise three linguistic communities (Flemish, French and German), along Luxembourg's eastern border (closely linked with Germany) and across Lorraine, a region with a distinctive place in French – and, indeed, European – history. Along the way, you will meet an interesting variety of people (including other walkers), observe different styles of architecture and sample diverse culinary traditions.

Statue of Queen Wilhelmina and Brielle Historical Museum (Stage 2)

Or your experience of the GR5 could be a museum tour. From the tugboat museum in Maassluis, passing the flint museum within the extraordinary Tour d'Eben-Ezer near Eben-Emael, to the salt museum in Marsal, there are interesting and often unusual museums beside the trail – not to mention world-renowned art museums such as the Centre Pompidou-Metz. You will also see many historic buildings along the way, both religious (such as St Étienne Cathedral in Metz) and secular (such as the picture-book castles at Beaufort and Vianden).

LANDSCAPE

In this guide, the Northern GR5 is divided into five sections: the Netherlands, Flanders, Wallonia, Luxembourg and Lorraine.

15

The Netherlands

Water surrounds you in the Delta region of the Netherlands: the North Sea, rivers, canals and lakes (not to mention the occasional rainstorm). The three great rivers that flow through the Delta area – Rhine (Rijn), Meuse (Maas) and Scheldt (Scheld) – gave this area its commercial and strategic importance over the centuries. It is difficult today to trace these rivers on a map, as they divide into numerous distributaries with different names (the Rhine changes names seven times within the Delta area), and canals have been built to divert their waters or to link them.

Approximately 25 per cent of the Netherlands lies below sea level, and the proportion is much higher in the coastal area and islands of South Holland, Zeeland and North Brabant. These are lands, known as polders, that have been reclaimed from the sea and inland lakes and are now protected by an extensive network of dykes, dams and canals. Carefully managed dunes, such as the Voornes Duin, shield some coastal areas from the sea.

The sea clay soil of the Dutch polders is well-suited to agriculture, ranging from cereals, sugar beets and potatoes to fruit and vegetables. You will see large greenhouses devoted to the intensive cultivation of vegetables. You walk along dykes and through polders, often on surfaced cycle paths, and pass through several picturesque towns and villages, including Brielle, Goedereede and Nieuw-Vossemeer, leading to the attractive, vibrant city of Bergen op Zoom.

Flanders

The GR5 turns inland after Bergen op Zoom and enters Flanders. The terrain is flat as it crosses the Kempen, an area of heath and forest. Historically,

Potato fields in polder near Brielle, protected by dykes

the Kempen was sparsely populated, as its sandy soil and marshlands were ill-suited to agriculture and it had few commercially valuable natural resources. The remoteness of the area and its relative lack of development made the Kempen an attractive area for monasteries during the Middle Ages.

All this was to change in the 20th century. The discovery of coal near Genk in 1901 led to large-scale mining until the mines were closed in the 1960–1980s. Some of the pine forests in the area were originally cultivated to provide pit props for the mines. Then farming, especially dairy farming, developed in the latter half of the 20th century, thanks to extensive drainage and fertilisation. Today, vegetables are grown in large greenhouses and asparagus is an important outdoor crop.

The GR5 crosses nature reserves that protect heathlands of the Kempen, such as the Grenspark De Zoom Kalmthoutse Heide and De Maten. Along the way, you will pass historic abbeys, such as Westmalle, Tongerlo and Averbode, and have a chance to savour the beer that they brew. You will also visit historic cities, such as Diest, and return briefly to the Netherlands to tour Maastricht before leaving Flanders.

Wallonia

The GR5 enters Wallonia in the valley of the Meuse River, north of Liège. For several days it passes through the Pays de Herve, east of the Meuse. The rolling, open country here is good land for cattle and orchards (apple, pear, cherry and plum). After crossing the Vesdre river, the route enters the Ardennes, an area of eroded mountains, forests and narrow river valleys. The trail is no longer quite as flat! An extension of the German Eifel mountains, the Ardennes continue south to Luxembourg and France.

This area once had extensive peatlands. Most have disappeared, as a result of agricultural development, but some remain. The GR5 crosses a peat bog, the Fagne de Malchamps, on a protective boardwalk. The Ardennes is another sparsely populated area, but the GR5 visits interesting towns, such as Spa (famous for its waters) and Vielsalm (famous for witchcraft). The final stages of the GR5 in Belgium cross a plateau and descend to the Our valley in the country's German-speaking area.

Luxembourg

Along the eastern side of Luxembourg, the route has a bit more variety. The trail first climbs, traverses and descends

Petite Suisse Luxembourgeoise

17

steep, wooded slopes beside the Our River to reach the historic town of Vianden. From there, it descends to the valley of the Sûre River and continues eastward to Beaufort, the gateway to the Petite Suisse Luxembourgeoise – Luxembourg's 'Little Switzerland'. The trail from Beaufort to Echternach, with its towering sandstone formations in dark forests, will be one of the highlights of the trek for many people.

The GR5 follows the Sûre south to its confluence with the Moselle and an entirely different environment. From Wasserbillig to Schengen (about 60km walking), the GR5 traverses the steep slopes of the vineyards of the Moselle valley, with occasional detours through forests and across the high, level ground to the west. Luxembourg specialises in the production of various white wines. There will be opportunities as you progress along the Wine Route to taste them all.

Lorraine

The GR5 enters Lorraine south of Schengen. The distinguishing geological feature of Lorraine is its côtes: the Côte de Bar, the Côte de Meuse and (most important for the GR5 trekker) the Côte de Moselle. These côtes are ridges running north-south that form the eastern edge of the Parisian Basin. Their western slopes are gradual, while the eastern slopes are steeper, more abrupt. The Côte de Moselle stands west of the Moselle river. To the east is the plateau of Lorraine bounded by the Vosges Mountains.

The GR5 approaches Metz from the northeast over the plateau of gently rolling hills and forests. It is worth pausing to visit this great city. It then crosses the

Moselle at Metz and turns south. From here it climbs and descends the slopes of the Côte de Moselle – and the river valleys that cut through the Côte – as far as Liverdun. Crossing the Moselle again at Custines it continues east, often on quiet country roads, across the plateau toward the Vosges mountains. The valley of the Seille river east of the Moselle is salt country, the Pays du Sel. Finally, the GR5 passes through an area of large ponds, the Pays des Etangs. These ponds were created when marshes were drained in the Middle Ages and were an important source of fish.

The landscape changes dramatically as you walk past those ponds. On the horizon are the Vosges Mountains. You climb one of those mountains, Le Donon (1008m), to reach Schirmeck and the end of the Northern GR5.

WILDLIFE

You will see (and hear) many birds along the Northern GR5. Some live permanently in the area; others visit to breed there. The Delta is an ideal habitat for aquatic birds such as mallards, coots, grey herons, Canada geese and mute swans. If you walk through this area in the spring, you will see many family groups. The chicks are learning how to navigate in the water – sometimes following mother in dutiful lines, sometimes paddling away in their first experiments with independence. An observation hide (blind) beside Breede Water in the Voornes Duin Nature Reserve identifies other birds that frequent the area, such as buzzards, little grebes, greylag geese, goshawks and cormorants.

Family of geese in Domein Bovy (Flanders)

The heathlands of Flanders are home to wood larks, willow warblers, nightjars and tree pipits, while the ponds and marshes in those areas welcome many species of ducks, sandpipers and grebes. There are woodpeckers, goshawks, wood warblers and redstart in the nearby forests. Many other species of birds inhabit the wilder forests and highlands of the Ardennes, including

Cattle near Wahlhausen (Luxembourg)

goldcrests, jays, blackbirds, starlings, pheasants, to name a few, and birds of prey such as kestrels and sparrowhawks.

As you cross the land of ponds in eastern Lorraine, you will again encounter aquatic birds such as the grey heron, mallard, cormorant and mute swan. Most notable are the white storks, which benefit from a programme to provide protected nests for breeding pairs beside the Etang de Lindre.

You will see many mammals along the Northern GR5, but most of them will be domesticated (cattle, sheep, horses). There are also wild mammals, but you may not see many of them. You are likely to see rabbits, brown hare, squirrels and perhaps foxes. A roe deer will occasionally bound across a forest trail and disappear before you can catch it in a photograph. There are wild boar, too, but they are unlikely to be out and about when you are walking. Instead, you may see the shallow trenches that they make as they dig with their snouts for insects, acorns and other delicacies.

HISTORY

From Caesar to the Carolingians

Julius Caesar's conquest of Gaul in 58–52BC brought the territory of the Northern GR5 into the Roman Empire. The Delta region remained a remote part of the Empire on its northern continental boundary. Lorraine, closer to population centres, produced grain, wine and salt for trade. Divodurum (Metz) became an important city, with a population of 15,000–20,000 in the 1st century AD. Major roads running north-south (linking Trier and Lyon)

and east-west (between Strasbourg and Reims) crossed at Metz. As Roman authority declined, migrating and invading Germanic tribes settled in the Empire's northern and eastern provinces. The linguistic border between Romance languages (French, Walloon) and Germanic languages (Dutch, Flemish, German) was established then and endures to the present.

On Christmas Day 800, Pope Leo III crowned Charles, the King of the Franks, as Emperor in the West. His place of birth in around 742 is unknown, but it was somewhere close to the GR5 (perhaps Liège or Aachen). At his death in 814, Charles ruled most of Western Christendom, apart from the British Isles. He had earned the name that posterity gave him – Carolus Magnus, or Charlemagne.

After Charlemagne's son Louis the Pious died, a succession dispute led to a division of the Carolingian Empire among Louis' three surviving sons (Treaty of Verdun, 843): West Francia for Charles the Bald, East Francia for Louis the German and Middle Francia for Lothar. Lothar's realm became known as Lotharingia (Lorraine). Eventually, the Duchy of Lorraine (including today's Lorraine) and various duchies and counties in the Low Countries (including today's southern Netherlands, Flanders, Wallonia and Luxembourg) emerged from Lotharingia. Most of these territories were part of the Holy Roman Empire. The County of Flanders lay outside the Empire and prospered in the Middle Ages. Flemish cities imported wool from England and produced fine cloth that was sold all over Europe.

Dukes, Kings and Republicans

In 1363, the Valois King of France, John II, granted the Duchy of Burgundy as a fief to his son, Philip the Bold. Philip and his successors – John the Fearless, Philip the Good, Charles the Bold – expanded Burgundian rule by conquest, marriage and purchase to encompass the counties and duchies of the Low Countries, as well as Burgundy itself. Charles the Bold sought to conquer the Duchy of Lorraine, which lay between these territories, and thereby re-establish the Carolingian Kingdom of Lotharingia. Charles commanded great resources, thanks to his rule over the rich cities of Flanders. His court was famous in Europe (and is remembered today) for its ostentatious luxury and high culture. However, ambition clouded his strategic judgement. Charles was defeated and killed at the Battle of Nancy in 1477, thus ending the rule of the Valois Dukes of Burgundy and their attempt to unite the entire area now crossed by the Northern GR5 into a single kingdom.

The political divisions of the modern age began to take shape in the 16th century. The Burgundian lands were divided (after a fight, of course). The Low Countries passed under Habsburg rule, while France gained the Duchy of Burgundy. The Duchy of Lorraine remained autonomous within the Empire, but in 1552, France took control of Metz, Toul and Verdun, starting a process that would lead – through many vicissitudes – to the incorporation of the entire Duchy within France in 1766. Philip II, Habsburg King of Spain (and briefly husband of Queen Mary of England), succeeded his father Charles V as ruler of the Low Countries in 1555. Philip's heavy-handed disregard of local laws and customs, and his harsh repression of Protestantism sparked rebellion against Spanish rule. The Spanish defeated the revolt in the south (the Spanish Netherlands, which remained Catholic), but the seven northern provinces, led by Holland, won independence as the United Provinces of the Netherlands (1648), a bastion of Protestantism.

This was the Golden Age of the Dutch Republic. Its maritime commerce prospered and spread across the globe. Amsterdam flourished as one of the leading commercial and artistic centres of Europe. The Republic's commercial rivalry with England led to a series of wars (1652–1674), during which a Dutch fleet shocked the English with its Raid on the Medway, but England acquired New Amsterdam – renamed New York.

The real threat to the Dutch Republic's existence came from Louis XIV's France. The Republic gained a new ally in that struggle when the Dutch Stadholder William III invaded England (at the invitation of English Protestant leaders) in 1688 and defeated King James II. As King of England, William III led coalitions of European states against France in a series of wars that lasted for 25 years. The Dutch Republic survived, but it was weakened by the struggle and declined in the 18th century. The Southern Netherlands, meanwhile, passed from Spanish control to Austrian, pursuant to the Treaty of Utrecht (1713).

From the French Revolution to the Industrial Revolution

On 5 May 1789, the Estates General of France convened in Versailles, raising the curtain upon the French Revolution. A priest from Lorraine, Abbé Grégoire, took a leading role in the overthrow of the Ancien Régime. He was one of the first clergymen to join the Third Estate. He contributed to the drafting of the Civil Constitution of the Clergy and supported the abolition of slavery. French armies eventually brought the Revolution and French rule to the Low Countries in 1795. The French occupation of the Low Countries ended in 1813–14 as the Napoleonic Empire crumpled, but two decades of French governance left an important legacy – for example, legal codes based upon the Napoleonic Code.

Napoleon met his Waterloo in, of course, Belgium – about 60km from the GR5. The victorious powers decided at the Congress of Vienna (1814–1815) to unite the former Austrian Netherlands with the Dutch Republic to form the United Kingdom of the Netherlands, under King William I of Orange. Luxembourg was established as a Grand Duchy in personal union with the Netherlands. Prussia annexed Saarbrücken and Saarlouis in north-eastern Lorraine.

The Vienna settlement did not endure. In 1830, the southern provinces of the Kingdom of the Netherlands rebelled and declared their independence as the Kingdom of Belgium. The western, Francophone part of Luxembourg was detached from the Grand Duchy and made part of the new Belgian state. The personal union of the Grand Duchy with the Netherlands ended in 1890, when the Dutch Queen Wilhelmina succeeded her father King William III, because women were

then excluded from succession in Luxembourg.

Lorraine shared the experiences of France after the fall of Napoleon: the restored Bourbon Monarchy, the July (Orléanist) Monarchy, the Second Republic and the Second Empire. The Franco-Prussian War of 1870 then caused traumatic change: The victorious, newly-established German Empire annexed part of Lorraine (today's Department of the Moselle) along with most of Alsace. France recovered those territories only after the defeat of Germany in World War I (1918).

The Industrial Revolution, which began in 18th century Britain, took off on the Continent in areas crossed by the GR5: In 1799, William Cockerill of Lancashire established a factory for the manufacture of textile machines in Verviers (in Belgium's Pays de Herve). Steel production and industrial manufacturing developed in the area, exploiting nearby coal and iron deposits. There were also large deposits of iron ore in southern Luxembourg and northern Lorraine, called minette, but excess phosphorous in the minette limited its utility. Sidney Gilchrist Thomas' invention in 1879 of a method to remove phosphorous from the iron in a Bessemer converter opened the way to exploitation of the minette. Luxembourg and Lorraine became major producers of iron and steel. These centres of heavy industry flourished after World War II, but declined and ceased production as they became uncompetitive in the global economy of the late 20th century.

War in Europe and its legacy
The 20th century, of course, brought even greater challenges and tragedies.

World War I began in the West with the German invasion of Belgium. The GR5 passes close to some of the forts that were meant to defend Liège. The GR5 crosses Bois-le-Prêtre in Lorraine, the scene of intense fighting between French and German forces in 1915.

In the 1930s, French and Belgian strategists prepared assiduously 'to fight the previous war' by constructing huge defensive fortifications in areas crossed by the GR5, such as Fort Eben-Emael north of Liège and the Maginot Line in Lorraine, which did not even slow the German offensive of May 1940. They neglected the Ardennes, judged to be too difficult for manoeuvring by modern, mechanised armies – but the German generals had other ideas. The central axis of their May 1940 offensive was a thrust through the Ardennes, and

their surprise attack in the same area in December 1944 led to the Battle of the Bulge. The GR5 will evoke memories of that battle in the forests and narrow river valleys of the Ardennes.

The conflicts and tragedies of the first half of the 20th century inspired Europeans to create new institutions of cooperation and friendship. The European Coal and Steel Community established a common market among its six member states in 1951. The Lorraine statesman, Robert Schuman (whose home in Scy-Chazelles the GR5 passes), proclaimed that the goal of the ECSC was to 'make war not only unthinkable but materially impossible'. The European Economic Community and the European Union grew out of the ECSC.

The GR5 leaves Luxembourg at Schengen and, after a few steps in

Former German bunker, now a vleermuisreservaat (bat sanctuary) in the Staelduinse Bosch (Netherlands)

Germany, enters France. In 1985, five European countries signed a treaty at Schengen that provided for the elimination of internal border checks. The Schengen Area now encompasses 26 European countries with a total population of more than 400 million. Unless circumstances change dramatically, you will not need to show a passport to cross any international border as you walk along the Northern GR5 from Hoek van Holland to Schirmeck (and beyond).

WHEN TO GO

An important factor in deciding when to walk along the Northern GR5 is, naturally, the weather. The Benelux countries have a marine west coast climate, but the oceanic influence diminishes as you move inland. Lorraine's climate is continental. Thus, the Netherlands and Flanders may offer walking weather in winter, but frequent rain and storms are likely. Cold, wet weather is common during the winter in the Ardennes and Lorraine, with occasional snow. Some years, people shake their heads and marvel at how cold and wet it was in April; other years, the weather then is glorious. The odds for good weather are better between May and mid-October but the long-distance trekker must still be ready for varied weather: It may be very hot and clear for a week and then rain heavily the next.

Another factor to consider is the calendar of festivals and other special events in the towns along your way. You may wish to time a walk in order to attend a particular event, for example: Nationale Molendag (National Mill Day) in the Netherlands, when windmills are open for visits (the second weekend in May); the Abdijentocht, a walk between two Flemish abbeys, Tongerlo and Averbode, on Ascension Day; the Sprangpressessioun (Dancing Procession) in Echternach on Whit Tuesday; the Fête de la Musique all over France and elsewhere on 21 June; or the Sabat des Macralles et Fête des Myrtilles (Festival of Witches and Blueberries) in Vielsalm on 20–21 July. Alternatively, you may wish to avoid an area because a special event puts pressure on local accommodation (for example, the Formula 1 Grand Prix at Spa-Francorchamps in late August). Tourist offices have information about these events and many others.

GETTING THERE (AND BACK)

The starting point for the GR5 is in Hoek van Holland, near Rotterdam. There is a ferry service from Harwich (UK) to Hoek van Holland. Those travelling on the Continent can reach Hoek van Holland by train to Rotterdam Central Station and then RET Metro Line B to the Hoek van Holland Haven stop. (This metro is scheduled to replace the railway in late 2018. Pending the completion of the new metro line, take a local train from Rotterdam Central Station to nearby Schiedam and then bus 711 to Hoek van Holland.)

The Northern GR5 ends in Schirmeck, a small town in the northern Vosges. The GR5 continues into the Vosges but if you want to stop in Schirmeck, there is a regular train service from there to Strasbourg.

Many walkers will start from, or stop at, intermediate points along the route.

Extensive public transport services make this easy to do. The stage descriptions in this book identify cities and towns with railway connections, as well as useful bus routes. Appendix D includes a list of websites with detailed information about public transport (including rail and bus routes, timetables and tickets).

ACCOMMODATION

There is a wide variety of accommodation on the Northern GR5, and if you travel far, you will probably sample the full range.

There are numerous hotels, but they are concentrated mostly in cities and larger towns. You will find B&Bs – *chambres d'hôtes* in French – in large cities and small villages. There are, however, sections of the route where accommodation is scarce, such as in Lorraine, south of Metz. The stage descriptions in this book offer solutions to this problem.

Youth hostels (Dutch: *jeugdherberg*; French: *auberge de jeunesse*) welcome trekkers of all ages. There are *gîtes d'étape* (similar to hostels) in several of the villages passed by the GR5 in Lorraine. Note that the term 'gîte' (or gîte rural) generally refers to a cottage that is rented as holiday accommodation for a week or more. Sometimes you will encounter a *gîte communal* – a gîte d'étape that is owned and operated by the local municipality.

Camping is an option, if you carry the necessary gear. The commercial and municipal campgrounds near the GR5 are oriented toward campers who travel by car or motorcycle, but they welcome trekkers as well. There are some campgrounds along the route that have hikers' cabins (*trekkershutten*), which are a good option if you are not carrying a tent. They vary in what they offer. As a minimum, they will have a bed (without blankets). Some also have a stove,

Trekkershutten at Kohnenhof Campground (Luxembourg)

refrigerator and running water. It is helpful to have a sleeping bag or liner (called a *sac à viande*). Few trekkers on the Northern GR5 wild camp (*camping sauvage*). Technically, it is not even permitted in most areas, but discreet camping is certainly possible. Daniel Graham, in his book *A Walk to the Water*, describes a trek with his brother from Bristol (UK) to the Mediterranean, mostly on the GR5, during which they often camped 'wild'.

Appendix C provides a list of accommodation along the GR5: hotels, B&Bs, chambres d'hôtes, gîtes d'étape, youth hostels and campgrounds with trekkershutten. You may find other accommodation using search sites such as booking.com, bedandbreakfast.eu, chambres-hotes.fr, gites-de-france.com and airbnb.com. Tourist offices often have lists of local accommodation that can be consulted online. Keep in mind that such lists (including Appendix C) are never definitive. Hotels and B&Bs open and close all the time.

In general, it is best to reserve accommodation in advance. In some places, there may be only one hotel or B&B (and a small one, at that). If it has no vacancy when you arrive (or if it is closed), you might have a long walk to the next place.

FOOD AND DRINK

You may burn many calories during a 20km walk with 10kg on your back, but you can easily restore them (and more) at dinner! You will discover and enjoy

Appeltaart met slagroom (apple pie with whipped cream)

regional and seasonal specialities along the GR5. For example, fresh asparagus appears on virtually every menu in the Netherlands and Flanders in May: try *asperges à la flamande* (especially good with salmon). For dessert, don't miss the delicious Dutch version of apple pie: *appeltaart*. Belgium is, of course, famous for its gastronomy – and especially its beers. A trek on the GR5 is not long enough to try them all, but beer lovers will not want to miss the Trappist and other beers brewed by the abbeys. A bowl of Belgium's famous stew, waterzooi, will restore you at the end of a long day. Among Belgium's cheeses, Herve (produced in the Pays de Herve east of Liège) is distinctive and delicious.

The GR5 takes you along Luxembourg's Wine Route beside the Moselle from Wasserbillig to Schengen, where fine white wines are produced. One of the national dishes of Luxembourg, *Judd mat Gaardebounen* (Smoked Collar of Pork with Broad Beans), is made with beans from Gostingen, a village west of Wormeldange near the GR5. It can be accompanied, naturally, with one of those Moselle wines.

You will want to sample *quiche lorraine* in its homeland. Lorraine has its own cheeses (such as *gros lorrain* and *géromé*) and wines (Côtes de Toul). The mirabelle (a yellow plum) is another one of Lorraine's specialties. Mirabelles are used, for example, in making pastries (*tarte aux mirabelles*) and liqueur. If eating a madeleine evokes fond memories of reading Proust, you will want to sample a lesser-known version of that delicious little cake, the Madeleine

de Liverdun (named after a city on the GR5).

Hotels and B&Bs in the Benelux countries generally serve copious breakfasts that include ham and cheese, eggs, yoghurt, cereal, fruit, bread, butter and jam, with coffee and tea. You can usually put together a good picnic lunch from the breakfast buffet. Traditions are different in France, where breakfast may be limited to bread (baguette or croissant) with butter and jam, fruit juice, coffee and tea.

As for the evening, if there is no restaurant nearby, your host at a chambre d'hôte may serve dinner (*table d'hôte*), but you should check this in advance. Some youth hostels offer meals but gîtes d'étape are self-catering.

CLOTHING AND EQUIPMENT

Extremes of weather are rare in the area of the Northern GR5. It is not necessary to be prepared for the rigours of mountain trekking. Nevertheless, you must be ready for days that are cool, windy and wet – storms that sweep in from the North Sea can be intense – as well as hot and sunny. Footwear depends upon individual preference, but most walkers will be comfortable in low-cut shoes (which should be water-resistant). Heavy hiking boots are unnecessary on the relatively flat, smooth paths and trails of the Northern GR5. You can travel light on this trail, since you can spend each night under a roof if you wish. It is easy to hand wash clothes in most places but it may be helpful to have a flat, rubber stopper for the sink in your room.

So the basic trekking kit in a medium-sized backpack should work well for you. You won't go far wrong if you use the trek packing list download-able from www.cicerone.co.uk/top-tips-for-european-trek-packing as a starting point, although you could probably get away with lighter shoes and leave the bothy bag behind.

The standard waymark for the GR5 is a pair of rectangles: white over red. This is the standard mark for all GR trails (except in Luxembourg and the Vosges), so be careful in some places to follow the GR5 and not another GR

trail. In many areas, a second, shorter pair of rectangles below the first points to a turn, while an X formed by white and red diagonal strokes indicates an incorrect route. Luxembourg has its own national system for marking trails. There, the GR5 follows a succession of yellow discs, green triangles and yellow rectangles. The stage descriptions in this book for Luxembourg tell you which waymarks to look out for. Finally, the waymarking for the GR5 changes to red rectangles at the Col de l'Engin, on the border between Lorraine and Alsace.

When walking in the Netherlands and Flanders, you will see many small signs indicating a 'knooppunt' (junction). The typical sign will display a number, plus one or more arrows below it pointing to other numbers. A pictogram of a walker or a footprint will identify this knooppunt as part of a network of walking routes: a *wandelknoopuntennetwerk*. (There are also networks of bicycle routes – *fietsknooppuntennetwerken* – with their own knooppunten signs.) The stage descriptions in this book include occasional references to the numbered knooppunten (KPx) where they could help to confirm your location.

MAPS

A walker today has several options for maps, including traditional paper maps and digital ones. Each has advantages and disadvantages. Paper maps do not need to be re-charged, unlike devices for using a digital map, but they must have a sufficiently large scale to be really useful. A collection of large scale maps to cover a long section of the GR5 would be expensive and bulky. One issue for both paper and digital maps is whether the route that you are following is actually marked on the maps – and, if so, whether it is up-to-date. GPX tracks of the Northern GR5 described here (accurate as of July 2017) can be downloaded free for registered owners of this guidebook on Cicerone's website (www. cicerone.co.uk/member).

Maps of various scales are available for each of the four countries covered by this guide. In addition to paper versions sold in shops and online, digital versions can be purchased. One convenient source for buying digital maps is ViewRanger (www.viewranger. com), which also offers GPX tracks on its site. The stage descriptions in this book include references to the maps that cover the relevant stage. For the Netherlands, Belgium and Luxembourg, these are 1:50,000 maps. Only the Luxembourg maps show the route of the GR5. Larger scale maps are available for these countries and may be preferred by those walking along a short section of the GR5. An old 1:50,000 series for France is now difficult to obtain, so this book refers to the 1:25,000 series, which shows the route of the GR5. See Appendix D for information about purchasing maps.

There are booklets, called 'topoguides', that combine maps showing the route with descriptions and practical information. Four topoguides

Opposite: A variety of GR waymarks (clockwise from top left): standard mark; mark indicating a left turn, with a knooppunt; old and new marks indicating the wrong way

cover the Northern GR5 and they are certainly useful, but there are complications. The topoguides for the Netherlands (Nederlands Kustpad Deel 1) and Flanders (GR 5 Noordzee – Middellandse Zee Deel Vlaanderen) are in Dutch, and they do not include information about accommodation. The topoguides for Wallonia and Luxembourg (Mer du Nord – Méditerranée Wallonie et Grand-duché de Luxembourg) and Lorraine (Les GRs de Lorraine) are in French. Both were published in 2009, so they do not include recent changes in the route and accommodation. (The publisher of the Wallonia/Luxembourg topoguide does post updates for the route, but not accommodation, on its website: www.grsentiers.org.) Moreover, the Lorraine topoguide is now out of print and difficult (or, at least, very expensive) to obtain.

Finally, it is important to note that the GR5 is not static. The route (which is managed and marked by private associations, with some involvement of local governments) is occasionally changed for various reasons. Sometimes, construction works in the area necessitate a change; sometimes, a better route is found. Two major changes were made in 2016: In Flanders, a 30km section of the GR5 was shifted (avoiding Grobendonk and following the delightful Kleine Nete into Herentals). The new route is shown in the 2017 edition of the topoguide for Flanders. A change in Luxembourg and Lorraine was even bigger: Previously, the GR5 crossed southern Luxembourg to Rumelange and entered Lorraine to approach Metz from the northwest, west of the Moselle River. Now, the GR5 leaves Luxembourg at Schengen, enters Lorraine and approaches Metz from the northeast, east of the Moselle (see Stage 36). The new route is more agreeable than the old (and nearly 50km shorter). Apparently, there are no plans to publish new editions of the two topoguides covering this section of the GR5.

Hence, the route shown on maps and in topoguides may not match the marked route on the ground. The general rule in that case is to follow the marked route.

GPX tracks

GPX tracks for the routes in this guidebook are available to download free at www.cicerone.co.uk/959/GPX. A GPS device is an excellent aid to navigation, but you should also carry a map and compass and know how to use them. GPX files are provided in good faith, but neither the author nor the publisher accept responsibility for their accuracy.

LANGUAGE

English is widely spoken as a second language in each of the countries crossed by the Northern GR5, so basic communication will rarely be a problem. If you can speak the language of the country, or at least manage a conversation, your experience will be greatly enriched.

The official language of the Netherlands is Dutch. (There are also regional languages and dialects.) Belgium is more complicated, with three linguistic communities (Flemish, French and German) and three regions (Flemish-speaking Flanders, French- and German-speaking Wallonia and bilingual Brussels). When you cross the almost-imperceptible international border from the Netherlands into Belgium, you enter Flanders, where the official language is Flemish. Dutch and Flemish are closely related and the written languages scarcely differ, but spoken Flemish is distinctly different from Dutch.

After crossing Flanders, the GR5 passes through a Dutch city, Maastricht, and then re-enters Belgium near the border between Flanders and Wallonia. The official language of Wallonia is French, except in the 'Eastern Cantons', where German is the official language. The last Belgian villages visited by the GR5 – Braunlauf, Burg-Reuland and Ouren – are in the German-speaking area. Luxembourg has three official languages: French, German and Lëtzebuergesch (a Germanic language). You may not have occasion to speak Lëtzebuergesch, but you will see place names and street signs in that language. Finally, the language of Lorraine is, of course, French. However, a German dialect, Platt, is also spoken by some people in the north-eastern part of the Moselle Department.

Appendix E is provided to give you a few useful words for travelling and trekking through French and Dutch-speaking areas.

MONEY

The four countries of the Northern GR5 (as well as nearby Germany, where you may venture in search of accommodation) share a common currency: the euro (€).

Most businesses accept payment with major credit cards, but there are exceptions. It can be difficult to pay with a foreign credit card in the Netherlands, even in large shops such as supermarkets. Some B&Bs and chambres d'hôtes along the Northern GR5 accept payment with a credit card, but many do not. You can generally pay by cheque in Lorraine, but it must be drawn upon a French bank.

Be prepared to pay for many goods and services with cash.

STAYING IN TOUCH

Mobile telephone networks cover most of the Northern GR5, but the strength of the signal will vary. Naturally, in more remote areas (such as the Ardennes), the signal may be weak or non-existent. A recent EU directive has eliminated roaming charges for European mobile telephone services.

Wireless internet (WiFi) is usually available in hotels, B&Bs and chambres d'hôtes, and occasionally available in gîtes d'étapes and campgrounds. Quality is variable. The WiFi in the upper floors of a large building may be weak. In cities and larger towns, many cafés and restaurants offer WiFi and train stations generally have it, too.

A generation ago, before the ubiquity of mobiles, email and social media, travellers often relied upon *poste restante* to remain in contact with the folks back home, and the service still exists today. Poste restante can be used to save weight by sending maps ahead to where you need them. Look up the address of a particular post office (see Appendix D for post office websites) and send the package to yourself at that address, marked 'poste restante'. Aim for it to arrive no more than about two weeks before you plan to pick it up. In the Netherlands, where private businesses now provide retail postal services, contact them in advance to confirm that they will hold poste restante packages. In France, many rural post offices have closed. Instead, postal services may be provided by an *agence postale* within the *mairie* (town hall) or tourist office.

HEALTH AND SAFETY

There are fewer risks to your health and safety on the Northern GR5 than, for example, crossing a 2500m pass in the Alps. All you should need to do is carry a basic first aid kit, and exercise ordinary caution and foresight.

There are, however, certain specific risks to anticipate. If the sky darkens and the wind picks up while you are walking upon a dyke in the Delta region, you should leave that high, exposed ground and seek shelter. The coming storm could be intense, with lightning. And as you walk along bicycle paths in the Netherlands and Flanders, you will observe that some cyclists ride at high speeds – they will pass you before you even hear them. So walk on the side of the path and look carefully behind you before crossing the path. Hunting is permitted in some areas, particularly in the autumn, so watch for signs announcing the dates and times.

Increasingly, we see warnings about ticks (carriers of Lyme disease). It is advisable to check carefully for ticks after walking through high grass and bushes. If you find one, remove it using the special tick remover that you have included in your first aid kit, and then watch the location of the bite carefully. If you develop a rash, swelling, pain or other indication, seek medical treatment immediately.

In this context, note that the standard European number for all emergency services is: 112.

European citizens and residents should obtain and carry a European Health Insurance Card. Supplemental personal insurance is advisable. Some alpine and walking associations (such as the Club Alpin Français) offer optional insurance with membership.

USING THIS GUIDE

This guidebook breaks the route into five sections: Netherlands, Flanders, Wallonia, Luxembourg and Lorraine. Each section begins with a short description of the GR5 in that region, followed by stages that correspond to daily walks. Essential information is provided at the start of each stage: start and end points, distance and walking time, total ascent and descent (except in the Netherlands and Flanders where those values are negligible), maps required, public transport available and accommodation. Places along the route where refreshments may be available are listed, but without the various weekly and daily closures. (Be prepared for Murphy's Law of Café Closures!) After a summary of the stage's highlights, there is a detailed description of the walk, including points of interest along the way.

The 1:100K stage maps in the text will help to orient you for each stage, supplemented by periodic maps of urban areas at the larger scale of 1:40K,

Vineyards above the Moselle River

Etang du Stock (Lorraine)

but neither of these are intended to replace large scale walking maps. The walking times are, of course, approximate. You will learn to estimate your own walking times against 'guide time' as you go along.

This guidebook concludes with five appendices: (A) a route planner that shows where facilities are available along the route, (B) some 5-day itineraries to fit into a week's holiday, (C) a list of accommodation along the route, (D) useful contacts, and (E) some useful words and phrases in French and Dutch. All telephone numbers are in the format for international dialling (which can be used inside the country), without the initial '0' that is not dialled when using the country code.

So let's go! *Op weg! Allons y!*

1 THE NETHERLANDS

18th century windmill in Maassluis (Stage 2)

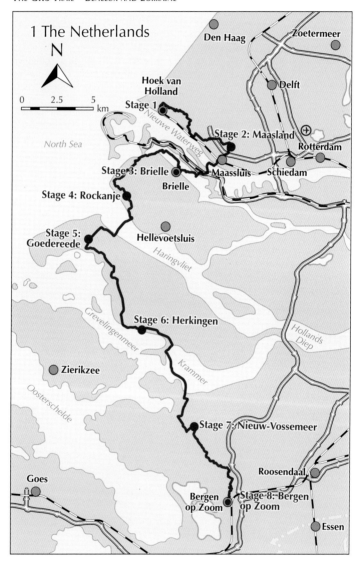

1 The Netherlands

N

0   2.5   5
         km

North Sea

Den Haag

Zoetermeer

Hoek van
Holland

Delft

Stage 1

Nieuwe Waterweg

Stage 2: Maasland

Rotterdam

Stage 3: Brielle

Maassluis

Schiedam

Brielle

Stage 4: Rockanje

Stage 5:
Goedereede

Hellevoetsluis

Haringvliet

Grevelingenmeer

Stage 6: Herkingen

Hollands
Diep

Zierikzee

Krammer

Oosterschelde

Stage 7: Nieuw-Vossemeer

Roosendaal

Goes

Bergen
op Zoom

Stage 8: Bergen
op Zoom

Essen

This first section of the Northern GR5 crosses the Delta region of the Netherlands (South Holland, Zeeland and North Brabant Provinces) in seven stages.

Here it offers numerous and varied encounters with water. You cross the Nieuwe Waterweg (New Waterway, built almost 150 years ago) on a small ferry and walk beside lakes, such as Brielse Meer and Brede Water (a bird sanctuary). A short walk upon a North Sea beach brings you to the Haringvlietsluizen, a major dam with 17 large sluice gates. After a long walk across two other dams (Grevelingendam and Philipsdam), you will enjoy the grassy path beside the Scheldt-Rhine Canal. You even walk through the moat around Fort De Roovere (near Bergen op Zoom) on a unique wooden bridge that puts the surface of the water at eye-level. And remember that Maastricht – named after a bridge over the Meuse (Maas) River – lies ahead, at the end of the Flemish section.

There is a lot of walking on paved and tarmac surfaces in the Delta, but it's mostly on bicycle paths. You will not be bothered by vehicular traffic. The bicycle, in all its forms, reigns supreme. You will see teenagers riding in small groups, checking their telephones as they chat with each other. Packs of more earnest cyclists sweep past on sleek road bicycles. Older people, riding 'city bicycles' (some equipped with electric motors), roll along at a stately, comfortable pace.

And the route is not all paved – far from it! The GR5 also leads through wooded dunes (in particular, Voornes Duin) and along grassy dykes (for example, 16km from Stellendam to Herkingen).

This section will give you a real feel for the rhythm of Dutch life in both agricultural and urban areas. You will find it easy to meet and talk with people here, as almost everyone speaks English.

SECTION SUMMARY TABLE

Start	Hoek van Holland
Finish	Bergen op Zoom
Distance	123.7km
Ascent/Descent	Negligible
Maps	Dutch Kadaster 1:50,000
Note	If you start early from Hoek van Holland, you could make it as far as Maassluis (21km) or Brielle (32km) for your first night.

STAGE 1
Hoek van Holland to Maasland

Start	Hoek van Holland Haven metro station
Finish	Maasland
Distance	18.5km
Time	4hr 15min
Map	37 West Rotterdam
Refreshments	None
Transport	Ferry from Harwich (UK) to Hoek van Holland; train to Rotterdam Central Station and RET Metro B to Hoek van Holland Haven
Accommodation	B&B in Maasland

This first stage of the GR5 is convenient for those who arrive in Hoek van Holland around midday. (Those who start earlier in the day may opt to walk an additional 2.8km to Maassluis, a city with more services.) The route to Maasland follows trails through woods and bicycle paths across polders. It is interesting to observe the intensive agriculture in large greenhouses and the spinning wind turbines beside active commercial waterways.

The GR5 starts at a tall pole, standing beside the Hoek van Holland Haven **metro station** and near the ferry terminal, with arms pointing in different directions. One points the way to 'GR5 Hoek van Holland – Nice 2289'. Cross the railway tracks here and follow Harwichweg. Turn left after 100 metres where a GR mark points into a wooded **park**. The GR5 wanders through this park, following a well-marked route. About 100 metres after entering the park, turn right beside a small pond, then left where the trail comes within sight of the road (on the right). Turn right at a field with exercise apparatus, right again to descend a short flight of steps and left on a paved path (Kerkhofweg). ◄ Turn right beside the pitch of a rugby club called 'The Hookers'. Emerging from the woods, the trail passes a football stadium.

There is a cemetery on the left side of Kerkhofweg with Commonwealth war graves, including those of RAF fliers who died during the Wehrmacht offensive in May 1940.

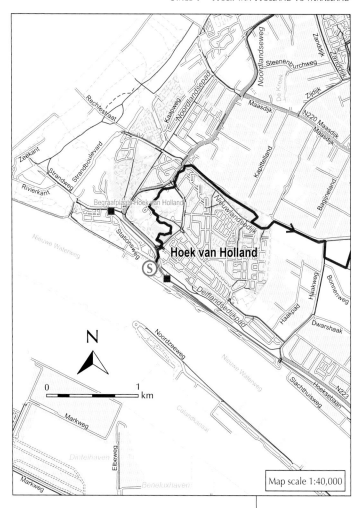

Map scale 1:40,000

The GR5 reaches Harwichweg: turn left and then right to walk on a path parallel to Dirk van den Burgweg, with a children's play area on the right. Shortly after passing the Hotel Noordzee on the left, the path enters a **forest** with a

39

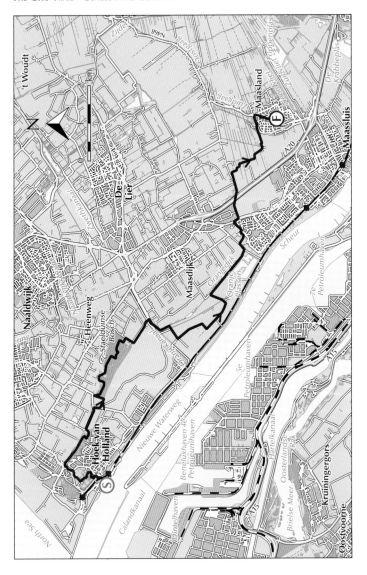

GR mark clearly indicating the route. The trail continues generally southeast, with well-placed GR marks – except at an unmarked T-junction about 15 minutes after entering these woods: turn right here.

After passing a canal and residential housing on the right, leave the woods and continue beside an open field on the right. At Haakweg, the GR5 follows three sides of a quadrilateral, rather than continue straight ahead on the path. Turn right on Haakweg, left on a path after 200 metres (KP29), and left again on a trail that runs along the west side of a wooded area, the **Staelduinse Bosch**. A sign identifies the trail as the 'Grote Rivierapad' (Great Riviera Path), confirming that you are indeed walking toward the Mediterranean Sea. The trail reaches the northwest corner of the woods and turns right into them. ▶ The GR5 meanders through the woods and is generally well marked, but there is one turn that is easy to miss. Watch for the GR mark indicating a right turn into the woods just after passing a house on the left.

Leaving the Staelduinse Bosch, turn right on Staelduinlaan. After crossing Bonnenlaan, turn left on a bicycle path. The path crosses the **Oranjekanaal** (KP78), turns right and continues southwest for 400m.

Residential neighbourhood in Hoek van Holland

Several concrete bunkers built here by the Germans during World War II are now bat sanctuaries (*vleermuisreservaat*). Their darkness and constant temperature create an ideal environment for bats.

You will see many **wind turbines** in the Delta area – and feel the wind that turns them! In 2017, wind power in the Netherlands produced more than 9.6 billion kWh of electricity, nearly 60% of the country's total production by renewable sources. The Dutch (like other Europeans) are increasing their wind power capacity. During Stage 6, you will pass the new Krammer Wind Park, where 34 wind turbines are being built (scheduled for completion in 2019).

Curving left, the GR5 follows a path beside the **Oranjedijk** and large greenhouses devoted to the cultivation of vegetables. Turn right after 500 metres (KP90) and walk on Polderhaakdwarsweg to Polderhaakweg. Turn left here and walk 1.3km to Spuidijk. The road curves left to join the Oranjedijk road after 500 metres. The GR5 turns right here and follows the road for 1.5km before reaching the end of the Oranjedijk itself.

At the end of Oranjedijk, pass an equestrian centre, Manege de Nieuwe Oranjehoeve, and continue on a bicycle path that enters **Maassluis** (KP16). The park here is a good place for a picnic. Leaving the park, walk northeast along a path beside a street. After crossing a main road, turn right and walk down a small road to a bridge on the

Friendly cattle guard a footbridge across a ditch in the Maasland polder

left. Cross that bridge and follow a road (Westgaag) beside a canal. This road passes under the **A20** motorway. About 500 metres after the motorway, the GR5 follows a bicycle path to the right. Then, 50 metres further, the GR5 leaves the path. It crosses a small bridge on the right and sets off across the fields upon a line of concrete paving stones. Maasland's two church steeples are visible on the horizon to the southeast.

Enter **Maasland**, a residential town, through a small park called 't hoenderpark. Cross a canal and turn left on Koningin Julianaweg for a tour of this quiet town. Wander through the town beside its canal and along bicycle paths. The general direction is south toward an intersection in the southwestern corner of the town, where you will find the GR5 if it has been temporarily lost. You can skip the walk through central Maasland by turning right on Koningin Julianaweg, which re-joins the GR5 at that intersection.

Services are limited in Maasland, but the town has what is needed for a comfortable overnight stay: a B&B, a supermarket and a restaurant.

STAGE 2
Maasland to Brielle

Start	Maasland
Finish	Brielle
Distance	12.8km
Time	3hr 30min (plus about 30min for the ferry)
Map	37 West Rotterdam
Refreshments	Cafés/restaurants and shops in Maassluis; cafés at Rozenburg ferry landing and beside Brielse Meer
Accommodation	B&B in Maassluis; hotels, B&Bs and campground with trekkershutten in Brielle
Transport options	Maassluis is on Rotterdam metro line B, so you could begin a walk on the GR5 there. Alternatively, combine Stages 1 and 2 (30.5km), departing early from Hoek van Holland to arrive in Brielle in the late afternoon. Connexxion bus 106 links Rozenburg with Brielle.

The walk from Maasland to Brielle passes through Maassluis, an attractive town, and includes a ferry ride across the Nieuwe Waterweg. The trek across three bridges, which may seem longer than its 2km length, is rewarded by a pleasant walk beside Brielse Meer. This relatively short stage allows you to arrive in Brielle with enough time to explore the city – or simply to relax in a café beside one of the canals or in the central Markt.

The GR5 leaves Maasland at the southern end of the town. Cross two bridges and then turn right and descend steps leading to a path along a canal. This turn is well-marked, but it helps to be watching for it. Walk southwest on this

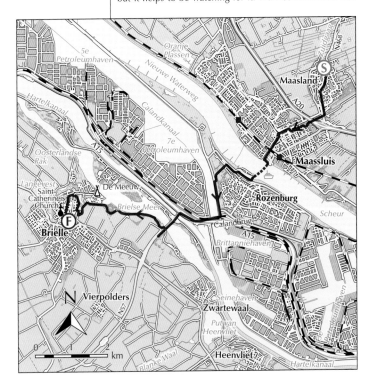

path under a motorway (**A20**) and beside an 18th century windmill. Go around the Lentiz Revius Lyceum and continue in the same direction on Zuidvliet ZZ, which enters the commercial centre of Maassluis. Turn right on PC Hooftlaan and left on Noordvliet, which becomes Veerstraat. Turn left on Hoogstraat (KP47) and then (after one block) right on Haven. ▶

The National Towage Museum (Nationaal Sleepvaart Museum, **www.nationaalsleepvaart museum.nl/en/** is beside the GR5 at Hoogstraat 1–3.

Haven, as its name indicates, leads to the harbour. Just before a railway line, a road to the left leads to the railway station. On the right, a monument records the height of water during the 1953 flood. Continue straight here and descend a flight of steps beside a bench with 'HOOFD' carved into it. The road, Burg de Jonghkade, ends at the quayside. Turn left and walk to the Rozenburg ferry (KP63). Ferries shuttle back and forth, carrying motor vehicles, cyclists and pedestrians a short distance across the **Nieuwe Waterweg**. ▶

The 20.5km Nieuwe Waterweg (New Waterway) was completed in 1872, in order to link Rotterdam to the North Sea as the Rijn and Maas Rivers silted up.

Disembark from the ferry, turn left and walk beside a café to steps that lead to a grassy dyke. Turn right and walk along this dyke for 400 metres, then shift to the left to walk in the same direction along a wooded path. Where the trail turns left (KP64), descend to a road and continue straight ahead on Zandweg (KP75).

Groote Kerk, Maassluis

The road curves left and rises to a line of trees. Cross a road here and turn left to walk beside a bicycle path along **Calandkanaal**. A vertical-lift bridge, **Calandbrug**, is 800 metres away. Upon reaching the bridge, walk under it and then climb steps on the left to a walkway that crosses the bridge.

This is not wilderness trekking, but it is interesting to walk through the heart of commercial Holland. There are two more bridges to cross, the Harmsenbrug and the Brielse Brug. The total distance across the three bridges and the paths between them is nearly 2km. The path continues 100 metres after the third bridge and then makes a hairpin turn back to the water (KP78). You are now on Voorne Island, beside Brielse Meer.

> **Brielse Meer** was formerly Brielse Maas, a branch of the Maas (Meuse) River. The construction of dams in 1950 transformed Brielse Maas into a lake, Brielse Meer, a popular site now for recreational boating.

LAW stands for Lange-Afstand-Wandelpad (long-distance hiking path). LAW 5–1 follows the coast from Sluis, on the Belgian border, to Hoek van Holland.

At the water's edge, turn left toward Brielle. This section of the GR5 coincides with a Dutch trail designated LAW 5–1; be careful not to follow the marker indicating a right turn on LAW 6. ◀

Follow the bicycle path to Brielle. You pass a grassy area, an excellent place for a picnic lunch, as well as a restaurant. It's a pleasant 3km walk, with fields and trees around the path, and Brielse Meer nearby. Soon, the tower of **Saint Catherine's Church** is visible on the horizon. Brielle's old ramparts, now grass-covered mounds, are surrounded by a moat. The GR5 curves left and skirts the moat before turning right to enter the old city over a bridge and through a gate on the southeast side of the town, **Kaaipoort**.

The GR5 meanders through Brielle towards the **Markt** (market place), giving the visitor an opportunity to observe noteworthy buildings, including the 17th century Brielle Historical Museum (Historisch Museum Den Briel, http://historischmuseumdenbriel.nl), which focuses on the Dutch war of independence, the 'Eighty Years War', and Saint Catherine's Church.

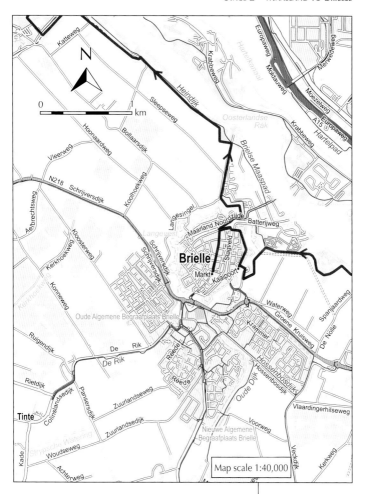

To reach the **centre** of Brielle directly, turn left on Kaaistraat after passing through the Kaaipoort and then right (still Kaaistraat) to cross a bridge (Kaaibrug). Ahead, Vischstraat leads straight to the Markt.

There are ample facilities for visitors in Brielle including hotels, B&Bs, cafés, restaurants and food shops.

SEA BEGGARS SEIZE BRIELLE

Monument commemorating capture of Brielle by the watergeuzen (sea beggars) in 1572

Conflict in the Netherlands (today's Netherlands, most of Belgium, Luxembourg and other territories) grew during the 1560s, as the Hapsburg King Philip II tightened Spanish rule: collecting taxes vigorously, combatting Protestantism and suppressing political opposition. A Spanish army, led by the Duke of Alva, crushed Dutch resistance led by William of Orange. Dutch privateers, contemptuously called 'watergeuzen' (sea beggars) by their enemies, remained active.

On 1 April 1572, they swooped upon Brielle (then an important seaport, known as Brill) and captured the city. This dramatic blow against Spanish rule inspired other successful attacks upon cities and reinvigorated Dutch resistance. The capture of Brielle was thus a decisive event in the Dutch war of independence. The Dutch celebrate the capture of Brielle each 1 April, and they recite a rhyming pun: 'Op 1 april verloor Alva zijn bril.' The Dutch word 'bril' means 'glasses', so: 'On 1 April, Alva lost his glasses.'

Brielle was one of several 'Cautionary Towns' that England occupied as security for repayment of the costs of its financial and military assistance to the United Provinces, pursuant to the Treaty of Nonsuch of 1585. Queen Elizabeth openly challenged Spain by supporting the Dutch revolt in this manner. Three years later, the Spanish Armada set sail for England...

STAGE 3
Brielle to Rockanje

Start	Brielle
Finish	Rockanje (Badhotel Rockanje)
Distance	18km
Time	4hr 15min
Maps	37 West Rotterdam
Refreshments	Cafés/restaurants in Oostvoorne and near Tenellaplas visitors' centre
Transport	Connexxion Bus 103
Accommodation	Hotels in Oostvoorne and Rockanje

This is perhaps the most attractive and enjoyable stage of the Dutch section of the Northern GR5, with very little tarmac. After leaving Brielle, you walk along a grassy dyke, with clear views in all directions. The latter part of the stage goes through forests and dunes, where you pass a bird sanctuary (Breede Water) and may encounter some Highland cattle.

To re-join the GR5 from the centre of Brielle, walk north from Markt on Voorstraat. Cross the Noord Spui canal and turn right on **Maarland Noordzijde**. You meet the GR5 just before the next bridge. A gate watch house (Poortwachterhuis) stands beside the bridge. Cross the bridge, walk 100 metres and turn left on a path going north (KP55). This tree-lined path follows the perimeter of Brielle's old ramparts.

The path leads to a road, **Langesingel**, which becomes van Bloys van Treslongweg (named after one of the leaders of the *watergeuzen*). When this turns right, the GR5 continues straight ahead on Oosterlandsedijk. The GR5 intersects a bicycle path after 300 metres. Do not follow that path, but instead turn left here on a path along **Heindijk**. Follow this for a kilometre. Eventually, the GR5 joins a bicycle path below the dyke. When the path intersects a road, the route shifts to the left and continues for another kilometre on the dyke (KP84).

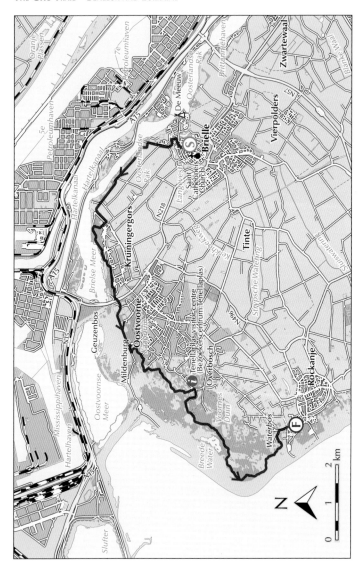

Turn left at an old watch tower (Stenen Baken), and then, 500 metres further, turn right and descend from the dyke. Cross the bicycle path and enter Molecaten Park (a recreational area). Initially a dirt trail through **woods**, the route becomes a broad, grassy path. The trail turns left, away from a sandy beach, then right through a parking lot and some woods. Opposite a café, turn right to follow another broad, tree-lined path.

Leave these woods, walk along a road with small cottages on the left and then cross an open area with major roads. About 200 metres after passing under a main road (**N218**), cross a road to the right and turn left to follow a bicycle path called 'Boulevard', entering **Oostvoorne** (KP13). The 'Boulevard' is a paved path with lanes marked for pedestrians as well as cyclists, with a grass verge for walking. A forest stands on the left. The cranes of the Maasvlakte container terminal are visible across the water on the right. At two points where a trail emerges from the forest, signs warn: 'Geen toegang via dit pad! – Dit is alleen een uitgang!' ('No entry via this path! – This is an exit only!'). These signs mark one-way bicycle trails in the forest, but soon (at a junction with a road where there is a hotel, KP16), a trail on the left for walkers enters the forest. ▶

This is the Kaapduin, a beautiful area of woods and dunes where automobiles and cyclists are excluded.

Voornes Duin

51

Walk along a well-marked trail of sandy soil through the forest and, eventually, through dunes with scattered, low-lying vegetation. The trail passes through cleverly designed gates (mounted upon tilted frames which mean they close automatically under gravity). The trail takes you to the **Tenellaplas visitors' centre** (Bezoekerscentrum Tenellaplas), with a restaurant nearby, and enters **Voornes Duin**.

The dunes of **Voornes Duin** protect the coastline. Shaggy Highland cattle graze here, limiting the growth of vegetation (a role formerly performed by rabbits, until their numbers were much reduced by disease).

One notable feature of Voornes Duin is **Breede Water**, a bird sanctuary. Access to Breede Water is restricted: Watch for two side-trails marked 'Uitkijkpunt' (lookout point) that lead to hides (blinds) where you can observe some of the many birds that live around Breede Water. The first is after KP71, the second after KP54.

Walk through woods and dunes for 4km after Breede Water. After leaving the dune area at Waterbos, turn right on a road (KP31) and walk into **Rockanje**. The GR5 soon reaches the Badhotel Rockanje which has a restaurant and a swimming pool – a comfortable place to end the day.

STAGE 4
Rockanje to Goedereede

Start	Rockanje (Badhotel Rockanje)
Finish	Goedereede (Markt)
Distance	13.2km
Time	3hr
Maps	37 West Rotterdam; 36 Oost Goedereede
Refreshments	There is a café just before the Haringvlietsluizen and several restaurants after it.
Transport	Connexxion Buses 103 and 104
Accommodation	B&B in Havenhoofd; B&Bs in Goedereede

This stage includes a walk along a North Sea beach, followed by a trek across one of the major components of the Delta Works, the Haringvlietsluizen. The final section of the stage (after 1km beside an open road) is a quiet walk along a tree-shaded canal to Goedereede, an attractive little town. It is possible to take a shortcut that would eliminate some road walking (but also Goedereede) by walking to Stellendam (where there are shops) after crossing the Haringvlietsluizen. To re-join the GR5 from Stellendam, walk through the town southwest on Voorstraat and then cross the fields on a path that leads to the dyke that you walk along in Stage 5.

Departing from the northern side of Rockanje, walk southeast on Duinrand to Waaldrift, then turn right and walk under the stately trees of this residential neighbourhood. Curving left,

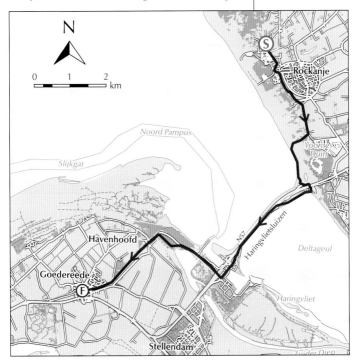

The European
Ramblers Association
has designated certain
long distance paths in
Europe as 'E-paths'.
E2, which starts in
Inverness, follows the
GR5 from Hoek van
Holland to Nice.

the route passes Badstrand Rockanje 1e Slag and then, 200 metres further, turns right on Duinzoom. Turn right off this road into the woods opposite No 48. When the trail emerges from the woods, it turns right on a road and crosses agricultural land. A sign identifies the trail as 'Europese Wandelweg E2 Noordzee – Riviera' (European Hiking Path E2 North Sea – Riviera). ◀

Turn right and enter **Voornes Duin** on a trail opposite a restaurant, de Houten Paardjes. Walk through dunes to the North Sea beach and turn left to walk along the beach for 1km. There is an exit from the beach to the left, with a GR mark. Follow a brick path, Zandloper, which passes under the motorway (N57) and arrives at a parking area with a café (KP99). Turn right here and walk toward the **Haringvlietsluizen** on a broad grassy area beside the water. After 1km, climb steps to the Haringvlietweg, a bicycle path that runs parallel to the main road. The walk across the Haringvlietsluizen is 2.5km long. You can measure progress with the numbers on the 17 huge sluice gates. Even when the weather is hot and sunny, there is likely to be a refreshing breeze blowing across this dam.

DELTA WORKS

The Watersnoodramp (flood disaster) struck Holland during the night of 31 January 1953. The combined effects of a North Sea storm, spring tides and high flow of water in the rivers breached dykes and flooded vast areas. Nearly 2000 people died, some 3000 houses and 300 farms were destroyed and many more damaged. In the aftermath of this disaster, the Dutch undertook a vast engineering project that would protect coastal areas against such flooding in the future and manage water resources.

The Delta Works comprise dams, sluices, locks, storm surge barriers and dykes that were constructed over a period of 40 years. These works shortened the total length of dykes open to the sea by 700km. Two waterways were left open because of their importance to shipping: the Westerschelde (access to Antwerp) and the Nieuwe Waterweg (access to Rotterdam).

The Haringvlietsluizen is major component of the Delta Works. It protects against floods and regulates the flow of water from the Rhine and Maas Rivers into the North Sea. The Haringvlietsluizen's environmental impact has been substantial, as it limits tidal flow and the Haringvliet has become a fresh water lake. The Dutch are considering whether to open several sluice gates permanently in order to restore the Haringvliet's estuary function with a tidal flow of salt water.

You are now on Goeree-Overflakke Island and likely to be ready for refreshment after crossing the Haringvlietssluizen. There are several options here: descending the long path from the dam to an intersection (KP60), there is a restaurant on the left (Zoet of Zout), followed by a fast-food restaurant (Eetcafe de Stelle). Then, 200 metres after turning right at a roundabout, there is a fish restaurant (Poisson and Cuisine) behind warehouses on the right.

The GR5 continues for 1km after the roundabout on a bicycle path beside a road and turns left across the road to enter the Duinen van Goeree. Orange-tiled roofs can be seen in the distance. Upon arriving at those houses, turn left and walk through **Havenhoofd**. Continue straight ahead on a tree-lined bicycle path, Noord Havendijk, where the road turns left. About 2km beyond Havenhoofd, **Goedereede** comes into view, starting with a bridge over the canal and an orange harbour buoy set beside it (KP46). The GR5 turns left and crosses that bridge, but Goedereede is a good place to end a stage, as it has B&Bs and other facilities. ▶ Continue along the canal without crossing the bridge to reach the central square, Markt.

Pope Adrian VI, born Adriaan Florensz, is the only Dutchman to have been Pope (1522–23). He served as pastor in Goedereede and lived in the building that is now the De Gouden Leeuw restaurant.

Goedereede

STAGE 5
Goedereede to Herkingen

Start	Goedereede (Markt)
Finish	Herkingen
Distance	18.5km
Time	4hr
Maps	36 Oost Goedereede; 42 Oost Zierikzee; 43 West Willemstad
Refreshments	None
Transport	It is possible to travel by bus from Goedereede to Herkingen, albeit with several changes.
Accommodation	B&B in Herkingen

This stage starts with a 2km walk on roads through farmland south and southwest of Goedereede. The GR5 then leaves the tarmac and mostly follows grass-covered dykes for the remaining 16km to Herkingen. The elevation of the dykes offers views of surrounding farmland and Grevelingenmeer (a lake formed by dams of the Delta Works), and the curving route of the dykes breaks the monotony. Paved bicycle paths, parallel to the dykes, are a good option in case of bad weather.

Departing from Markt, in the centre of Goedereede, cross a bridge over the canal and turn left on ZZ Haven.

Walk along the canal to the next bridge and turn right on Hoofpoortstraat to re-join the GR5. There is a GR mark beside the bicycle shelter ahead of you. Walk across a road at a traffic light and then turn left on a bicycle path toward Stellendam and Middelharnis. Continue straight a short distance and then follow a right fork where a path to **Stellendam** and Middelharnis (off map to the east) branches left. There is an arrow pointing to KP44 here, but no GR mark to indicate this turn.

The GR5 now follows a road across farmland, first south and then southwest on Oude Westerloose Dijk. Turn left on Korte Wegje and walk along a dyke (Kliene Zuid Polderse Dijk). The path forks after 800m: turn right on a path that is marked as a dead end, 'uitgezonderd' (except for) bicycles.

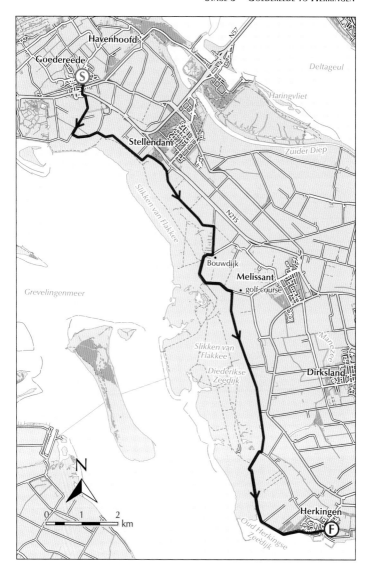

Stay on the bicycle path as it descends below the crest of the dyke, and then return to the top of the dyke at a fork to the left. Turn right where there is a sign for a 'Theetuin' (tea garden), with an arrow pointing to KP56 but no GR mark, and walk on the grass-covered dyke.

The path continues along the crest of this dyke, heading generally southeast for about 2.5km. Stellendam comes into view on the left. Stay on the dyke where a paved path descends to the left. The trail bends to the left and continues east for 400 metres. Turn right at a gate and continue walking on the dyke due south. After 750 metres, the trail arrives at a junction with a road (Bouwdijk) beside a blue metal bench. ◄

This is the only bench that you will encounter on the dykes during this stage, so it is a good place to stop for lunch.

Climb over a fence here on a stile, turn right and continue on another dyke. For the next 1.8km, the trail follows the dyke on a gradual arc to the left. When it reaches a gate, with a **golf course** on the left, turn right and walk south on the Diederikse Zeedijk for 4.6km. ◄

On the right, the mudflats of the Slikken van Flakkee lie between the dyke and Grevelingenmeer.

Do not be distracted by the bicycle paths that cross the dyke at several places. Continue straight ahead on the dyke.

After climbing over a fence on a stile (or going through a gate), follow the trail on a dyke (**Oud Herkingse Zeedijk**) that curves along the coast of the **Grevelingenmeer** for

Cyclists passing cattle in the Slikken van Flakkee

another 4km. The masts of sailboats come into view, moored in Herkingen harbour. Walking east now, descend from the dyke to the left and enter **Herkingen**, where there are several restaurants and an excellent B&B.

> The **Grevelingen** was once part of the estuary of the Rhine, Meuse and Waal rivers. The Delta Works included two dams – Grevelingen and Brouwers – that cut the Grevelingen off from the North Sea, making it a lake, Grevelingenmeer. By blocking tidal flows, the closure of the Grevelingen wreaked environmental havoc. In 1978, a lock was built in the Brouwers Dam to re-connect the lake with the North Sea. The Grevelingenmeer is now brackish salt water with some tidal flow. It encompasses nature reserves and recreational areas.

STAGE 6
Herkingen to Nieuw-Vossemeer

Start	Herkingen
Finish	Nieuw-Vossemeer
Distance	24km
Time	5hr 15min
Map	43 West Willemstad
Refreshments	None
Transport	Connexxion Bus 102 runs from Oude-Tonge across Grevelingdam and Philipsdam to Sint Philipsland
Accommodation	Hotel in Oude-Tonge (3.5km off the GR5); B&B in Nieuw-Vossemeer

This stage starts with 6.4km along a bicycle path beside Grevelingenmeer and then 9.6km across two linked dams: Grevelingdam and Philipsdam. You leave the tarmac when you turn onto pleasant trails through the wooded Slikken van de Heen and along the Schelde-Rijnkanaal (Scheldt-Rhine Canal). Finally you cross a bridge over the canal and walk a short way along the road into Nieuw-Vossemeer.

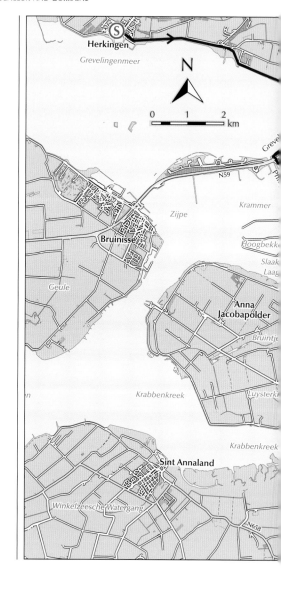

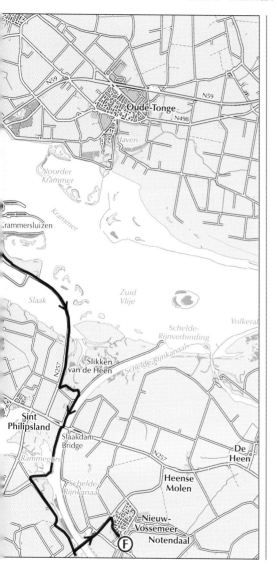

From Herkingen harbour walk through an open gate in the dyke with the inscription '1953', a reminder that this area was badly flooded that year. Turn left and walk east on the bicycle path, between the paved dyke (topped by wind turbines) and the **Grevelingenmeer**.

About 2.3km from Herkingen, pass a small marina, Battenoord, and continue on the bicycle path to the right. As the path approaches the main road (N59) crossing the **Grevelingdam**, it moves to the top of the dyke. Turn right on the bicycle path that runs on the Grevelingdam parallel to the road. To walk instead to Oude-Tonge (where there is a hotel), continue straight and walk through a tunnel under the main road. Then turn left and walk 3.5km along a bicycle path. ◀

You are likely to see many mute swans in the Krammer, the body of fresh water on the left. The swans generally eschew the salty Grevelingenmeer on the right.

After walking southwest on the Grevelingdam for 1.3km, turn left (southeast) at a large intersection to cross the Philipsdam. The GR5 leaves the province of Zuid Holland (South Holland) here and enters Zeeland. Just after the Krammersluizen (locks) in the middle of the Philipsdam, there is an observation tower that provides a good view over these dams, locks and the bodies of water around them. The GR5 follows a side-road from the observation tower for a short distance before re-joining the main road. ◀ Finally, the GR5 leaves the tarmac and turns left into a beautiful wooded area, the Slikken van de Heen.

An information post beside the trail explains that this area is part of the Nationaal Park Oosterschelde (Eastern Scheldt National Park).

> The **Krammersluizen** (Krammer Locks) operate in a way that minimises the flow of salt water from the Oosterschelde (on the western side) into the fresh water Volkerak (on the eastern side), and vice versa.

Walk from the path over a hill and enter the **Slikken van de Heen** through a tilted gate. The trail meanders through these woods and heath, heading generally east. There are not many GR marks here, but enough (along with waymarks for other trails) for guidance. The destination is the line of trees to the east, where there is a fence. Walk through another tilted gate and turn right onto a paved path beside the **Schelde-Rijnkanaal** (Scheldt-Rhine Canal). After 100 metres, branch left on a pleasant, grass path that continues beside the canal. Walk under the **Slaakdam Bridge** and climb onto a dyke that runs parallel to a bicycle path.

About 2km after the bridge, pass a white gate (KP48), climb over a stile and continue straight (southeast) on a dyke. Turn left at an intersection of roads, and follow the dyke. One kilometre ahead, there is a bridge across the canal. ▶ The trail passes under the bridge, descends from the dyke beside an old, white pump house and then doubles back toward the bridge. Walk up a slope to reach a bicycle path that crosses the bridge. The GR5 leaves Zeeland here and enters Noord Brabant (North Brabant) Province. Continue straight across the bridge and along a road for 1.4km to Nieuw-Vossemeer. At an intersection, beware of a GR mark that points left where you should turn right into town!

The GR5 skirts Nieuw-Vossemeer along its southwestern side. The town is a convenient place to stop: there are restaurants, cafés, a grocery store and a B&B here.

Walking in the Slikken van de Heen

There are many birds in residence around that bridge enjoying the shallow water.

STAGE 7
Nieuw-Vossemeer to Bergen op Zoom

Start	Nieuw-Vossemeer
Finish	Bergen op Zoom (Grote Markt)
Distance	18.7km
Time	4hr 30min
Map	49 West Bergen op Zoom
Refreshments	None before the outskirts of Bergen op Zoom
Transport	Connexxion Bus 102; extensive bus and railway service at Bergen op Zoom
Accommodation	B&B in Lepelstraat; hotels, B&Bs and youth hostel in Bergen op Zoom

This is a transitional stage. From a small village in North Brabant, you walk across quiet polders beside the Schelde-Rijnkanaal (Scheldt-Rhine Canal) to one of the largest cities on the GR5: Bergen op Zoom. You will scarcely notice urban sprawl, as the GR5 enters the city through parks and attractive residential neighbourhoods. Bergen op Zoom is an interesting city and a good place for a rest day.

Departing from the commercial centre of Nieuw-Vossemeer (KP83), walk a short distance southeast and then turn right on Veerweg. The route quickly enters the countryside, turning southwest to pass a small fire station ('Brandweer') and go through a tunnel under a road.

Shortly after passing a windmill at the entrance to a campground, turn left on Zeeweg and walk beside a dyke. Where the road forks opposite the Zoutesluis pumping station (KP12), bear right and walk along the dyke. At the crest of the dyke, turn right and walk through a white gate and down to a paved path between the waterway and the dyke. There is a broad grass verge beside the paved path. After 1.4km, the path turns left away from the waterway, crosses over the dyke and descends to a road on the other side. Walk on the road to a T-junction: turn right here on **Rubeerdijk**.

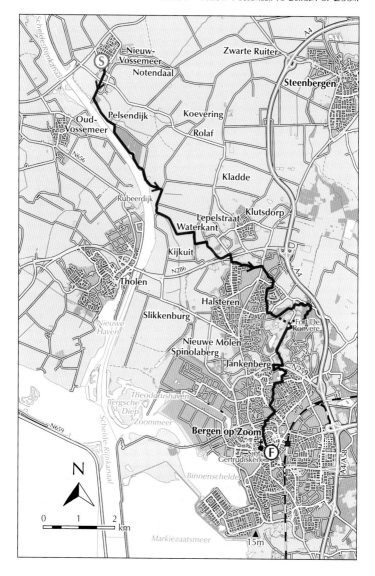

Windmill near Nieuw-Vossemeer

The waymarking over the next few kilometres is uneven. At KP21, Rubeerdijk runs into Noorderkreegweg. Continue on that road as it curves left and then right. Where the road crests slightly, descend to the left to a dirt path that runs southeast bounded by woods on the right and a dyke on the left. There is no GR mark facing you at the beginning of this path, but there is one on a post facing in the opposite direction. After nearly 1km on that path, you reach a corner of the dyke and the fence beside it. There is a weathered, barely recognisable GR mark on a fence post (but again a more prominent GR mark on a tree facing the opposite direction).

Turn left here and walk east beside the fence where the route finally passes a good GR mark. After 500 metres, turn right at a T-junction with Heenweg (KP56) and then left on Jan Bodenweg. ◄ Turn right on Blindenstraat beside a house. It seems as if the trail leads into someone's driveway, but there is a discreet GR mark here and the trail continues into the field behind the house.

The GR5 skirts Lepelstraat, a village with a B&B.

The path through the field leads to a road, which the GR5 follows to the left. After 150 metres, turn right on Erasmusweg and walk under a major main road (**N286**). Here, a sign marks the city limit of **Halsteren**, a suburb of Bergen op Zoom. Turn left, climb up a small rise and go around a guard rail to reach a road that runs east. Walk 300 metres on this road, with stables on the left and residential houses on the right. Again, there is no GR mark facing you until you reach a double street sign: Daansbergen to the left (your direction) and Léharstraat to the right.

The waymarking improves here in the approach to Bergen op Zoom. Daansbergen leads to Steenbergsweg: cross this busy street to reach Schannsbaan. Continue on that road until it crosses Vang then follow Molenwieken to the right. Walk past neat, brick houses, then turn right on Grondmolen into a housing estate with broad green spaces. Turn left to walk past a primary school. Then, after curving right, turn left to walk beside a canal and rows of modern houses. The path enters a wooded area on a dirt road (Zoutendamseweg) and then turns left beside a paved road. After just 150 metres, turn right to enter a forest.

The GR5 sets off here on a big loop through the forest to the northeast and then south and southwest, principally to visit the ruins of **Fort De Roovere**.

> **Fort De Roovere** was completed in 1628. The leading feature of recent restoration work in the ruins of this fort is an open wooden structure that crosses the moat mostly below the level of the water, called the 'Moses Bridge'.

If you prefer to skip the fort and follow a more direct route into Bergen op Zoom, saving 2.2km, bear right at the first fork in the trail after entering the forest. Walk southeast 150 metres to a paved road. Turn right on that road and, 50 metres on, the GR5 joins the road from the left (KP93).

Continue on the road and then, after 150 metres, turn left into the woods on a dirt path called Ernst Casimirweg. That path leads to a small, paved path, Prins Mauritsweg, beside a major main road (**N259**). Turn right here (KP92) and then cross the main road to the left at a traffic light.

You are now in Bergen op Zoom. The route from here to the centre of the city goes through parks and past an attractive lake that is home to many geese and other birds. The route is well-marked and easy to follow. Alternatively, use a map to plot a more direct route to the **Grote Markt** or some other destination in the city. Bergen op Zoom, with its many services (hotels and B&Bs, restaurants and cafés, shops),

Grote Markt,
Bergen op Zoom

museums and other attractions, is a good place to spend a night or longer.

There are records of the Lord of Breda granting privileges to **Bergen op Zoom** around 1212. It became an important commercial centre in the Middle Ages, with fairs attracting merchants from all over Europe twice a year. As new commercial methods displaced fairs and silting limited sea access to its port, Bergen op Zoom's prosperity waned. Its strategic location and natural defences made it an important fortress in early modern times. In the 19th century, industrial manufacturing developed around Bergen op Zoom (sugar, metallurgy), most of which is now gone, replaced by chemical industries and services. To learn more about Bergen op Zoom's history, visit the Markiezenhof (www.markiezenhof.nl) which houses the tourist office.

2 FLANDERS

Windmill in Diest (Stage 14)

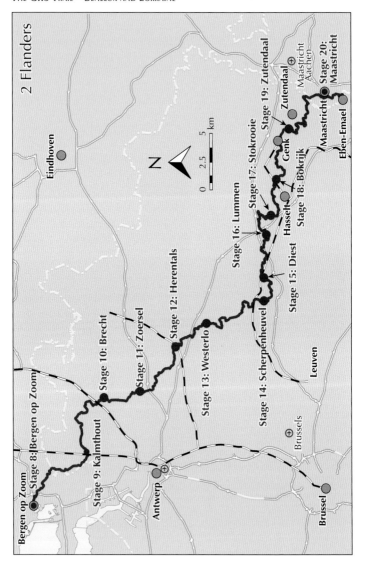

This section describes the GR5's route across northern Flanders, from the Dutch border near Bergen op Zoom to Eben-Emael in Wallonia (with a short return to the Netherlands to visit Maastricht).

The Flemish Kempen landscape is flat, like the Dutch Delta, and you walk beside canals, rivers, lakes and ponds, but it's different. The Kempen's distinctive features are the heathlands, dunes, conifer forests, marshes and ponds that you encounter during the first stage in the Grenspark De Zoom Kalmthoutse Heide and later in the Averbode Bos en Heide and De Maten Nature Reserve.

The strategic and commercial importance of the Low Countries has drawn foreign armies to this area over the centuries, where they clashed in battles such as the Golden Spurs (1302), Ramillies (1706) and Waterloo (1815). Today, most of all, 'Flanders Fields' evokes memories of the terrible battles of World War I, in particular around Ypres. The GR5 crosses Flanders well to the north-east of those battlefields, but if you hike along the trail in late spring, you will see many of the red poppies that inspire remembrance of the sacrifices and losses in armed conflicts.

There are many long walks through forests and across farmland in Flanders. These sometimes include paved roads and paths, but there is not too much of that. A glance at the map will show that the route has often been designed to avoid tarmac, even if that requires a longer walk through a forest. You are likely to sample the full range of accommodation in Flanders: hotels, B&Bs, youth hostels and campgrounds with trekkershutten. In addition to Diest, there are interesting places worth visiting along the way, such as the Bokrijk Open Air Museum and Maastricht. And the beer is excellent!

SECTION SUMMARY TABLE

Start	Bergen op Zoom
Finish	Eben-Emael
Distance	248.9km
Ascent/Descent	Negligible
Maps	(to start Stage 8) Dutch Kadaster 1:50,000; (from the Belgian border) Belgian NGI 1:50,000
Note	Some of these stages could be combined, for example Stages 14 and 15, if you are prepared to sacrifice time exploring the interesting city of Diest.

STAGE 8
Bergen op Zoom to Kalmthout

Start	Bergen op Zoom (Grote Markt)
Finish	Kalmthout
Distance	27km
Time	6hr
Maps	49 Oost Bergen op Zoom (Dutch Kadaster 1:50,000); 1/7 Brasschaat
Refreshments	None after the youth hostel near Bergen op Zoom
Transport	Railway service at Bergen op Zoom and Kalmthout. To skip some urban walking at the beginning of this stage, take the No 11 bus from the train station to the hospital (Ziekenhuis).
Accommodation	B&Bs in Wouwse Plantage and Kalmthout

Walking inland from Bergen op Zoom, you are immediately aware of the transition to a different environment. The land is still flat, but you have left behind the dykes and polders of the Delta. The first part of this stage passes through pine and oak forests and across farmland. You leave the Netherlands and enter Belgium across a virtually unmarked border. The stage concludes with a long walk across the heath and dunes of the beautiful Grenspark De Zoom – Kalmthoutse Heide.

Departing from the Grote Markt in the centre of Bergen op Zoom, walk east on Zuivelstraat and continue straight to the **train station**. Walk through a tunnel under the railway line and continue in the same direction on Lepstraat. The route to the eastern side of the city is well-marked. Familiar GR5 marks on lamp-posts, walls and trees lead to the **hospital**. After passing the hospital on the right, walk through a tunnel under the **A4** motorway – and step into another world.

The GR5 continues straight ahead on a bicycle path through a forest. After 650 metres, you arrive at a big signpost beside the **youth hostel**. Arms of the signpost point to different trails, all marked with the white-and-red blaze. Be sure to follow the marks for the GR5 and not, for example, the GR12

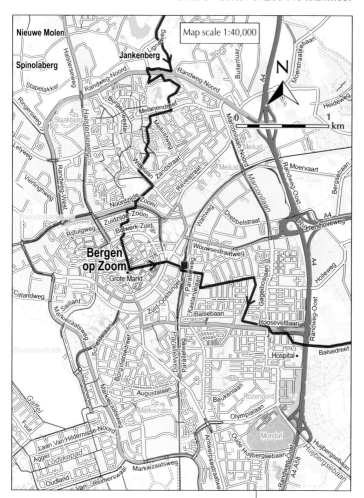

Map scale 1:40,000

(Paris-Amsterdam)! The GR5 turns right at the signpost, with the GR12, and then remains on a road when the GR12 forks right into the woods. The GR5 crosses an open area and then bends left on a sandy path into the forest.

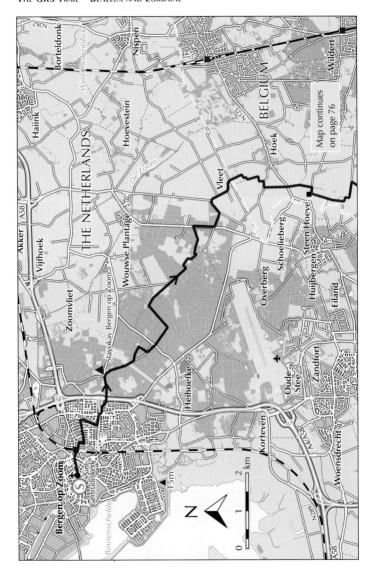

Map continues
on page 76

Continue on this path for more than 5km through the forest. It is pleasant, easy walking, and the route is generally well-marked. You are walking here through the **Wouwse Plantage**. Most of the surrounding area is closed to the public as private property or a nature reserve. Signs proclaiming 'Verboden Toegang' (entry forbidden) and variations on that theme bar many of the side trails. At one place (KP61), notices – including 'PRIVE GEEN VRIJ TOEGANG' – make it clear that you are not allowed to continue straight, but there is no GR mark in sight. Turn left here. There is a GR

Pillar (grenspaal) No 243 marks the border between the Kingdom of the Netherlands and the Kingdom of Belgium

75

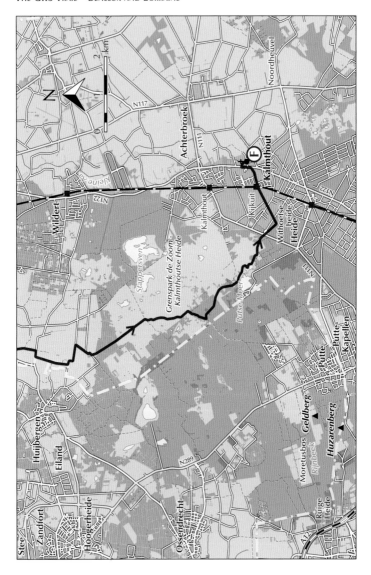

mark 100 metres after the turn. The GR5 then twists and turns around fields and through forests, with adequate waymarking.

The trail comes to a road (Plantagebaan) with traffic that seems rather fast after the calm of the forest: Turn right here and walk along a bicycle path. Then, after 600 metres, turn left on a road. Where that road leaves the forest (KP15, beside a bench), follow Schouwenbaan to the left and then right on Hollandsedreef to farmhouses in a place called **Vleet**. Where the main road curves left, continue straight and immediately fork left where a sign with a GR mark indicates a dead-end. Pay close attention now: somewhere in the next 50 metres, you will cross the international border and enter the Kingdom of Belgium. The only tangible evidence of the frontier is a lonely border pillar (*grenspaal*), No 243, in a field, surrounded by high grass.

> Belgians celebrate their independence from 1830, but the Dutch did not immediately accept the loss of their Belgian provinces, and some fighting took place. The strategic location of the Low Countries drew the Great Powers into the conflict. The **Treaty of London** (1839), signed by Great Britain, Austria, France, the German Confederation and Russia, as well as Belgium and the Netherlands, recognised Belgian independence and its neutrality. (German Chancellor Bethmann-Hollweg dismissed this treaty as a 'scrap of paper' in August 1914, as his troops marched into Belgium.) The delineation of the new Dutch-Belgian border – a complicated job, as a glance at a large-scale map shows – was completed in 1843. Pillar No 243 here is one of 369 that mark the border.

The route follows roads through open farmland here, and you will notice the striking difference from the polders of the Netherlands. The route is generally well-marked, but in May 2017 there was a little problem south of a farmhouse called 'Steen Hoeve': The track after KP68 had been ploughed over and planted with maize. Future walkers may find the old route restored – or a new one marked. Currently, after walking across those fields, turn left on Achterstehoevesraat and then right on Groenendriesstraat (KP67), which leads to the

A pond in the Grenspark de Zoom – Kalmthoutse Heide

wonderful **Grenspark De Zoom – Kalmthoutse Heide** (the Zoom – Kalmthout Heath Border Park).

The **Grenspark De Zoom – Kalmthoutse Heide** is an area of heath and sand dunes, interspersed with pine forests. At first glance, it appears to be an arid landscape, but there are, in fact, marshes and ponds that form an important part of the park's ecology.

Follow a well-marked path through the Grenspark for 7.5km. The trail leads to an exit from the park at a main road (**N111**). Cross the main road, pass a tourist information office on the right and turn left to walk 1.7km through residential neighbourhoods to the **church** at the centre of **Kalmthout**. Along the way, pass a train station, **Kijkuit**. The Kalmthout train station is further north. Kalmthout has everything you need for an overnight stay: B&Bs, restaurants and a supermarket.

STAGE 9
Kalmthout to Brecht

Start	Kalmthout
Finish	Brecht
Distance	22.8km
Time	5hr
Maps	1/7 Brasschaat; 2/8 Turnhout
Refreshments	Cafés/restaurants, bakeries and supermarkets in Wuustwezel
Transport	Railway service in Kalmthout and Brecht; De Lijn buses serve Kalmthout (670), Wuustwezel (640, 641) and Brecht (440, 600, 602, 605 and 620)
Accommodation	Hotels in Brecht

Walking from Kalmthout to Brecht, you might forget that the Kempen region, with its infertile soil and poor communications, was for a long time less developed than nearby areas. The Kempen still lags by some economic measures, but you will notice highly mechanised dairy farming and other agricultural activities as you walk through the fields. Both Kalmthout and Brecht – as well as Wuustwezel – are busy little towns.

The GR5 starts off north from the church in the centre of Kalmthout and then heads northeast on a bicycle path. Turn right at a junction, following a sign for Wuustwezel. Continue straight ahead on the path for 1km. ▶ Turn right at a main road (**N117**) and then immediately left on Dr J Goosenaerts Straat. Here, you enter a residential neighbourhood with well-trimmed lawns and hedges.

One of the dairy farms along this path offers fresh milk from a vending machine.

Following GR marks on Heiken and Witgoorsebaan, leave the village (**Achterbroek**) and cross fields devoted to cattle grazing and crops such as potatoes. After 2.5km, turn left on Bleekvenweg and then right into a forest, the **Pastoorsbos**, on a broad trail (KP27). ▶

Panels along the trail through the forest describe the local plants and animals.

Leaving the Pastoorsbos, walk along a road, Wouwerstraat, and after 350 metres turn left on Ponydreef.

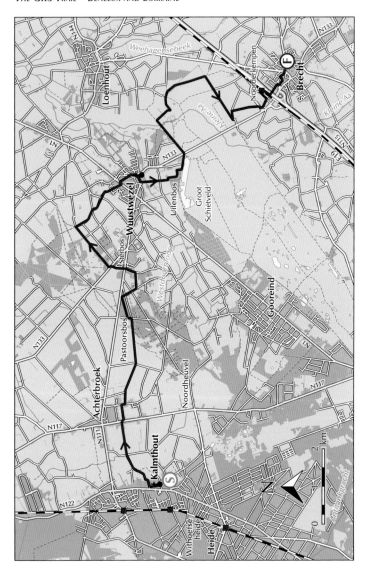

Dairy farm near Kalmthout

At the next intersection, turn left on Blekenberg. Skirting a village, **Sterbos**, cross a main road (**N111**) and continue straight to the next main road (**N133**). Cross this, turn left and then immediately right to enter woods on a broad dirt path. A pleasant, 1.5km walk through the woods and open fields brings you to a crossroads (KP11), where a right turn is clearly marked. Follow a road here for 2km through fields and past large farm buildings. Walking on Hageldruisakker, enter a residential neighbourhood with stark, modern architecture. In the commercial centre of **Wuustwezel**, which you reach at the N1, there are supermarkets, cafés, restaurants, bakeries and other shops.

After crossing the main road, the waymarked route leads you along a quiet path between apartment buildings.

> In May 2017, that path was blocked by a construction project. It was necessary to take a **detour** on a road to the left, Kloosterstraat, parallel to the GR route. After 300 metres, that road curves to the right in front of a church. About 100 metres further, the road intersects the GR5 and you turn left on Gaasthuisdreef to rejoin the trail.

Walk south on a bicycle path for 800 metres in open country and then enter a forest, the **Uilenbos**, on the left. Follow the well-marked trail through those woods. You may hear loud gunfire here. The Groot Schietveld, an army training area, covers a vast expanse of territory to the south, so stay on the marked trails!

The GR5 does not, of course, enter the Groot Scheitveld: At the edge of the Uilenbos, turn left on a broad, dirt road. Reaching a main road (**N133**), continue straight (northeast), first in forest and then open country. Cross a small river (the **Kleine Aa**), and after 150 metres turn right on a dirt road and then a narrow path shaded by trees along it. The path turns left in the woods after 500 metres and then curves gradually to the right. Walking through open fields now, turn right (KP59) and head southwest. After 1.5km, turn sharply left onto a paved road and, 150 metres further, right on Kleinheikensweg.

As you approach a busy road (Papbosstraat), leave Kleinheikensweg and cross the road at a convenient point opposite a hotel. ◄ Follow the small road beside the hotel and then turn left on Oudaenstraat, which leads to Brecht's **Noorderkempen** railway station.

At the time of writing, the Hotel Boshoeve here had recently closed.

Bovine welcome committee outside Brecht

To reach the centre of Brecht, go through a tunnel under the railway line and follow GR marks through the city (1km). Brecht offers full services for food and lodging. A comfortable hotel (with a good restaurant) is within a converted windmill.

STAGE 10
Brecht to Zoersel

Start	Brecht
Finish	Zoersel (youth hostel)
Distance	13.5km
Time	3hr
Maps	2/8 Turnhout; 16 Lier
Refreshments	Cafés at Brug 11 and Westmalle Abbey
Transport	Train service at Brecht; De Lijn buses serve Westmalle Abbey (410) and Gagelhoflaan (for youth hostel) (411, 414)
Accommodation	Youth hostel and hotels in Zoersel

The GR5 leaves Brecht and follows a bicycle path beside the Dessel-Turnhout-Shoten Canal. You cross the canal on a drawbridge and walk across fields and through a forest to Westmalle Abbey, one of the best known of the Belgian abbeys. Since this is a short stage, you may have time to pause at the café near the abbey to sample the fine Trappist beer that is brewed there. Then it's a short walk to the youth hostel or on along the road into Zoersel for other accommodation.

This stage begins at the intersection of Hofstraat and Gasthuisstraat (the **N115**) in the centre of Brecht. Walk a few paces southwest on Gasthuisstraat and then turn left into a narrow passage that leads to a park. Walk through the park beside the *gemeentehuis* (town hall), a large brick building, and continue through a parking lot. Turn left on Vaartstraat and then right on Eyndovensteenweg. At a fork in the road, turn left on Van Pulstraat. Walk through a residential area and turn right on Duivelstraatje, which leads into the countryside. At the end of this road, continue left on Paepestraat.

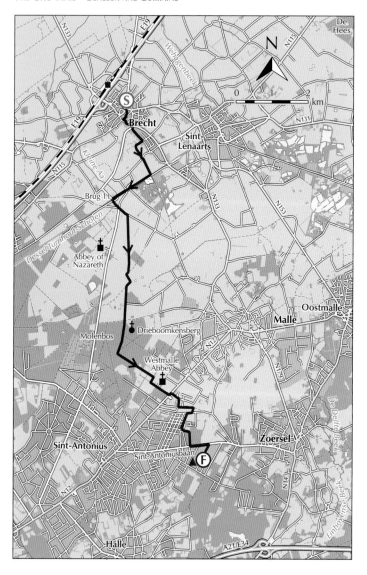

After a kilometre on Paepestraat, you reach the Dessel-Turnhout-Shoten Canal. Turn right here and walk 1.5km on the cycle path beside the canal to a drawbridge, **Brug 11**. Painted notices on the pavement, with pictographs, remind you that: 'Het jaagpad is er voor iedereen!' (The towpath is for everyone!): walkers, runners, cyclists and service vehicles.

A quiet path between the Dessel-Turnhout-Shoten Canal and the Molenbos

Cross the canal over Brug 11 (after pausing, perhaps, for refreshment at the café beside the bridge) and walk 300 metres straight ahead on Westmallebaan. Turn right at a brick farmhouse called 'Scheve Zuid Hoeve' (KP48) and walk 3.5km along a dirt road through agricultural fields. ▶ The path continues straight ahead for 800 metres after it enters a forest (**Molenbos**), passing a shrine (and a good bench for lunch) called **Drieboomkensberg**. This is pleasant walking, on a broad dirt trail, with a chorus of birds singing in the trees. After a left turn (not well marked), the walls of **Westmalle Abbey** appear ahead of you. The trail goes around two sides of the abbey and reaches the N12.

In the distance to the right, the tower of the Cistercian Abbey of Nazareth rises above the treeline.

The **Abbey of Our Lady of the Sacred Heart of Westmalle** was founded in 1794 by a group of monks from La Trappe in France, who had fled the Revolution. It acquired the full status of a Trappist

85

Abbey in 1836. In the same year, the monks began brewing beer – initially for their own consumption, later for sale to the public. Westmalle Abbey now belongs to the International Trappist Association and conforms to its requirements: a 'Trappist' beer must be brewed within or near a monastery under the management of the monastery, and profits from sales of the beer must provide for the needs of the community or be devoted to social services.

Cross the road and follow GR marks to the left of the Trappisten Café and then right on Lacroixlaan into a residential neighbourhood. At a fork in the road, follow Oude Kastanjedreef to the right. Where the road curves right, bear left on a dirt path that leads to Rode-Kruislaan. Continue on a residential street and again a dirt path in the woods. Turn right at KP54, then right on Mostheuvelstraat and left on Wilgenlaan. This road leads to a roundabout: Bear left on Essendreef, which becomes Boslaan where it curves to the right. After 500 metres on Boslaan, turn left to walk beside a busy road, **Sint-Antoniusbaan**.

Turn right after 600 metres onto Gagelhoflaan, and walk another 100m. The Zoersel youth hostel, **Jeugdherberg Gagelhof**, is on the right. The friendly, volunteer staff of the youth hostel offer dinner – and Trappist beer. Being on the GR5, Jeugdherberg Gagelhof is a convenient place to stop, but there are other options 3km east along Sint-Antoniusbaan in **Zoersel** or 3km west in **Sint-Antonius**. See Appendix B.

STAGE 11
Zoersel to Herentals

Start	Zoersel (youth hostel)
Finish	Herentals
Distance	21.5km
Time	5hr
Map	16 Lier
Refreshments	Cafés along the route – Boshuisje and Manege de Heide – have irregular opening hours.
Transport	De Lijn buses serve Zoersel (411, 414) and Herentals (numerous lines); rail service in Herentals
Accommodation	Hotels in Herentals

The GR5 continues along easy paths through forests. When the trail emerges in open country, you will see horses grazing on lush grass. The urban stretches of this stage are interesting, particularly the striking modern architecture of some houses, but the best walking comes at the end of the day: a delightful stroll along the tree-lined banks of the Kleine Nete.

Starting from the youth hostel, turn right on Gagelhoflaan. At the end of the road, turn left on Antwerpsedreef and then right into a forest where there is wooden shelter and picnic table. The trail starts as a broad, sandy path and then, after turning left (KP48), narrows as it winds through the woods (**Zoerselbos**).

The GR5 intersects two other GR trails here, and the waymarking (including a signpost) is ambiguous.

Three kilometres from the start, you arrive at the **Boshuisje** (forest cottage), built in the early 19th century. ▶ Carry on in the same direction and bear left when you pass a bench. The trail follows a path beside a road and then the road itself as it crosses a bridge over a motorway (A21/E34). After the bridge, continue straight through an intersection. The GR5 marks here identify the trail clearly: 'GR5 Noordzee Riviera'. ▶

Turn left at the **N14** and walk beside it on a bicycle path for a short distance, then turn right on a dirt road (Zandbeekstraat) into the woods. The road becomes paved, but the route soon turns right on another dirt path. After

In addition to these new waymarks, you will see some old ones: fading white-and-red blazes painted on trees.

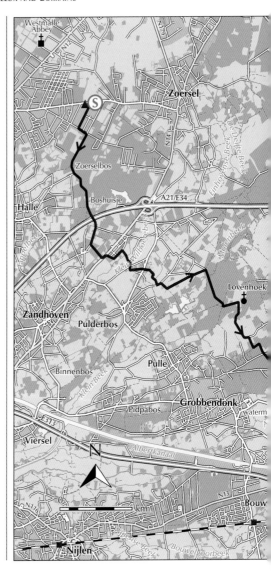

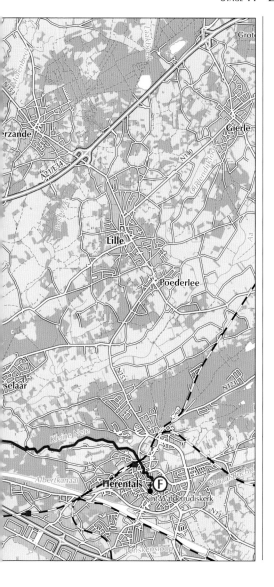

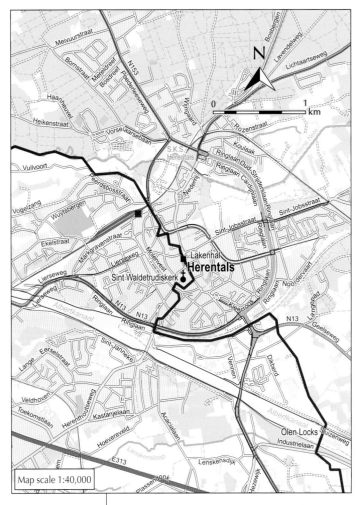

passing under high-voltage power lines, you will see a wind-mill (Molen Pulderbos) in the distance. Turn left, cross a road and continue straight ahead on Masternbaan. Walk around the Pulderbos football pitch and follow a trail to a road.

Turn left here (KP14) and then right at the first road, Boskant, where there is a picnic table. The trail curves left and continues northeast for 1.2km to a crossing in the forest. It turns right here (KP17) and continues for another 1.1km in the forest. Near KP73, turn right on Heirbaan and then immediately left on a path into the woods. Turn right at the **Kapel van Lovenhoek** (KP74) and follow a dirt road through cultivated fields. At a group of farm buildings (KP76), turn right and re-enter the woods. After left and right turns, cross a road and continue in the same direction (southeast). Leave the woods at KP38 and enter a residential area on Grensstraat, which becomes Korentenbossen. Pass the ruins of the Neerhof castle on the left. Then, near the confluence of the Kleine Nete and the Aa Rivers, turn left on Watermolenweg, which leads, as its name implies, to the old **Grobbendonk watermill**.

> There are records of a **watermill** at Grobbendonk from the 11th century. In 1254, the mill was the property of Saint Bernard Abbey of Hemiksem. It was used to grind grain and press vegetable oils. The current structure dates back to the 17th century – and is still in operation today.

After walking 1.2km on Watermolenweg, turn left on a road (Troon). Another 1.2km brings you to an intersection:

A pleasant path beside the Kleine Nete

You may see young people going downstream in kayaks and on rafts. Give them a wave!

turn left here, cross the **Kleine Nete** and turn right on a narrow dirt path that follows the stream. Apart from one 500m section, where the trail turns away from the stream and crosses an open field, the GR5 follows the Kleine Nete for 3km, all the way to **Herentals**. This is a charming, tranquil walk. ◄

From the point where the GR5 crosses a bridge and leaves the Kleine Nete, it's 1.5km to the centre of Herentals, passing the **railway station** along the way. The route is well-marked, but you could just follow signs to the centre, where you will find all services, including hotels, restaurants and shops.

STAGE 12
Herentals to Westerlo

Start	Herentals
Finish	Westerlo (youth hostel)
Distance	16.5km
Time	3hr 45min
Map	16 Lier
Refreshments	Cafés/restaurants and food stores in Olen; café/restaurant near Tongerlo Abbey
Transport	Rail service in Herentals; De Lijn buses serve Herentals (numerous lines), Olen (305, 540 and 542), Tongerlo (540) and Westerlo (490 and 491)
Accommodation	Youth hostel, B&B and Tongerlo Abbey in Westerlo

This stage combines a variety of interesting elements: a walk along one canal and over a major lock complex of another canal. As is common in Flanders, you walk beside agricultural fields and through forests. There is a town midway through the stage, Olen, where you can pause for refreshment. Shortly before arrival in Westerlo, you pass Tongerlo, one of the great abbeys of Flanders. Tongerlo Abbey offers accommodation and boasts an excellent copy of Leonardo da Vinci's mural 'The Last Supper'.

Starting at the 16th century Lakenhal in the centre of Herentals, walk south on Bovenrij. Turn right after 170 metres

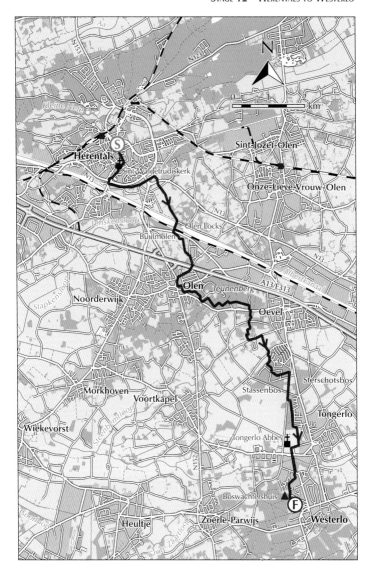

on Paepestraat and pass a church, Sint-Waldetrudiskerk, on the right. Follow GR marks along Sint-Waldetrudiskerkstraat and then Noorderwijksebaan. Pass a supermarket (closed on Sundays) and then turn left on Herenthoutseweg, which leads to an intersection with the **N13**. Cross the **Bocholt-Herentals Canal** here and turn left to walk along a path beside the canal.

> The **Bocholt-Herentals Canal** and the **Albert Canal** meet in Herentals. The former was one of several canals constructed in the 19th century to connect industrial areas in the Meuse River valley with the Scheldt River and its port, Antwerp. The construction of the Albert Canal in the 1930s, linking Liège to Antwerp, reduced the commercial role of the Bocholt-Herentals Canal. The Albert Canal is 160km long, with six sets of locks rising 56m.

Walk along the Bocholt-Herentals Canal for 1.3km, passing under a main road bridge along the way. The GR5 then turns right on a trail. Cross the N13 and continue straight ahead on Vennen into the countryside. At the **Olen Locks** (Sluizencomplex Olen) cross over the **Albert Canal** and walk past a modern wind turbine in a field with an old windmill, the **Buulmolen**. The trail continues to the left of the windmill and winds through fields and woods. It passes under the **A13/E313** motorway and enters **Olen**. There are shops, cafés and restaurants here, as well as benches well-suited for a picnic lunch.

> A **fountain** in the centre of Olen in the form of three large beer tankards recalls a legendary tale about Emperor Charles V. Ask someone to explain why one tankard has a single handle, another has two and the third tankard has three handles…

At the traffic light in the centre of Olen, turn left on Bulestraat and then, after 150 metres, right on a narrow path, Schoolpaddeke. Follow the waymarks as the GR5 enters the woods and meanders through the **Domein Teunenberg**. After crossing a road, continue straight ahead on Beverstraat. Turn left at the next road and walk beside it for 400 metres. Then turn right on a dirt path, Hommelstraat, which enters

Trienekant. Turn right on the road at the end of Hommelstraat and then, 100 metres further, left on Prior Backxlaan. After 125 metres, turn right beside a bench into a forest, the **Sterschotsbos**.

The path through the Sterschotsbos leads to a bicycle path, Oevelse Dreef. Turn right here and walk south, parallel to a road. The GR5 turns left after 800 metres and then right to continue in the same general direction through a residential area. Soon, with a football pitch on the left, the belfry of **Tongerlo Abbey** comes into view, rising above the trees to the right. Approaching the Abbey, the trail turns right to pass before its main entrance.

> Tongerlo Abbey (www.tongerlo.org) is a Premonstratensian monastery founded around 1130 by Norbertine monks from Saint Michael's Abbey in Antwerp. The Abbey's museum has a fine copy of Leonardo da Vinci's 'The Last Supper', painted around 1520, with details that are no longer visible in the original.

The GR5 turns left in front of Tongerlo Abbey and follows a path south, beside a road leading into Westerlo. It passes a café that, naturally, serves Tongerlo beer (and many others).

Tongerlo Abbey

At the end of the road, continue straight ahead on a path (Boerenkrijglaan) past a football pitch and through woods. Continue on Papedreef to the youth hostel, **Jeugdherberg Boswachtershuis**, at the edge of the forest. This is a convenient place to spend the night, but there are other options for accommodation in the area, including Tongerlo Abbey itself and a B&B.

STAGE 13
Westerlo to Scherpenheuvel

Start	Westerlo (youth hostel)
Finish	Scherpenheuvel
Distance	24km
Time	5hr 15min
Map	24 Aarschot
Refreshments	Cafés and shops in Averbode and off the GR5 in Blauberg and Zichem
Transport	Rail service in Zichem and Testelt; De Lijn buses serve Westerlo (490, 491), Blauberg (491, 492), Averbode (36), Zichem (36) and Scherpenheuvel (35, 36)
Accommodation	Hotel in Testelt; B&B in Scherpenheuvel
Note	If the Demerbroeken is flooded and you need to take the variant path, this will add 2.3km to your day.

This stage combines several of the best elements of hiking across northern Flanders: pleasant trails through forests and across heathland, a path beside a small, meandering river and a visit to one of the great abbeys, Averbode. If you happen to walk this stage on Ascension Day, you could join an organised walk between Tongerlo and Averbode Abbeys, the Abdijentocht.

The GR5 continues directly into the forest from the youth hostel. A broad, straight path runs southwest 500 metres to a crossroads called De Ster (The Star). The GR5 turns obliquely to the left here and continues straight through the forest for 1km, crossing a wooden bridge over a road along the

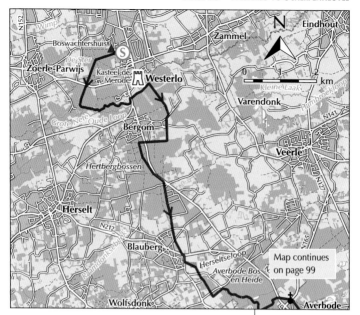

way. ▶ The trail bends to the left and reaches a paved path beside the **Grote Nete**, a river that is not much bigger than the Kleine Nete that you walked along at the end of Stage 11. Turn left on the path (shared with cyclists and runners) and

The route is well-marked, and there are benches here and there beside the trail.

Map continues on page 99

Grote Nete

The large building
on the other side of
the Grote Nete is
the Kasteel (Castle)
de Merode, the
oldest elements of
which were built in
the 14th century.

enjoy the 2.3km walk beside the river, interrupted only by crossing the **N19**, where the GR5 changes from the right to the left bank. ◄ The river meanders through a forest and lush, long grass covers its banks.

Finally, at a bridge beside the remains of an old sluice and dam, Het Trammeke, it is time to leave the Grote Nete. Do not cross the bridge, but instead turn right. Upon reaching a road, turn right and walk a short distance before turning left (Berglaan). Walking south, skirt the town of **Bergom**. Turn right (KP27) and enter the **Hertbergbossen** (Hertberg Woods). About 150 metres after crossing a road, turn left and continue walking through the woods (south and southeast). Along the way, the trail passes a picnic area with parking stands for dozens of bicycles and an impressive 'insect hotel'.

Leaving the woods, walk past a residential neighbourhood of Blauberg and a football pitch on the right. At a main road (**N212**), pause to observe the striking modern design of a chemist (drug store). Then cross the main road and continue south for a short distance before turning left into the forest.

This is the route of the **Abdijentocht**, a walk between Tongerlo and Averbode Abbeys that attracts thousands of participants each year on Ascension Day (39 days after Easter Sunday). In odd-numbered years, people walk from Tongerlo to Averbode; in even-numbered years, they walk in the opposite direction.

Averbode Abbey is
a Premonstratensian
abbey that was
founded about 1134.
A recent renovation
of the courtyard
installed a beautiful
reflecting pool in front
of the abbey church.

On a sunny day,
ice cream vendors
will be busy here.

The trail leads to the **Averbode Bos en Heide** (Averbode Woods and Heath), an open area of heath, marshland and ponds. Watch for a right turn at a fork in the trail near a pond (KP104). The trail meanders through a forest of towering pine trees. Finally, after a right turn, **Averbode** comes into view. Leave the forest here: cross the N212 again and follow a paved path toward **Averbode Abbey**. ◄ Take a moment to step inside and admire the baroque church and its courtyard.

The GR5 bends to the right in front of the abbey entrance and crosses a park. ◄ There is a café-restaurant near the southeast corner of the park. Approaching the end of the park, the GR5 turns sharply right and follows a road, Judocus Pauwelslaan, two blocks to the N212. Cross and continue

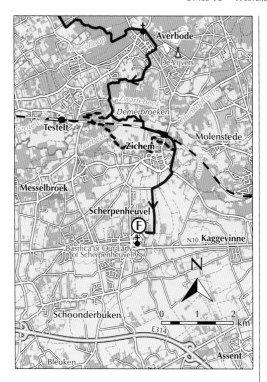

straight ahead on what has become Melkerijstraat. Turn left at the end of that street and, following the GR marks, walk through a residential neighbourhood with an interesting variety of architectural styles and a distinctive memorial modelled on a miner's lantern.

The route enters a forest interspersed with open fields. After passing ponds that are part of a water treatment system, turn left behind a building with the words 'TER ELZEN' on it, and then right. Follow a good trail for a short but pleasant walk through the woods. When you reach a road, turn left and walk along it passing ponds on your left.

There is an important fork in the trail here (KP298): the main GR5 takes the left fork and goes through a protected area, the **Demerbroeken**. There are ponds and scattered trees in this heathland and cattle graze here to keep the vegetation down. Leave the Demerbroeken area by walking toward and then along the railway line.

The Demerbroeken may be flooded after heavy rain, in which case the **Demer Variant** (the right fork at KP298) is the preferred route. Just follow the clear signage until you rejoin the main route. (The Demer Variant is 4.9km long, compared with the main GR5's 2.6km between the same two points.)

Basilica of Our Lady of Scherpenheuvel

When you reach the N212 (yet again), turn right and walk past the **Zichem** railway station. Immediately after crossing the tracks, turn left, walk a short distance beside the railway and then follow a trail on the right that enters the woods. ▶ Cross a bridge over the **Demer** river, where the Demer Variant trail re-joins the main GR5.

Follow a dirt path for a few hundred metres, then turn left on a road, followed shortly by a right turn on another road (Bredeveldstraat). The dome and belfry of **Scherpenheuvel Basilica** appear on the horizon to the left. The GR5 branches slightly to the left off the road and onto a bicycle path. Just a couple of hundred metres further (KP139), turn left onto a dirt road (Peerdskerkhofstraet) and walk south. Take a road to the right 400 metres before the main road that leads to the northern side of the city and then turn left off that road after 450 metres to reach the centre of Scherpenheuvel.

Continue straight ahead at the railway station on the N212 for refreshments in Zichem.

The Spanish Archdukes Albert and Isabella commissioned the **Basilica of Our Lady of Scherpenheuvel** – the first baroque church in the Netherlands (1627) – to give thanks for the expulsion of Protestants from the Southern Netherlands. Scherpenheuvel is now a popular pilgrimage destination.

STAGE 14
Scherpenheuvel to Diest

Start	Scherpenheuvel
Finish	Diest (Grote Markt)
Distance	10km
Time	2hr 15min
Maps	24 Aarschot, 25 Hasselt
Refreshments	None until the shopping centre on the outskirts of Diest
Transport	Rail service in Diest; De Lijn buses serve Scherpenheuvel (35, 36) and Diest (numerous)
Accommodation	Hotels, B&Bs and campground with trekkershutten in Diest

This is a short, easy stage. Diest is one of the most attractive and interesting cities in the Flemish section of the GR5, so you might aim to arrive in Diest in time for lunch and some exploration of the city in the afternoon. If you prefer not to pause here, you could combine this stage with the next one, ending in Lummen: the walk from Scherpenheuvel to Lummen is about 25km.

Scherpenheuvel Basilica stands in the centre of the town, surrounded by a park and a seven-sided road with shops, restaurants and a hotel. To reach the GR5 from here, walk southeast on Diestsestraat to the **N10**. Turn left and walk 200 metres east to where the GR5, coming from the north,

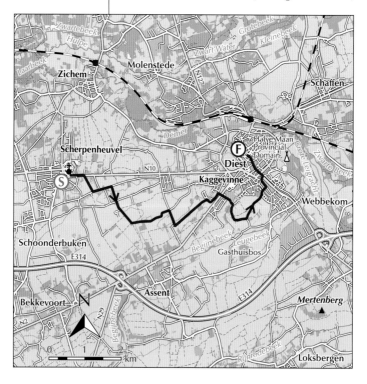

intersects the N10. Turn right here and walk along a pleasant, grass path between fields. At the end of the path, turn left on Groenstraat. About 350 metres after passing a small chapel, turn right on a path through an open field. Watch carefully for this turn, as the GR mark on a power line pylon is easy to miss.

After crossing a road, continue straight ahead on Roeterstraat, which soon becomes a dirt path. After a slight rise in the path, the GR5 intersects the GR512. Turn left here and enjoy the view over the undulating fields, interspersed with woods. ▸ Walk a kilometre to a road: Turn right here and walk 400 metres along the road. Just after the road curves right, turn left on Galgenberg. The paved path runs northeast above fields. A shaded bench offers a place to pause and admire the view.

You are likely to see horses grazing.

Enter **Kaggevinne**, on the outskirts of Diest, and turn right to cross a busy main road (the **N2**). ▸ Continuing straight ahead on Reustraat, pass a shopping centre with a supermarket and a restaurant.

The GR512 separates from the GR5 just before this turn and follows a more direct route to the centre of Diest.

The GR5 then curves around the southern side of **Diest**, first turning right (south) after the shopping centre and then left. Walk up a dirt road on a hill with a view of Diest. Parts of this route have few GR marks. Continue straight past a path to the right, beside some apartment buildings, and then walk

The GR5 follows a path upon the old ramparts of Diest

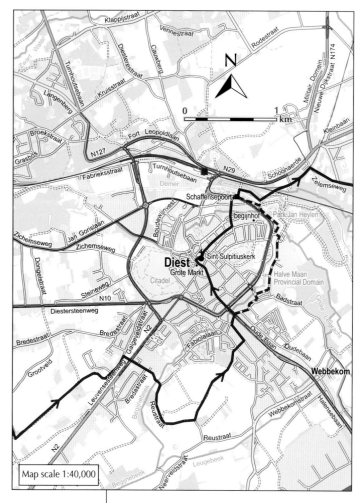

past a primary school on the left. Entering a residential area, the route is better marked. Cross the N2 and continue on Wijngaardstraat in the same direction. Arrive at a café beside the **Begijnbeek** river.

Here the GR5 turns right and follows a broad path along the eastern side of Diest passing the **Halve Maan Provincial Domain** (a large recreation centre with a swimming pool and *trekkershutten*) on the right.

To reach the **Grote Markt**, leave the GR5 and cross the river to walk straight ahead to the centre of the city.

The earliest record of **Diest** dates back to 877. With its strategic location on the Demer river and the trade route between Bruges and Cologne, Diest prospered with the cloth industry in the Middle Ages. The town came under the control of the Counts of Nassau in 1499 and later the princes of Orange-Nassau, the ruling family of the Netherlands. Dutch monarchs still hold the title 'Lord of Diest'. Diest's history has left noteworthy buildings in the city, such as St Sulpitiuskerk. Most interesting, perhaps, is the *begijnhof*, one of 13 Flemish béguinages (lay religious communities) on a UN World Heritage List and once home to 400 women and five convents.

STAGE 15
Diest to Lummen

Start	Diest (Grote Markt)
Finish	Lummen
Distance	16.5km
Time	3hr 30 min
Map	25 Hasselt
Refreshments	None, until a restaurant on the N725 main road 2km before Lummen
Transport	Rail service in Diest; De Lijn buses serve Diest (numerous) and Lummen (35c)
Accommodation	Hotel and B&B in Lummen (or Viversel, c2km further on)

This stage does not manage to avoid all major roads – a motorway cuts across its path – but there is a lot of good forest walking between Diest and Lummen. Indeed, there is one place where it would be easy to get lost in the woods. As if to make up for the pavement, some sections of the forest trails may be flooded or muddy, requiring little detours.

The logical place to rejoin the GR5 on this stage is the Schaffensepoort, an old fortified gate on the northern side of Diest. Walk from Grote Markt on Koning Albertstraat and Schaffensestraat to the **Schaffensepoort**.

If you are coming from the Halve Maan accommodation, follow the waymarked GR5 around the northeastern edge of the city. Turn left on a bridge and then immediately right on a trail that climbs onto a tree-lined path on the old city ramparts. Descend from the ramparts beside an old sluice gate, turn left on the bridge there and then right on a trail beside the Demer river. (You could turn right on this bridge and join the GR5 on the other side, thereby skipping the Schaffensepoort.) Descend to the inner side of the ramparts and walk along a bicycle path a short distance to the Schaffensepoort.

An old bridge offers a possible shortcut across the Demer

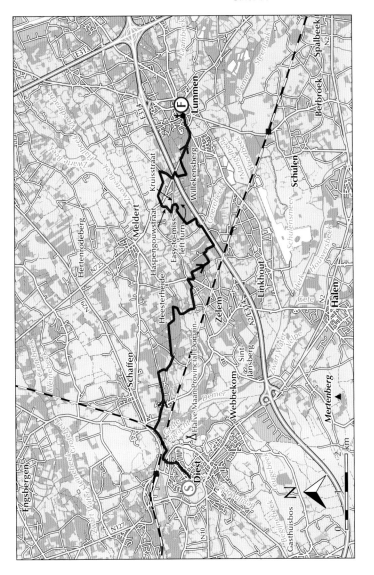

There is a large signpost here with arms indicating the 'NOORDZEE – RIVIÈRA' trail. Follow the arm that points to 'BOKRIJK – VISE – ARDENNEN'. Walk through the Schaffensepoort – a tunnel under the ramparts – and over a bridge to join a trail that enters the woods on the right. This trail leads to a road near the sluice gate bridge.

Turn left on the road, cross a bridge over a railway line and then bend to the right onto a bicycle path that runs parallel to a disused railway line. The GR5 turns its back on the railway after 500 metres and enters the woods to the right. Emerging from the woods, continue in the same direction on a busy street (Zelemseweg) for 350 metres and then fork left on a quieter street (Barenbergseweg). Pass a sign indicating the exit from Schaffen and enter another forest. Turn right on a trail and then, after a short distance, turn left on a road (Herzerheiweg, which soon becomes Molenstraat). Where the road forks, turn left on Heesstraat and then, 100 metres further, right on a trail into the woods (called the Heesterheide). The trail continues straight (east) for 800 metres and then turns on a diagonal to the right, followed shortly by a left diagonal (heading east again). Finally, the trail turns sharply right, leaves the woods and crosses a stream called **Zwarte Beek**.

Here, the GR5 enters a village called **Zelem**. Turn left on a road and follow waymarks through a residential neighbourhood and then right on a larger road. After walking along this road for a short distance, turn left on a trail that enters the woods. There are some gaps in the waymarking in these woods, starting with a right turn 150 metres after you enter the woods, which is not marked. Walk in the woods to a road. Turn right here and then left at a T-junction with a wide road. A motorway (A2/E314) – audible but not visible – runs parallel to this road. ◀

A short side-trail leads to a memorial to the six crewmen of an RAF Lancaster bomber, shot down here in February 1945.

Turn left at the end of this road and then immediately right on a dirt road. Enter a forest, curving left at a fork and then right on a smaller trail. The conditions of this trail make it a bit of an adventure, as there are flooded and muddy sections that you avoid by walking along parallel tracks. Watch carefully for GR marks, which are not always in clear view.

There is one place that is particularly problematic. A standard GR mark for a left turn is painted on a tree just before the trail appears to fork. However, trees on both trails in that fork have the standard mark indicating the wrong direction (a red-and-white X). So where is the trail? It turns out that you should push through high grass on the left and pick up a faint trail through trees leading to a road (Kruisstraat), where there is a reassuring GR mark to the left.

Walk 200 metres along the road and turn sharply right on Haspengouwstraat. Follow that road to a main road (**N725**): Cross the main road and continue in the same direction on a dirt road. After 150 metres, the GR5 curves gradually to the right where there is also a trail to the left. There is a GR mark on a tree in the distance, confirming that you are headed in the right direction. The trail passes a venerable tree, 'De Duizendjarige Eik' (the Thousand Year Oak).

The GR5 continues on a grassy path through open fields. At the end of a field, turn right and then right again on a road. The road leads back to the N725. Turn left to cross a bridge over the motorway (A2/E314). Immediately after crossing the bridge, turn right onto a dirt road that enters the forest. This is another trail that may be flooded and muddy in places. It turns left twice to return on a diagonal (northeast) to the N725.

Turn right and walk beside the main road. It is not a good place to walk, but you do not have to stay on it for long. Just after a grove of enormous rhododendrons on the left, the GR5 follows a trail into the woods on the right side

Rhododendrons near Lummen

of the main road. Watch carefully for this turn to escape the verge-walking. The trail leads to a secondary road. Turn left here to walk into the centre of **Lummen**. If you are planning to spend the night in Lummen, bear in mind that some hotels and other accommodation are located on the eastern side of the city and further on in Viversel (just off map to the east).

STAGE 16
Lummen to Stokrooie

Start	Lummen
Finish	Stokrooie
Distance	18.5km
Time	4hr 15min
Map	25 Hasselt
Refreshments	Cafés/restaurants and food stores in Viversel and Bolderberg; none in Stokrooie
Transport	De Lijn bus 35c serves Lummen, Thiewinkel, Viversel, Bolderberg and Stokrooie by a circuitous route
Accommodation	Hotels in Viversel and Bolderberg; B&Bs in Stokrooie

This stage passes through an area with a lot of commercial activity, two motorways, a canal and a motor racetrack (which is very noisy on a race day). The meandering GR5 manages to avoid most (but not all) of that. The best part of this stage is the walk through the Bolderberg Nature Reserve, an area of forests, heath and sand dunes. The trail passes numerous ponds and, in one case, crosses one on a wooden walkway. Overall, then, this makes for an enjoyable day's walking.

Connect with the GR5 in the southwest corner of Lummen's central square. Walk southeast from here on Neerstraat, then bear right on Schulensebaan when the road forks. Go straight through a roundabout (pausing, perhaps, for coffee at the café here) and then follow Burgemeester Briersstraat at an angle to the left. Soon you are in the country, walking through fields and woods. Within 200 metres, the GR5 leaves the pavement and forks to the right on a dirt road beside a picnic table.

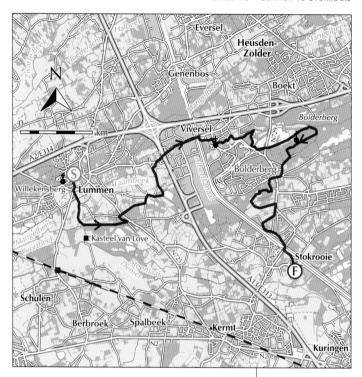

This road arrives in front of the ornamental gate of
the **Kasteel van Loye**. Turn left (east) here and walk 1.8km
through a forest on a broad dirt path. The path approaches
a major road but does not yet cross it: Turn left on
Nessesheidestraat, right on Muggenhoekstraat and then cross
the road (**N725**). Continue straight ahead on Kievitstraat into
another forest. Turn left at a T-junction with a paved road.
The route becomes dirt again and it's a pleasant walk in the
woods. Turn left at a large pond. The trail leaves the forest
and enters a residential area, first on Vijverstraat and then
Watermolenstraat. Turn right on Lammbeekstraat and right
again on a busy, commercial street, Rekhovenstraat.

A 1.5km walk on Rekhovenstraat (which passes under
the **A13/E313** motorway, not far from an interchange with

the **A2/E314**) leads to the GR5's second crossing of the **Albert Canal**. Just after the canal, descend an embankment on the right and then turn left on a small road, Laarstraat. The road enters **Viversel**, which has a café, restaurant and food store.

Viversel is also the home of the **Zolder race track**. If it's a race day, you will hear the roaring engines, but you will not see them: the GR5 wisely avoids the track and wanders off into the forest.

Turn left after the **church** in Viversel on a trail beside a small stream. The trail through the forest is well-marked. Pass a pond where men sit quietly and tend long fishing poles resting upon little stands. The trail leads to the N729. Cross,

Kluis van O.-L. Vrouw van Loreto near Bolderberg

turn your back to the Zolder racetrack entrance and walk into the forest on a wide dirt path.

Soon, the land opens into an area of trees (dominated by towering conifers), open heath, marshes and ponds. This is the **Bolderberg Nature Reserve** (Natuurgebied Bolderberg). It is a lovely place to walk, and the GR5 provides a full opportunity to appreciate it as it takes a long loop – first northeast and then back southwest. On that return leg, pass the **Kluis van O-L Vrouw van Loreto** (the Hermitage of Our Lady of Loreto) and walk over a sand dune that rises above the surrounding forest. ▶

The Kluis van O-L Vrouw van Loreto was built in 1673 for Lambert Hoelen uit Diepenbeek who had been impressed by the hermitage in an Italian town, Loreto.

Leave the nature reserve by the southwest and enter **Bolderberg**, a small town. Walking along a road that crosses the N729 again, you pass hotels, restaurants, cafés and other services that may be convenient. Turn left into Het Domein Bovy. For a trekker, the leading feature of this recreational area is the boardwalk that crosses two ponds. Walking across those ponds, you are likely to see families of geese and other birds enjoying their own promenade on the water.

Leave the Bovy Domain after the second pond on a path that curves left, past a tennis club, to a road. Headed northeast through a residential area, the road meets the N729 again. Turn right but then almost immediately continue straight ahead on a smaller road (Pannewinning, opposite a supermarket) as the N729 curves left. Take the first road on a diagonal to the right, Bruynebossstraat, which then curves left after 400 metres.

The road approaches the Albert Canal and becomes Schuurstraat. Just after passing a B&B on the left (a good place to spend the night if you are not continuing on to the centre of Stokrooie), you reach Bredestraat. Turn right here and walk a short distance to the Albert Canal. Turn left and walk along the bicycle path to the bridge visible in the distance.

For another crossing of the Albert Canal, walk under the road bridge and then up to the road. Cross the **canal bridge**, turn left and walk a short distance on the bicycle path beside the canal before bending right on a road into the centre of **Stokrooie**, where there is a B&B with a café, but no other services.

STAGE 17
Stokrooie to Bokrijk Provincial Domain

Start	Stokrooie
Finish	Bokrijk Provincial Domain (Open Air Museum)
Distance	16km
Time	3hr 45min
Map	25 Hasselt
Refreshments	Cafés/restaurants at Herkenrode Abbey and the Kiewit Domain
Transport	De Lijn bus routes 35c (between Stokrooie and Hasselt), G4 and 46 (serving Bokrijk); train service at Bokrijk train stop
Accommodation	B&B in Hasselt (2km from GR5) and youth hostel (2.7km from GR5, see map for direct route)
Note	If you take the variant route via Hasselt you will add 2.5km to today's walk.

Most of this stage passes through open country and forests. There is only occasional walking in built-up areas. Along the way, there is a variant that provides the option of walking through Hasselt. This would be useful if you wish to use public transport. In addition, of course, Hasselt is an interesting destination in its own right. If you prefer to stay on forest trails, continue on the main GR5. There is currently no accommodation within the Bokrijk Provincial Domain, but there are good options nearby.

In the centre of Stokrooie, walk west on Sint-Amandusstraat and then turn left on Schabbestraat, a small road that soon becomes a dirt trail in the woods. Continuing straight through fields, you will see **Herkenrode Abbey** on the left. Turn left to pass the abbey entrance, where there is a picnic area, a café and a shop.

Herkenrode Abbey was founded in 1179 and transformed into a Cistercian nunnery in 1217. Herkenrode became an important pilgrimage site, owing in part to acquiring the relics of St Ursula and

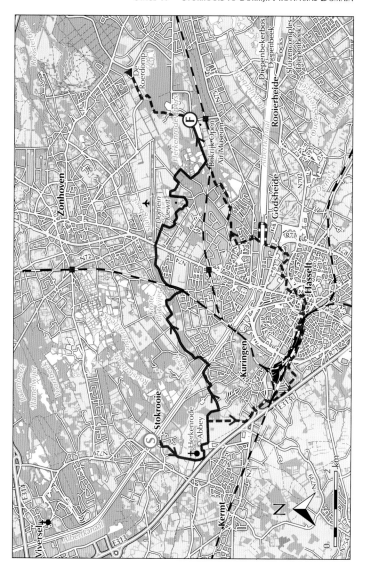

her 11,000 virgins. In 1796, French Revolutionary forces closed the abbey and expelled its nuns. The French sold the abbey and its furnishings. Herkenrode's stained glass windows, bought by an English collector, are now among the Treasures of Lichfield Cathedral in England.

The GR5 turns right after passing the abbey and then left, just before a large parking lot.

About 600 metres after the parking lot, a trail branches to the right (south) off the main trail. This is a **variant** that passes through Hasselt and re-joins the main trail at the Herkenrodevijvers near Bokrijk.

The GR5 continues east, following the edge of the forest and then curving to the right. Turn left on a small, paved road (Rode Rokstraat), which crosses the now-familiar Demer. At a T-junction with Albertkanaalstraat, turn right and then left on a dirt road. Walk through a residential area of **Kuringen** with striking modern architecture before entering a small wooded area.

The road leads to a bicycle path beside the **Albert Canal**. Turn right here and walk to the nearby bridge for the GR5's fourth crossing of this canal. Cross the bridge and continue straight to a roundabout. Turn left here and then, a short distance further, turn right on a small road (Semmestraat) that enters the woods. A trail continues for 1.4km through woods and beside ponds and then forks left at a picnic table beside a large pond (**Grote Platwijer**).

The path soon turns right, in a southerly direction, and leaves the woods. Pass an old boundary stone, the Paalsteen, and turn left on Slangbeekweg after crossing a **railway line**. After 500 metres beside the railway, Slangbeekweg bends right on a diagonal and becomes Ranonkelstraat, which leads to the **N74**. Cross and continue straight ahead on Kiewitdreef, a bicycle path. Watch for a right turn through a gate that leads into **Kiewit Domain**, a protected area of heath and woods. The trail is easy to follow (particularly where you walk upon a protective boardwalk), but it lacks GR marks in a few places where they would be helpful. Pass through another gate and turn left on a road, followed immediately by a right turn on a path into a forest.

Herkenrodevijvers, near Bokrijk

The GR5 goes through the forest and past some peaceful ponds. ▸ Along the way, it passes through a popular recreational area, with a children's farm (*kinderboerderij*), a visitor's centre and a café. A big GR5 signpost points to destinations as far as 210km in both directions.

With so much water here, there may be many mosquitoes in some areas.

Continue north in the forest after the recreational area and then turn right to cross an open field. At the far side of that field, pass through a gate and turn left on a trail that runs beside a road. After 200 metres, turn right, cross the road and continue straight into a forest. There is another right turn, just before a road, which is not signalled in advance. The trail runs parallel to a road for 350 metres and then turns left. Walk here beside a group of large ponds called, collectively, the **Herkenrodevijvers**.

After walking southeast 650 metres, you reach a small parking area. The GR5 turns left here, but there is also a GR trail on the right. ▸ After the left turn, walk northeast into the Bokrijk Provincial Domain. The view over the ponds and the distant forest early in the morning on a still, clear day is magical. Further on, the large parking area on the right signals the approach to the **Bokrijk Open Air Museum**.

This is the Hasselt variant of the GR5. Follow this 2km southwest for a handy B&B.

The **Bokrijk Open Air Museum** (Openluchtmuseum, www.bokrijk.be) presents traditional, pre-industrial life in Flanders with more than 100 restored buildings and their furnishings in an area of about 50 hectares. Groups of buildings represent rural life in different regions of Flanders (East and West

Flanders, Kempen, Haspengouw and Maasland), along with a village. There are demonstrations of traditional activities and crafts, with opportunities for hands-on participation. During a visit to Bokrijk, I was invited to clamber onto a scaffold and help with the wattle-and-daub construction of a farmhouse. If you notice an egregious flaw in a building, that may be my work!

There is a youth hostel (Auberge de Roerdomp) 2.7km northeast of the big roundabout near the entrance to the museum (follow the GR564). Alternatively, trains run from the Bokrijk **train station** (Treinhalte Bokrijk) to Hasselt and Genk, major cities with hotels. The station is on the GR5, just 400 metres south of the roundabout. Train service is frequent, and the distances to Hasselt and Genk are short.

STAGE 18
Bokrijk Provincial Domain to Zutendaal

Start	Bokrijk Provincial Domain (Open Air Museum)
Finish	Zutendaal
Distance	20.6km
Time	4hr 45min
Maps	25 Hasselt, 26 Genk
Refreshments	Cafés/restaurants in the Bokrijk area, Termien, Kattevenia (Sports Centre) and Wiemesmeer
Transport	De Lijn bus routes serve Bokrijk (G4 and 46) and Zutendaal (10, 45, G7); train service at Bokrijk train stop
Accommodation	Hotels in Genk (about 1.5km on a variant from the GR5) and Zutendaal

This stage takes you back to the Albert Canal. You do not cross the canal this time, but walk beside the Diepenbeek Locks where it is interesting to watch barges and other vessels pass through. Turning away from the Albert Canal, you explore the magnificent De Maten Nature Reserve. The GR5 then follows a route though forests south of Genk and on to Zutendaal, a convenient place to stop.

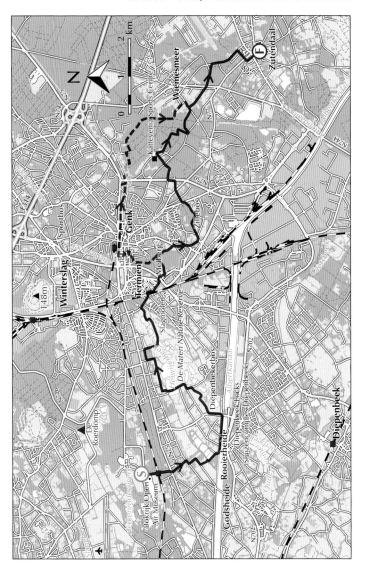

This stage begins at the entrance to the Open Air Museum. Turn south and walk through a large roundabout, leaving the GR564 trail on the left. Continue straight ahead on a path beside the road, passing the Bokrijk **train station**, to reach the **N75**. Cross and continue southeast on Halveweg. At the end of that road, turn right.

Pass a memorial to the Free French crew of an RAF Halifax bomber, shot down near here on 15 March 1945, and then turn left on Langwaterstraat. Follow the marked route on a paved road and then a dirt path, leaving the residential area and entering the countryside. ◄ After passing a pond, turn right on a road that immediately curves left, leading to the **Albert Canal**.

Turn left and walk along the bicycle path beside the canal towards the **Diepenbeek Locks (Sluizencomplex Diepenbeek)** 1km ahead. ◄ Along the way, a side-trail branches off to the left and runs parallel to the path. Follow that side-trail or simply continue up the bicycle path for a closer look at the locks. Upon reaching the road that crosses the canal, turn left (north, away from the canal) and then immediately bend right to follow a trail that descends into the woods, parallel to the road.

The trail turns right 400 metres from the canal bridge and enters **De Maten Nature Reserve** (Natuurreservaat De

There is one enclosure here where you may see some rather excitable ostriches.

Diepenbeek comprises three locks: the largest is 200 metres long and 24m wide; the two smaller locks are 136m x 16m. They rise 10.1m.

The Diepenbeek locks in operation

A pond in the Maten Nature Reserve

Maten). A well-marked trail passes through this beautiful reserve, a 300-hectare area of heath, dunes, marshland, ponds and forest – quintessential Kempen land. ▶ After an initial walk through part of De Maten, pass through a gate and stroll along a road for a while. This is one of the most agreeable sections of road-walking to be found on the GR5, as you are surrounded by trees and birdsong.

Many species of birds nest or rest here during their migrations.

At a point where the paved road turns left, continue straight into the forest on a dirt trail. At the end of that trail, turn left on a road (Heiweier), then right on Kneippstraat where there are benches and a religious shrine. Take the first road on the right, Drijtrap, back to De Maten. After passing through a gate before a small pond, follow a trail to the left between two ponds. Walk 800 metres, go through another gate and continue through heath and forest. Next to a large pond there is a poster with pictures, names and descriptions of two dozen different types of birds that can be seen in De Maten.

Finally, the GR5 leaves De Maten and approaches the urban area around Genk. Turn right on Slagmolenweg and pass an old watermill, **Slagmolen**.

The **Slagmolen** was built as a wool fulling mill around 1523. In 1612, it was converted to the production of vegetable oils, and from 1834 to 1955 it was used to grind grain. The area around it is now protected as a 'green lung' in the urban area of Genk.

At the end of the road, turn left beside a café, walk under a **railway line** and then turn right on a road at the city limits of Genk. At a T-junction just before a main road (**N75**), turn left and immediately right on a road that passes under the main road. Finally, leave the pavement by turning left into a forest on a dirt path.

The well-marked trail leads to an important junction where there is a signpost with three arms.

One arm points back the way you have come (Hasselt, Bergen op Zoom); another arm, identified as the GR5, points to 'Genk Centrum'; and the third arm, identified as a GR5 'Variante', points to Zutendaal. In fact, the organisation that marks the GR5 in Flanders (Grote Routepaden) recently changed the designation of the trails here, as shown in a new edition of their topoguide (2017). The trail leading to Genk is now the **variant**, and the trail going to Zutendaal is the **main GR5**. Perhaps the signpost will eventually be modified. If you wish to walk to Genk (a city with all facilities, including railway service), turn left at this sign.

Turn right and continue toward Zutendaal. The walk through this forest is charming: a smooth path, shaded by trees and enlivened by the singing of birds. Leaving the forest, walk through a residential area and turn right on a road near a large water tower. Where the road forks, turn left on Langerloweg (signposted for Langerlo). The road leads to a small chapel (Kapel Langerlo) and several shaded picnic tables. Turn left across a field and then cross the road on the right to follow a dirt road for another pleasant walk in the woods. Watch for a left fork in a small clearing beside a power line pylon. Turn right at a group of tennis courts and walk beside them. The turn here is not well marked.

Walk through a built-up area and across several major roads before returning to the calm of the forest. At the first road (Sledderloweg), turn left and then right on Daalstraat after just 50 metres. Continue straight and cross a main road

(**N77**) to walk on a narrow road in the woods. Soon, the GR5 reaches a major main road (**N750**): turn left and walk beside the main road for 200m then turn right and cross it to walk on Drogegwijerstraat.

Back in the forest, you may find the waymarking difficult to follow. Stay on the road as it curves left and then right to reach the entrance of the large **Kattevenia Sports Centre**. The route is clearly marked from here: Walk straight through the centre (passing a café along the way) and then turn right after exiting on the other side. The GR5 first follows the perimeter of the centre and then turns left into the forest. After some meanders, the trail emerges from the forest, where it turns left and immediately right on a road (Veugenstraat) beside a café. ▶

The Genk variant re-joins the main GR5 here.

The road crosses another main road (**N744**) and continues straight ahead on a smaller one (Boenveldstraat). The GR5 then makes one more passage through woods before entering **Zutendaal**. Walk along Pandenstraat, then turn right on Kerkstraat to cross the busy N77 again. Continue in the same direction on Onze-Lieve-Vrouwestraat, which soon turns left and leads to the centre of Zutendaal, a small city with all you need for an overnight stay.

STAGE 19
Zutendaal to Maastricht

Start	Zutendaal
Finish	Maastricht
Distance	30km
Time	7hr 30min
Maps	26 Genk, 34 Tongeren; 61 Oost Maastricht (Dutch Kadaster 1:50,000)
Refreshments	Cafés/restaurants and shops in Lanaken
Transport	De Lijn buses serve Zutendaal (10, 45, G7), Stalken (45, G7), Lanaken and Maastricht (20a, 45, 63); railway service in Maastricht
Accommodation	Hotels and B&Bs in Lanaken and Maastricht
Note	If you want to shorten this stage, you could stop in Lanaken which has plenty of facilities.

On this longer stage you walk through forests and across fields, with very little tarmac under your boots, from Zutendaal to Lanaken. Prior to 2017, the GR5 passed west of Maastricht along the Albert Canal but now it enters the city. The route between Lanaken and Maastricht is not very interesting, but the inclusion of Maastricht on the GR5 was certainly a good idea: It's a vibrant, interesting city (and would be a good place to spend a rest day if you have time).

Walk from the centre of Zutendaal southwest on Daalstraat, then turn left through Vijverplein, with the 18th century classical-style *pastorie* (presbytery or priest's house) on your right. Continue straight ahead on Schoolstraat and then Blookbergstraat, passing a cemetery, football pitches and

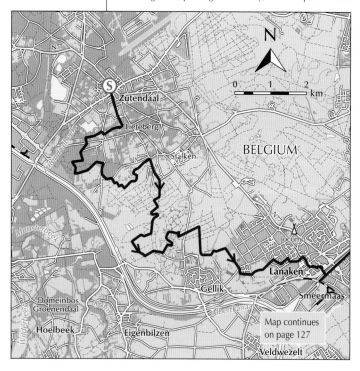

Map continues on page 127

tennis courts on the right. The GR5 soon enters the woods. The trail forks to the right (without clear waymarking) just before the **Lieteberg** visitors' centre (part of the Nationaal Park Hoge Kempen).

When you reach a road, turn right and then (after 100m) left. Walk along a dirt path for 600 metres and then turn left (south). After crossing a road (Broekmollenweg), the trail slants to the right (southwest) and then returns to a more southerly line. Shortly, there is a right turn that is easy to miss. Turn left after 300 metres and left again 350 metres further. Continue straight, northeast, past a picnic table to a paved road.

Turn right on the road and walk past another picnic table under a shelter. The GR5 soon leaves the road to follow a trail to the left, continues briefly on another road and then turns right on a forest trail. The GR5 zigzags extensively through the grid of paths in this beautiful conifer forest. When you reach a monolithic stone monument on the outskirts of **Stalken**, dedicated to the writer Jeroen Brouwers, you will have walked more than 6km from the Lieteberg visitors' centre. (The direct route on a paved road is about 1.5km!)

Turn sharply right beside the monument and return to the forest on Hoogkantstraat. Watch carefully for waymarks that indicate the route and the turnings. Occasionally, there are helpful blazes (a white-and-red X) indicating that a particular trail is not the correct route, but not always. ▶ Where Hoogkantstraat curves left, continue straight ahead on a dirt path, then turn right at a junction and left at the next junction (where there is no GR mark until after the turn). The path curves to the left and then the right before reaching a bench, where it turns sharply right. Turn right at another bench.

Reach an intersection after 600m, turn left and then left again after a further 600m. Continue through the forest and turn right on a paved road (Gellinkenheide). After 100m on Gellinkenheide, turn left on a forest trail and walk around a group of homes on the left. After curving to the right and making sharp right and left turns, the GR5 crosses a road and continues straight. Turn right (south) on a bicycle path and, after 700m, left on a path that passes beside a meadow. Turn right at a junction.

The waymarking remains sparse in the approach to **Lanaken**. Leaving the forest, the route passes a hotel on

If you walk beyond a crossroads or fork in the trail and don't see a GR mark for 100 metres or so, consider retracing your steps to see whether you missed one.

*Sint-Ursulakerk,
Lanaken*

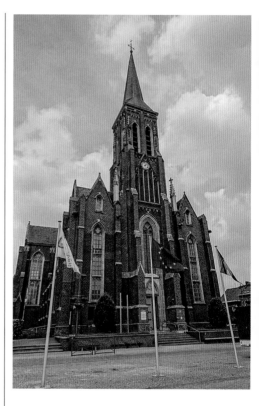

Kiewithstraat. Go through an intersection and continue straight ahead on Kounterstraat, then turn left on a narrow path (Kleine-Hofstraat). Turn right on Op de Puin and then immediately left on a dirt road through fields. Enter a residential area and follow a road that becomes Jan Van Eyckstraat. Continue straight across Pannestraat and then turn right on PP Rubensstraaat. (No GR5 mark shows this turn, but there is a mark further on.) At the end of the street, turn right on Hellingstraat, then left on Arkstraat. Finally, at a T-junction, turn right on Bessemerstraat, which enters the centre of Lanaken (Kerkplein), where there are cafés and other facilities.

Departing from Kerkplein, walk on Jan Rosierlaan to the right of the *gemeentehuis* (city hall). The street curves left. After passing a small parking lot, turn left on Breulsstraat. Turn right at a large signpost indicating directions for the GR5 and the GR561 and then right on a bicycle path that goes through a tunnel under a main road (**N78**). Cross the **Briegden-Neerharen Canal** on a small bridge and turn right on Industrieweg. After a short walk on that road and just before a railway line, make a hairpin turn to the right to descend to a gravel path beside the canal.

Walk northeast along this path for 2km. Shortly after passing under a road bridge, the GR5 takes a diagonal to the right beside a paved road. Turn right after 300 metres onto a dirt road through open fields. After left and right

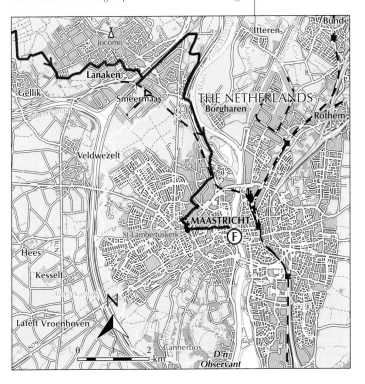

turns, the path merges beside a bench with a path that becomes a paved road, Kanaaldijk. Walk past **Smeermaas** to a bridge over another canal, the **Zuid-Willemsvaart**. Cross the bridge to the left and walk a short distance on

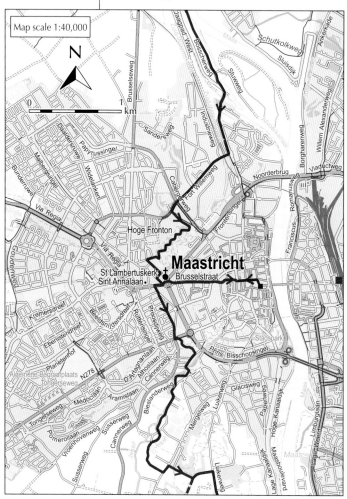

Brugstraat. ▶ Heading southeast, leave the road and walk on a path through grassy fields beside a quiet branch of the **Maas** river on the left.

The path beside the river joins a road (Oude Smeermaeserweg), which leads to a busy road (**Bosscherweg**). Turn left here on a path beside the road. Cross the canal at a lock that is operated by what look like large bicycle chains and then enter Maastricht after crossing another bridge. Opposite a supermarket on the left, turn off the road on a small trail to the right. After a short walk on that trail, turn right to cross a bridge over an old canal lock. Follow **Fort Willemweg** through a commercial district to a major inter-section with a traffic light. Continue straight through that intersection and then turn left on a path that leads to the **Hoge Fronten**.

The **Hoge Fronten** are vestiges of 17th century ramparts. These ramparts were insufficient to pro-tect Maastricht when besieged by Louis XIV's army in 1673: the city capitulated after a two-week

Somewhere here – probably without noticing it – you cross the border into the Netherlands. A large road sign giving the speed limits on Dutch roads provides a hint.

MAASTRICHT

Stadhuis, Maastricht

Maastricht, the oldest city in the Netherlands, is known for the treaty that was signed here in 1992, estab-lishing Europe's common currency. The city's name is derived from Traiectum ad Mosam ('crossing at the Meuse'), referring to a bridge across the river built by the Romans. During the Middle Ages, Maastricht was a centre for trade and leather manufacture. Maastricht and the surrounding Province of Limburg were included in the United Kingdom of the Netherlands in 1814. When Limburg was divided between the Netherlands and Belgium in 1839, Maastricht remained part of the Netherlands. Today, Maastricht has a distinctive culture, influenced by Belgium and France, that sets it apart from the rest of the Netherlands. The city has many attractions for visitors, including its museums and fine restaurants. The Preuvenemint is a popular festival in late August, featuring food, drink and music.

siege. Charles Ogier de Batz de Castelmore, Comte d'Artagnan (the inspiration for Alexandre Dumas' d'Artagnan in *The Three Musketeers*) was killed during this siege. Fighting beside the Comte d'Artagnan that day was young John Churchill, the future Duke of Marlborough.

The path upon the ramparts is sometimes closed, in which case there is an alternative route on the outer side of the ramparts.

The GR5 follows a zig-zag path atop the ramparts, with good views of the city. ◄ After leaving the Hoge Fronten, walk a short distance on Acht Zaligheden and turn left on Pastoor Habetsstraat. A right turn on Sint-Odastraat and a left on Victor de Stuersstraat lead to Sint-Annalaan (beside a large church, St-Lambertuskerk). The GR5 turns right here. To reach the centre of **Maastricht**, turn left on Sint-Annalaan, walk past the large roundabout and continue in the same direction on Brusselstraat, or take a bus into town.

STAGE 20
Maastricht to Eben-Emael

Start	Maastricht
Finish	Eben-Emael
Distance	13km
Time	3hr 15min
Map	61 Oost Maastricht (Dutch Kadaster 1:50,000)
Refreshments	Café in the ENCI-groeve; cafés/restaurants in Kanne
Transport	Bus routes 20a, 45, 63 (Maastricht) and 18, 62 (Kanne and Eben-Emael); train service in Maastricht
Accommodation	Hotels in Kanne; B&B in Eben-Emael

This short stage begins with a pleasant walk along the Jeker River to leave Maastricht. It then climbs to high ground around the ENCI-groeve quarry, which is being converted into a nature reserve. If the project goes according to plan, the GR5 will pass through the old quarry; if not, the trail will skirt the quarry area and go more directly to Kanne in Belgium. The GR5 leaves Flanders after Kanne and enters Wallonia. There, the Maas becomes the Meuse River.

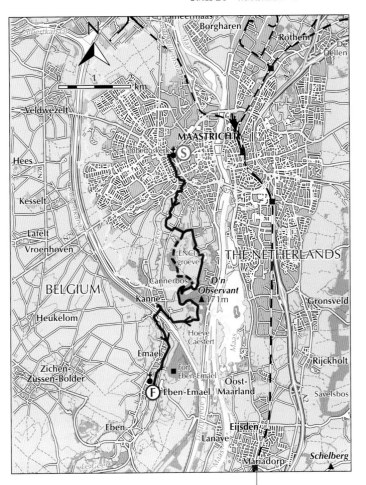

Walk from the centre of Maastricht to Sint-Annalaan to connect with the GR5. After passing the church on the right,
turn left on Volksplein. This road passes through a residential
neighbourhood and forks to the right beside a small park. At
a major intersection, turn left and then right to enter a park
(Waldeckpark). The route curves around a swimming pool

131

on the right to a road. Turn right here and follow Champs Elyseeweg to a modest wooden bridge on the left. Cross the bridge and follow a path to the right beside a tranquil stream, the **Jeker**. This pleasant walk takes you into open country. The path turns left (southeast), away from the Jeker, and rises to a road (**Mergelweg**). Turn left here and then (opposite a café) right on a trail that climbs steeply a short distance in the woods.

The trail ends at a broad path that runs in both directions, left and right. Here you have a choice of two routes, which is complicated by other GR trails that pass through this area and the changing status of **ENCI-groeve**.

> **ENCI-groeve** is a limestone quarry that began operations in 1926. Plans are now being implemented to end all quarrying here and to convert the area into a nature reserve. ENCI-groeve was briefly open to the public – including GR5 trekkers – in 2017, but then closed due to overcrowding. New arrangements for visiting ENCI-groeve are expected in 2018. Check with the tourist office in Maastricht (see Appendix C).

A stairway descends from a viewing platform to the ENCI-groeve quarry

The current route of the GR5 runs to the left (east) on the broad dirt path. After a few hundred metres, turn right on a paved road (there is a refreshing water fountain just to

the left of this turn). The road leads to a spectacular viewing platform over the ENCI-groeve. ▸ A metal stairway attached to the side of the vertical cliff descends to the floor of the quarry. Walk past a swimming pond and a café, and then around a small lake. The GR5 climbs on a path with two switchbacks back to the level of broad dirt path, which it re-joins by turning left.

> This is the end-point of the Pieterpad, a 498km trail from Pieterburen in Groningen through the eastern part of the Netherlands.

The alternative route
The alternative route, avoiding ENCI-groeve, turns right (southwest) at the top of the trail and follows the broad dirt path as it turns and curves. Along the way, two trails intersect this path: first, the old route of the GR5, which climbs from the valley to the right (west), and second, the new GR5, which joins the path from the left after its tour of ENCI-groeve as just described. Continue on this path.

The GR5 meanders here along the Dutch-Belgian border, finally crosses it and turns right beside an old farmhouse, **Hoeve Caestert**, to approach **Kanne** from the southeast. Here (without entering the centre of Kanne), the GR5 crosses the Albert Canal again. Descend from the bridge by stairs on the right and continue on a short path to Rue Avergat. Turn left on that small road and then right on a larger one (N619). After passing a sign that welcomes you into the Province of Liège, leave the road on a dirt path to the left. ▸ This pleasant path runs through fields and forest, below the back gardens of homes. Eben-Emael's **church** appears on the high ground to the right. Continue straight across a road, Rue du Fort, beside a bridge over the **Geer** river. A road to **Fort Eben-Emael** branches to the left here.

> You are now in Wallonia.

> Fort Eben-Emael was constructed in 1932–1935 to guard strategic bridges over the Albert Canal. With its natural defences, reinforced concrete construction, powerful armament and garrison of 1200 men, Eben-Emael was considered impregnable. However, the German army captured the fort in a carefully planned, daring assault at the beginning of their offensive in the West. At 5.30am on 10 May 1940, 9 gliders carrying about 80 paratroopers landed on the roof of the fort. They disabled Eben-Emael's principal armament in about 15 minutes.

Approaching Eben-Emael

The German paratroopers defended their positions on the roof until reinforced by infantry the next morning. The Belgian garrison then surrendered the fort.

At the second Geer bridge, the GR5 turns left and crosses the bridge. A right turn here on Rue du Garage leads to the centre of **Eben-Emael**. There is a comfortable B&B in Eben-Emael and a restaurant nearby.

3 WALLONIA

In dappled sunlight on a trail near Eben-Emael (Stage 21)

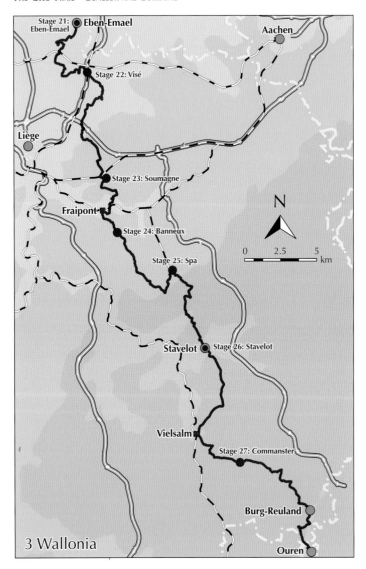

This short section crosses Wallonia, one of Belgium's three regions, from Eben-Emael southeast to Ouren. The entire route lies within the Province of Liège. The city of Liège itself is a short distance to the west, accessible by a variant trail, the GR57.

The route is described here in seven stages. The first is a transitional stage from Eben-Emael to Visé across open, level terrain. The next two stages explore the rolling, bucolic countryside of the Pays de Herve. South of the Vesdre River, the GR5 enters the Ardennes. In four stages, the trail then goes through an interesting variety of terrain: open plateaus cut by narrow river valleys, high peat lands and mountainous forests. At the same time it visits several noteworthy towns in the Ardennes: Spa (a renowned source for curative waters since Roman times), Stavelot (the seat of a historic abbey and the venue of a colourful carnival) and Vielsalm (where

a celebration of sorcery and blueberries takes place in July).

The Ardennes are a great area for outdoor sports. Walking on the GR5, you will encounter other trails, such as the GR56, the Sentier des Cantons de l'Est (Eastern Cantons Trail), which passes through the Hautes Fagnes-Eifel Natural Park. You will also cross the route of the legendary Liège-Bastogne-Liège bicycle race, a one-day classic dating back to 1892 that is held every year in late April. The hills that you climb and descend between Spa and Vielsalm are part of what makes that race such a challenge. After your trek through the Ardennes, you might want to return in the winter for cross-country skiing.

The official languages of Wallonia are French and, in three 'Eastern Cantons', German. (Walloon is also recognised as a regional language.) The final stage passes through this German-speaking area.

SECTION SUMMARY TABLE

Start	Eben-Emael
Finish	Ouren
Distance	143km
Ascent/Descent	3350m/3089m
Maps	Belgian NGI 1:50,000
Note	At this point, the trail is no longer flat, as in the Netherlands and Flanders, so the information at the beginning of each stage now includes cumulative ascent and descent.

STAGE 21
Eben-Emael to Visé

Start	Eben-Emael
Finish	Visé
Distance	19km
Ascent/Descent	263m/270m
Time	4hr 30min
Map	34 Tongeren
Refreshments	Café in Wonck
Transport	TEC bus routes 16, 76 (Eben-Emael), 67 and others (Visé); railway service in Visé
Accommodation	Hotel and B&Bs in Visé

The GR5 enters an area of hills and plateaus, a foretaste of the more varied topography that awaits you in Wallonia and beyond. The highlight of this stage is the extraordinary flint castle, the Tour d'Eben-Ezer. Climb to the roof to enjoy a broad view over the countryside you will be crossing on the circuitous route to Visé. After Eben-Ezer, there are long sections of level walking across open country.

Re-join the GR5 from the centre of Eben-Emael by walking southeast on Rue du Garage, which leads to a bridge over the **Geer** river. Continue across this bridge and, when the road rises to the left, turn right on a small path into the woods. A short distance further, bear right where the path forks. This pleasant trail runs along the edge of a forest, with fields on the other side, and then follows a paved bicycle path and road through the village of **Eben**.

Walk a short distance beside the **N619** and then (before reaching a roundabout) turn right on a small path that leads to Rue du Geer. Follow that road through a residential area to a T-junction and turn left on Rue du Village. Continue straight through an intersection, where the road becomes Haie de Wonck and passes under a main road bridge.

Soon, the striking **Tour d'Eben-Ezer** emerges from the woods a few hundred metres away.

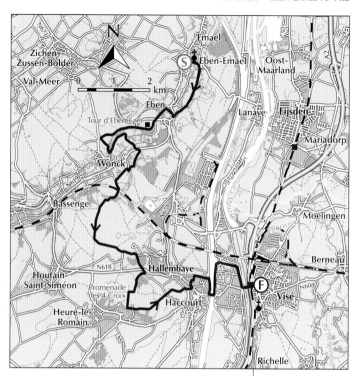

The **Tour d'Eben-Ezer** was built of flint by Robert Garcet, with help from friends, in 1948–1966. Garcet (1912–2001), who worked as a stone mason, was a conscientious objector and a militant for social justice and peace. His castle is impregnated with religious and esoteric symbolism, including most dramatically the winged sculptures on its roof that represent the four cherubim of the Apocalypse. The castle houses a flint museum (www.musee-du-silex.be) and offers a great view from its roof.

The GR5 continues past the Tour d'Eben-Ezer into the open on a ridge between fields. About 500 metres after passing under high-voltage power lines, look for a poorly-marked

The Tour d'Eben-Ezer, surmounted by the four cherubim of the Apocalypse

A short distance beyond that turn, there is a group of trees and a bench – a good place for a rest on a hot, sunny day.

turning to the left (southeast) onto a dirt road. ◀ There is eventually a GR mark confirming that you are going in the right direction. The road crosses open fields and then, as a sunken road, descends to the edge of **Wonck**, a small village. The GR5 does not enter Wonck so (unless you want to detour to the café 250 metres further on) make a hairpin bend to the left on Rue Pachlauw. The road leads to a turnstile at the entrance to a nature reserve. Walk here along a pleasant, shaded trail beside a stream. After passing through another turnstile, turn right on a bicycle path and cross the Geer on a small, arched bridge.

Follow a gravel path to cross a main road (**N619**) and climb gradually. Turn right on a narrow trail that passes through a small wooded area and then enters open country. Turn right again on a dirt road that soon becomes paved, then turn left, descend to a T-junction, and turn left again.

The GR5 crosses a bridge over a **railway line**, continues straight (not left) at a fork, and climbs gently to a broad, open plateau.

Cross this plateau, a distance of more than 2km (which may seem longer on a hot, sunny day). At the first crossroads, continue straight (south) toward an isolated group of trees. Continue past those trees and turn left at the next crossroads (east-southeast). Finally, at a fork in the road, bear right and descend to reach a shelter with picnic tables. The GR5 continues to descend through a forest and then reaches a main road (**N618**).

You could simply turn left on this main road and walk to Visé (3.5km), but it would not be as pleasant as the official route which describes a loop south of the main road before heading into town – a total of 7.5km (of which about 1km can be omitted in a shortcut described below). To stay on the GR5, cross the main road and continue on a paved path into the country, then turn right on a dirt road that climbs gradually beside a forest and fields. Turn right at a T-junction and then left on a path that is part of the **Promenade des 4 Croix** (the cross here is the second one).

The path ends in **Heure-le-Romain**. Here you turn left on a road that leads back into the countryside. A white, arched bridge over the Albert Canal and, beyond it, Visé are visible on the horizon. Pass pear orchards and descend to a roundabout to turn left. A short distance further you reach the N618 again. Counterintuitively, the GR5 crosses the main road and turns left (away from Visé). Within a few metres, however, it turns right on a small street and finds its way toward Visé.

The route passes playing fields and a sports centre (where there is a café) and turns right again to walk toward the **Albert Canal**. Turn right at the canal and walk to the bridge. ▸

This is the GR5's sixth and final crossing of the Albert Canal.

After crossing the canal, the GR5 follows three sides of a quadrilateral (turning left, right and right) to reach the bridge over the Meuse. ▸ Cross the bridge. The Visé train station stands at the other end (with a hotel across the street), and the commercial centre of the city beyond that.

At this point, you may prefer to walk directly (east-southeast) to the bridge and save a kilometre.

STAGE 22
Visé to Soumagne

Start	Visé
Finish	Soumagne (Aux Cosmos chambre d'hôtes)
Distance	24.5km
Ascent/Descent	457m/329m
Time	6hr 30min
Map	42 Liège
Refreshments	Shops in Dalhem; café in Saint-Remy; restaurant on N642 (between Wandre and Barchon)
Transport	TEC bus route 67 (Visé, Dalhem, Feneur, Saint-Remy, Barchon and Saive)
Accommodation	Chambres d'hôtes in Argenteau, Evegnée-Tignée and Soumagne

This stage takes you into the Pays de Herve, the area of Wallonia east of the Meuse river and north of the Vesdre river. While there are long stretches of level walking across the open plateau, the trail also climbs and descends hills in forests. Your pace here is likely to be a bit slower than in the flat terrain of the Netherlands and Flanders. Enjoy the scenery as you walk more slowly! And if you like cheese with a strong flavour, be sure to try the local specialty, Herve.

The GR5 follows the railway line south from the Visé station, passing the *hôtel de ville* (town hall), and then turns left before reaching a bridge. A quick left/right leads to steps that climb to a square with a church, the **Collégiale Saint-Martin et Saint-Hadelin**. Continue straight across the square and follow a tree-lined path into open country, with views in all directions. The trail descends from the plateau, past houses and an apartment building, and turns left on a road.

Turn right on a grass path before a large farmhouse, the Ferme de Cronwez. ◄ The grass path becomes faint as it crosses a field. At the end of that field, turn right to follow a narrow trail beside a stream, the **Berwinne**. Turn right on a

Do not continue straight here, where another GR marker is visible. That is a mark for the GR563, the 'Tour du Pays de Herve', which joins the GR5 here.

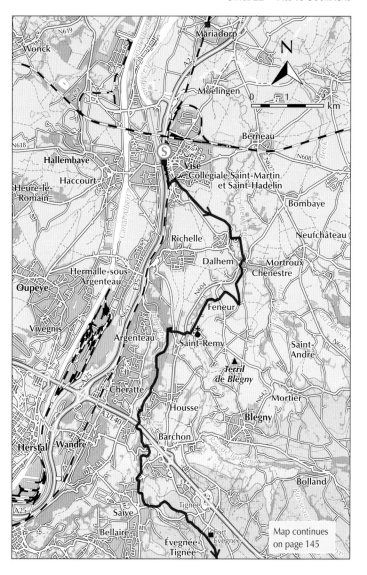

Map continues
on page 145

Clear skies ahead after a morning rain storm near Visé

Dalhem is an attractive village dating back to the 9th century.

road to cross the stream and enter **Dalhem**. ◄ After walking uphill on Rue Général Thys, turn right and walk through a passageway in a building, the 'Wichet de la Rose'. On the other side, descend steps to a road and then immediately turn left on a trail that goes back up.

Where the trail reaches a road, turn right and continue straight when the road enters a farm on the left. After passing the farm, turn left to walk behind it. Cross the Chemin des Moulyniers and continue straight ahead on what is marked as a dead-end road. The road passes through fields, and Saint-Remy, dominated by its church, comes into view. Turn right to descend toward **Saint-Remy** and then join a road to the left. Turn right again at a T-junction toward the **church**. After perhaps pausing for refreshment at the café opposite the church, cross the road and then turn right to ascend a narrow path, Voie Marion.

The right fork is the GR57, which leads to Liège and continues south through the Ardennes. The GR5 meets the GR57 again in Gilsdorf, Luxembourg. See Stage 31.

The Voie Marion leads to a beautiful trail in a forest that follows the sinuous **Julienne** river – first above it, then beside it – in a generally southern direction. The trail joins a road in more open country, passes several houses and then, after a hairpin turn to the right, re-enters the forest. Soon, the sound of traffic can be heard: it's a motorway (**A3/E40**). The GR5 passes under the motorway and, at a fork in the trail, bends left. ◄ The trail climbs in a forest and then follows a dirt path

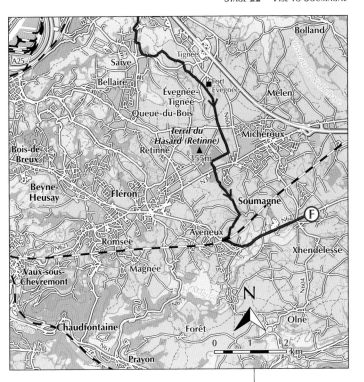

in open country. Turn left at a main road (**N642**), beside a restaurant, and then immediately right on a small road, which leads to a trail in the woods and then a road through a residential area. After the houses, the GR5 forks to the right on a trail that returns to the woods.

Emerge from the woods to turn right on a road that leads to **Saive**. At a fork in the road, bear left on Chemin du Frise, cross a small stream and then turn right at an inspiring signpost. ▶ Leave Saive by turning left at a T-junction and then left on the village's principal road.

The next destination is Tignée, a small village where there is a chambre d'hôtes. Turn left on a road 100 metres beyond Saive that becomes a sunken trail and climbs through trees. When you leave the trees, walk past a farm and turn

The signpost shows destinations and distances along the entire length of the GR5, from Hoek van Holland, 302km one direction, and to Nice, 2115km in the other.

145

Walking across a field near Soumagne

right on a road that enters **Tignée**. Turn right beside the chambre d'hôtes, cross a road and continue on a road called Their Hamal. Follow this road straight ahead through the next two junctions to reach a small village, **Evegnée-Tignée**.

The GR5 is still following the same route as the GR563 (which joined our trail back in Dalhem). At an intersection with a larger road, a third trail, the **GR412** (the 'Sentier des Terrils', the slag heap trail), joins the GR5 and GR563. The large slag heaps in this area are a reminder of the importance of coal mining here for many years.

In Evegnée-Tignée, follow a left fork on a path, cross a road and continue straight ahead on Rue de la Chapelle.

Fort Evegnée, a short distance east of the GR5, was one of 12 forts built in the late 19th century to defend Liège. These forts bore the brunt of the German army's offensive into Belgium in August 1914. The heroic – but doomed – resistance of these forts (and the state of war between France and Germany's ally, Austria-Hungary) inspired the French to change the name of a popular dessert from *café viennois* to *café liégeois*.

After 750 metres, the three GR trails turn right into a park on a bicycle path. (A variant of the GR412 turns left here.) Then, 500 metres into the park, the GR5 (along with the GR563) turns left, while the GR412 continues straight. This brings the GR5 into a residential area. Cross a main road (**N3**) and continue straight ahead on a small road. Pass through a gate, cross a series of fields and then follow a tree-lined path. After another gate, you reach a small road, Rue des Carmes. Turn right here (poorly marked), and then, after a short distance, turn left off the road to follow a trail beside a fence on the right.

The trail passes under a **railway line** and leads to a paved road which is well-marked from here down to Chaussée de Wégimont (the N621). Walk 1.5km northeast along this road to reach a comfortable chambre d'hôtes, along with a restaurant and other services. ▸

The GR5 was modified in 2017 to follow the route described here from Rue des Carmes to the N621. New construction in the area may lead to additional changes.

STAGE 23
Soumagne to Banneux

Start	Soumagne (Aux Cosmos chambre d'hôtes)
Finish	Banneux
Distance	15.5km
Ascent/Descent	455m/331m
Time	4hr 30min
Maps	42 Liège; 49 Spa
Refreshments	Fast food (friterie) in Olne; café/restaurant and shops in Nessonvaux
Transport	TEC bus routes 69 (Soumagne, Saint-Hadelin and Olne); 31 and 188 (Nessonvaux and Fraipont); 64 and 727 (Banneux); railway service in Nessonvaux and Fraipont
Accommodation	Chambres d'hôtes in Olne and Fraipont; hotels in Banneux
Note	This stage could be extended another 7.3km to La Reid, where there is a chambre d'hôtes.

This stage marks the transition between the Pays de Herve and the Ardennes. You begin by continuing to walk across the open, relatively level terrain of the plateau. You then cross the Vesdre river, and the terrain becomes more varied, with ascents and descents in forests. The transition is fairly abrupt, in fact, where a forest trail climbs quite steeply south of Fraipont. Welcome to the Ardennes!

From the chambre d'hôtes walk 1.5km (southwest) on the N621 and turn left (south) when you reach the GR5. Walk to the left of a brick building into open country. A grass path between fences leads to a road. Turn right here and take the right fork at Rue Mitoyenne.

Turn right on a dirt path and then branch to the right on a narrow, sunken trail that descends the slope. The trail soon broadens into a pleasant forest trail, then emerges from the forest and descends to a road in the village of **Saint-Hadelin**. Turn left here and left again on Chemin du Rouau, which climbs to an intersection with Au Château de Saint-Hadelin. Continue straight ahead on the dirt road across an open plateau that leads to **Olne**.

The waymarking through Olne leaves something to be desired. The goal is to walk through the centre of the village, past the church, and then turn right (south-southeast) on a road that returns to the open country of the plateau. Take another right 700 metres after leaving Olne and walk down a dirt road. Soon, it branches right on a sunken, rocky trail shaded by trees. Turn right in **Vaux-sous-Olne**, then left beside a stream and left again on a road after a bridge over that stream. After 300 metres, leave the road where it turns right and turn sharply right on a trail that climbs steeply in the woods. **There is currently no GR mark for this turn.**

At the top of that climb, the GR5 emerges from the woods and turns left on a road. Further on, the GR5 and the GR563 finally separate: the GR563 turns left, while the GR5 continues straight ahead on a gravel road. When that road curves to the right, turn right on a grass trail through trees. The trail crosses open country and then descends in a forest to **Nessonvaux**. Enter the town by walking down a series of steps and across a small bridge.

A left turn leads to a bridge across the **Vesdre** and then a T-junction with a main road (**N61**). Turn right here and walk

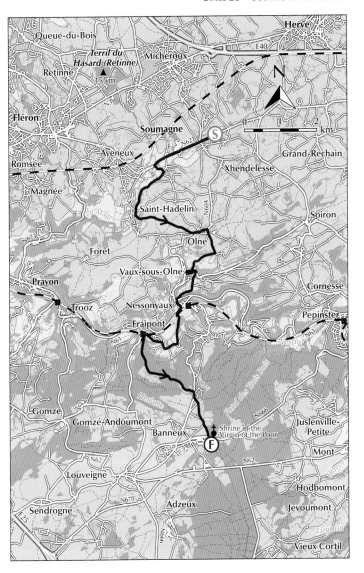

Inviting countryside between Olne and Nessonvaux

past a café and a supermarket. After 300 metres, the GR5 turns left under a **railway viaduct** and joins a trail that climbs through a forest. The trail levels off and traverses the edge of the forest, with open fields to the right – a pleasant walk that leads to Fraipont.

Descending from the forest, the GR5 avoids a road that leads directly to **Fraipont**, opting instead for a path to the left that enters the village through a wooded park. Turn left on Rue Havegné before the entrance to a tunnel under the railway line and then immediately left again on a trail that climbs steeply (first with steps, then as a forest trail). When the trail levels off, it broadens and continues among trees that provide welcome shade on a sunny day. There are good views from this high point over the countryside to the left (northeast).

After 2.5km, when the trail reaches a T-junction with a road, turn right and then, 150 metres further (opposite a sign indicating entry into Louveigné), turn left on a dirt path and pass sports fields on the right. Turn left on a paved road, then left on a gravel road that enters **Banneux**, a pilgrimage centre with hotels.

In 1933, an adolescent girl living in Banneux, Mariette Béco, reported that the Virgin Mary had appeared to her on eight separate occasions. These apparitions, and healing miracles associated with a spring in Banneux, led to the **Shrine of the Virgin of the Poor** becoming a place of pilgrimage.

STAGE 24
Banneux to Spa

Start	Banneux
Finish	Spa
Distance	17km
Ascent/Descent	429m/486m
Time	5hr
Map	49 Spa
Refreshments	Café/restaurant and shops in La Reid
Transport	TEC bus route 64 passes through Banneux; route 388 links Becco, La Reid and Spa; railway service at Spa.
Accommodation	Chambres d'hôtes in La Reid; hotels and chambres d'hôtes in Spa

A crow flying directly from Banneux to Spa (about 10km) would scarcely see the route of this stage. Following a south-easterly line from Banneux, the GR5 passes well to the west of Spa and then approaches the city from the southwest. The route is well-chosen: It climbs and descends through picturesque, narrow valleys cutting into the plateau and concludes with an enjoyable walk through a forest into Spa.

Leaving the centre of Banneux, walk east beside the **N666**. Turn right into the woods after 200 metres and walk along a broad trail beside the sanctuary of Notre Dame de Banneux. The trail narrows and becomes rougher. At an intersection of two main roads, cross the first one (**N62**), turn left to cross the second one (**N606**) and then follow a diagonal into the woods. Turn right on a dirt road beside a brick cabin. Walk past a dirt road on the left and then turn left on a narrow trail

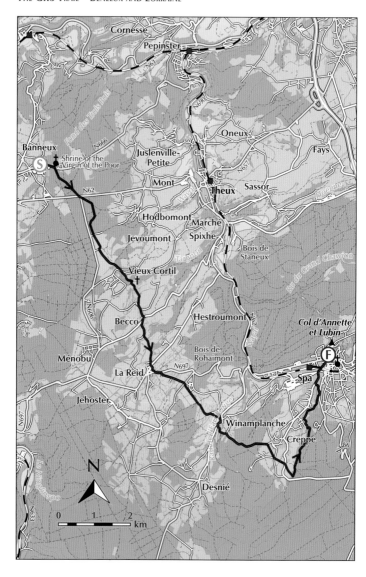

into the woods. There is a mark indicating this turn, but a distinct lack thereafter for more than 200 metres (probably because of forestry work). Just keep following the trail!

A forest trail southeast of Banneux

After emerging from the forest, cross a small paved road and continue straight ahead on a path through open fields that offer views over the surrounding countryside. Turn right at a T-junction with a paved road and then immediately left on a gravel path that leads to a small village, **Vieux Cortil**. At a crossroads, follow a small trail to the right that descends into the woods. Leave those woods and cross a small bridge to the right and then turn left (beside a white **cross**). ▶ The GR5 follows a road uphill to **Becco**.

The GR5 intersects two other GR trails here: the GR573 and the GR576.

From Becco, descend steeply to La Reid, first on Chemin de Baudrifosse and then, having turned off left, on a dirt path. As it reaches **La Reid** (a good place to pause for refreshment or an overnight stay), the GR5 turns left on a small path that leads to a main road (**N697**), where it turns left. After walking 200 metres beside the road, turn right on a smaller one that climbs to an intersection.

Continue straight here on a dirt road into open country and descend again. The GR5 leaves that road on a narrow trail to the right that leads to a road. Turn left here. After

The GR15 joins the GR5 here and remains with it to Spa.

just 100 metres, turn right on a path that goes downhill to another small village, **Winamplanche**. ◄

Turn right to walk through the centre of Winamplanche, then left on Clos des Marteleurs to a trail that climbs through woods back to the plateau. After turning right on a road that runs beside the woods, note the sign on the left that warns: 'Domaine Militaire Accès Interdit' (Military Area Entry Prohibited). The GR5 approaches the village of **Creppe** but turns right just before it on a dirt road, then left on a paved road and finally straight across another road to a trail.

Enter the forest here and turn left (north) toward Spa. This is a delightful trail, meandering through the dense forest beside a small stream, the Rau du Vieux Spa. Occasional

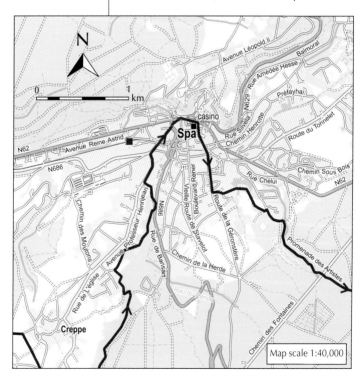

gaps in the waymarking (you may see some blazes on fallen trees) matter little. The general direction is downhill near the stream as far as a bridge. Cross that bridge to the left and then walk uphill to a road. Leave the forest briefly and then return to it on a dirt trail that descends to a road, **Rue de la Barisart**. Walk just a few metres on this busy road before turning left on a quieter one, Chemin de Bahychamps. Finally, turn right on **Avenue Professeur Henrijean**, which leads into the centre of **Spa**.

To the Romans Spa was 'Aqua Spadanae' and, in his *Natural History*, Pliny the Elder described 'a spring of great renown, which sparkles as it bursts forth with bubbles innumerable, and has a certain ferruginous taste, only to be perceived after it has been drunk. This water is strongly purgative, is curative of tertian fevers, and disperses urinary calculi.' Spa's renown as a site for **mineral-rich thermal waters** grew over the centuries. It became the fashionable place for royalty and other elites to visit for a cure. A casino, restaurants and other diversions occupied them when they were not taking the waters. The city's name became a generic term for a resort with a mineral spring that is believed to have healing powers.

STAGE 25
Spa to Stavelot

Start	Spa
Finish	Stavelot (Place Saint Remacle)
Distance	16km
Ascent/Descent	567m/528m
Time	5hr
Maps	49 Spa; 50 Malmédy
Refreshments	None
Transport	Railway service in Spa; TEC bus routes 744 and 294 link Spa and Stavelot.
Accommodation	Hotels and chambres d'hôtes in Stavelot

The walk from Spa to Stavelot is very enjoyable and interesting. Highlights include the 'Promenade des Artistes' in the forest southeast of Spa and then the peatland of the Fagne de Malchamps. Peatlands hold a lot of water, as you will notice when walking on sections of the trail that are generally quite muddy, regardless of the weather. You also cross open plateaus with views over beautiful countryside before descending to Stavelot.

Departing from the centre of Spa, walk east on Rue Royale past the imposing **casino** and turn right on Rue Henri Schaltin. Continue straight, passing a church. The road becomes Rue du Wauxhall and later **Route de la Géronstère**. Turn left on Chemin de la Roche, which climbs gradually and then levels off to enter a forest as a dirt path. Leaving the forest, turn right on a road and then, 250 metres further, turn right again into the forest to walk along the **Promenade des Artistes**. This is an easy, well-marked trail that winds its way gradually uphill through the forest beside a small stream, the **Picherotte**, and crosses the stream five times on wooden bridges that are named after artists.

A forest walk along the Promenade des Artistes

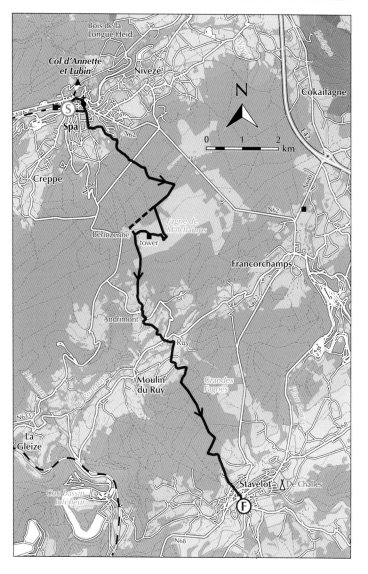

A sign here warns that the spring's water is non-potable.

The GR5 continues in the forest after crossing a road, the **Chemin des Fontaines**, and passes a spring called the Pouhon Delcor. ◄ Turn right on a dirt road and, at a crossroads after 300 metres, turn left (east-southeast) to walk along a long, straight road through a forest of towering conifer trees. At a T-junction, turn right and continue on another straight road. Then, after 750 metres, the GR5 turns left beside an informational panel to enter the **Fagne de Malchamps**, an area of protected peatland. A red and white pole bars the way to motor vehicles. ◄

When access to the Fagne is barred, there is a clearly-signed detour (continue straight ahead on the road toward Bérinzenne), which knocks about 1.2km off your distance.

Peatlands once covered tens of thousands of square kilometres in north-western Europe. Exploitation of the peatlands for agriculture, forestry, fuel and even (in coastal wetlands) salt has left only a small remnant undisturbed or in a natural state (with active peat accumulation). Peatlands that are supplied by rainwater are called bogs (*tourbières*), while those supplied by groundwater, runoff and rivers are fens (*bas-marais*). The Fagne de Malchamps is a raised bog, with a total area of about 360 hectares.

Most of the GR5's route through the Fagne de Malchamps is on a protective wooden boardwalk. You pass a monument to the seven crew members of an RAF Lancaster bomber shot down here during World War II, near the highest point of the GR5 in Belgium (576m), and then follow a meandering route toward a 22m observation tower.

Leaving the Fagne de Malchamps, turn sharply to the left on a dirt road and pass the Bérinzenne Domain, which includes a museum of the forest and waters (Musée de la Forêt et des Eaux, www.berinzenne.be/fr/musee.htm). Continue straight as the road becomes a trail. A section of this trail is likely to be muddy and slippery so this is one place where you might welcome a paved road, such as the one that descends here to **Andrimont**.

Turn right on a small road that forks to the left and continue to descend on a very rocky path, enclosed by trees and hedges. There are no services in **Ruy**, the small village at the bottom of the slope, but there is a bench that offers a welcome rest after negotiating that rocky trail.

*View over to
Andrimont*

Turn sharply right after crossing a small bridge over a stream and then left on a path between houses. Cross a bridge over another stream (the **Roannay**) and follow a trail that climbs back to the plateau. This is a pleasant trail beside a stream – shaded and not as rocky as the one down to Ruy.

Emerging from the woods, the trail continues to climb in open country. After crossing a road, turn left on another trail. Turn right at the next road and then left to continue climbing. The trail passes a modern wooden house on the right.

This is a magnificent section of the trail, with a coni-fer forest on the right and an open field descending to the left, affording **views** over the rolling coun-tryside. You can measure progress by looking back across the valley to Andrimont.

The GR5 now enters an area called the **Grandes Fagnes**. Walk first along a broad, grass trail through conifers. There follows another section of bog, where the trail is narrow and rather slippery but soon the trail enters a more open, drier forest, and you turn left (southeast) on a dirt road. This then zigzags: right after 200 metres, left after 500 metres and finally right again to return to the original direction.

The trail descends to **Stavelot**. Walk along the lower edge of a hill, traverse a slope with pine trees, and continue downhill through a deciduous forest. Turn left on a road and then, after 50 metres, turn sharply left on a narrow trail that leads down to… a tunnel! After the tunnel (under a road), continue downhill on a road to the right of a fountain. Cross a main road (**N68**) and walk to Place Saint Remacle in the centre of the town. Stavelot is a good place to spend the night, with various options for accommodation and dining.

Stavelot's famous **carnival,** drawing upon traditions that date back to the early 16th century, takes place on the fourth Sunday of Lent. The Blanc Moussis, disguised with white cloaks and long, red noses, roam the streets of Stavelot, creating mischief and fun. The former **abbey** houses three museums (www.abbayedestavelot.be/fr/musees) that cater to diverse interests: the Museum of the Principality of Stavelot-Malmédy, the Guillaume Apollinaire Museum and the Spa-Francorchamps Racetrack Museum.

STAGE 26
Stavelot to Commanster

Start	Stavelot (Place Saint Remacle)
Finish	Commanster
Distance	25km
Ascent/Descent	705m/483m
Time	6hr 30min
Maps	50 Malmédy; 56 Sankt-Vith
Refreshments	Cafés, restaurants and shops in Vielsalm
Transport	TEC buses (294 and 142) link Stavelot to Vielsalm, where there is also railway service; no public transport in Commanster.
Accommodation	Hotels and chambres d'hôtes in Vielsalm; chambre d'hôtes in Commanster

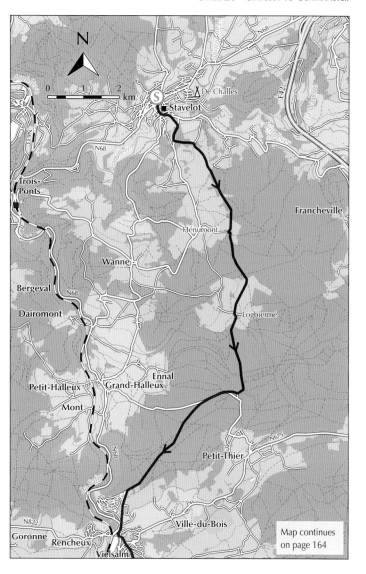

Map continues
on page 164

This is a very pleasant, easy stage, combining trails through forests and dirt roads across high, open countryside. Memorial plaques recall the area's violent experiences during World War II. Along the way, you pass through Vielsalm, famous for its festival of witchcraft in July.

The GR5 leaves Stavelot from the southern corner of Place Saint Remacle on Rue Général Jacques, which becomes Rue du Châtelet as it passes the **abbey**.

On the left, there are several **plaques** dedicated to the memory of the American army units that liberated Stavelot in September 1944 and others that fought here during the Battle of the Bulge, as well as Belgian civilians from this area who lost their lives during the war (in particular, 133 victims of Nazi massacres in December 1944). Stavelot, with its bridge over the Amblève river, was a contested, strategic point during that battle.

THE BATTLE OF THE BULGE

Before dawn on 16 December 1944, the German army launched an offensive into the Ardennes. Their goal was to divide the Allied armies and advance to Antwerp. The American forces here were caught by surprise. They considered this to be a 'quiet sector' that they could use for training new units and resting battle-weary ones. Bad weather prevented Allied air forces from operating for several days. The Germans broke through the American lines and nearly reached the Meuse river, creating a bulge in the lines that gave the battle its name. The Germans encountered stubborn resistance, however – most famously at Bastogne where they surrounded but could not defeat the American forces. Allied counterattacks stopped the Germans' advance and then pushed them back.

A walk through the narrow valleys and steep, wooded hills of this area, where there are few roads (and even fewer in 1944), gives some idea of the difficulty of fighting here – compounded by the intense cold and deep snow also suffered by the Belgian civilians caught in the middle of it.

The GR5 continues after the abbey on Rue Gustave Dewalque and crosses the bridge over the **Amblève** river. The

GR14 (the Sentier de l'Ardenne) joins the GR5 to cross the bridge. Then, while the GR14 turns right on Route de Wanne, the GR5 bears left and goes up Chemin du Château. After 250 metres, the GR5 turns right off that road and follows a dirt path uphill. ▸ This narrow, sometimes overgrown path leads to a road: turn right and continue uphill. Just before the B&B Villa Stavelot, turn left on a dirt road that soon becomes a pleasant trail in the woods.

The trail emerges from the woods beside a large, modern farm that practices organic ('bio') farming. Turn right to walk between the farm buildings and then left on a road beside a bench. The tree-lined road runs beside broad, open fields where cattle graze, offering splendid views over the high plateau. Cross a road and follow a trail into the woods, passing the Croix de la Belle Ferme (525m) 1.5km after the organic farm. Continue straight through a crossroads beside a picnic table. At another crossroads (1km after the cross), the church and château of **Wanne** are visible 4km to the right (southwest). A left turn here is not marked, but white-and-red Xs on trees indicate that the roads to the right and straight ahead are not the correct route. Soon, the road turns right (with a proper GR mark) and then (after 300m) reaches a triple fork, where the GR5 bears right.

A view of Stavelot from the south

This turn is not well-marked.

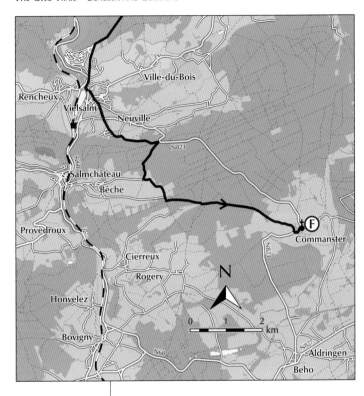

Leaving the forest 1km after the triple fork, the GR5 descends another kilometre across open country to **Logbiermé**, a small village. Turn right on the road here, left beside a war memorial, and then right to walk past a gîte operated by the Amis de la Nature. The dirt road enters the forest and (as it reaches some houses) turns right. Pass a sheltered picnic table and walk for several hundred metres on a paved road before re-entering the forest on a dirt road to the left. Continue straight through a crossroads (and pass another sheltered picnic table). The road turns left at a gate and then immediately follows a right fork, crosses a road and continues on a dirt path downhill. The GR5 passes a chapel and reaches a road. Turn left here to enter Vielsalm.

Vielsalm welcomes visitors with a statue of a witch (*macralle* in Walloon). The **Sabbat des Macralles takes** place each year during the evening of 20 July. It is a sound-and-light spectacle in which witches present amusing anecdotes and 'enthrone' local personalities, making them drink a potion, ride a broom and recite a spell. The fun continues next day with the Fête des Myrtilles (Blueberry Festival).

There are gaps in the waymarking through Vielsalm. Approaching the centre of the town, walk past the church and a fountain in the Place Paulin Moxhet. Leave the square on Rue Général Jacques and continue through an intersection with a traffic light. Bear right at a war memorial and go straight through a roundabout. ▶ The road curves left, narrows and enters a forest. Where a paved road descends to the left, the GR5 continues straight ahead on the dirt road. After a section of level walking below the edge of a forest and above open fields, the GR5 turns right on a trail into the forest.

The forest trail leads to a gravel road, which climbs gently and joins a road to the left. Just before reaching a paved

Turn right here for Vielsalm railway station.

Welcome to Vielsalm!

road (**N823**), make a hairpin turn to the right on a gravel road. After 500 metres on that road, turn left on a road going downhill and continue to another road, with a large farmhouse on the opposite hillside. Turn left here and follow a road, enclosed by fences, that runs through a field. At an intersection where the road continues straight and another road turns left, the GR5 enters the woods on a trail diagonally to the left. It crosses a stream on a small footbridge, turns left on a dirt road and then (after 150m) takes the right fork on a path that may be muddy.

The GR5 now meanders pleasantly through these woods (generally east and southeast), finally emerging for its final approach to **Commanster**, a small village where there is a comfortable chambre d'hôtes (which offers table d'hôte) near the church.

STAGE 27
Commanster to Ouren

Start	Commanster
Finish	Ouren
Distance	26km
Ascent/Descent	474m/662m
Time	6hr
Maps	56 Sankt-Vith; 61 Limerlé
Refreshments	Cafés/restaurants and other services in Burg-Reuland
Transport	Very limited: TEC bus routes 848 (Braunlauf–Sankt-Vith (off map to NE), weekdays only) and 496 (Burg-Reuland–Ouren, weekdays during the school term only)
Accommodation	Chambre d'hôtes in Braunlauf; hotels in Burg-Reuland and Ouren

A large portion of this stage follows paved or other hard surfaces. However, it is much better than average road-walking and really quite enjoyable. You cross broad plateaus with attractive views to distant horizons, walking at a comfortable, steady pace. Burg-Reuland is a good place to pause for refreshment. Thereafter, the GR5 rewards you with 7km of pleasant forest trails.

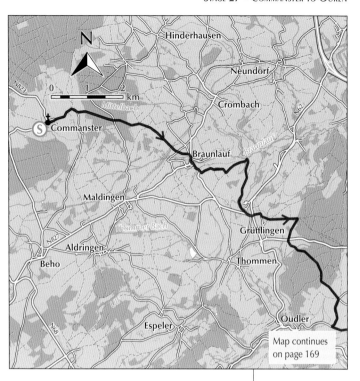

Map continues on page 169

As you face the church in Commanster, the GR5 departs on the road to the right and passes the village cemetery on the left. After 800 metres and just before a sign indicating the end of the village, turn right. Then, a short distance further, turn left on a road that enters the forest. A road sign bars vehicle traffic 'Bei Schnee, Eis und Tauwetter' (in case of snow, ice and thaw). You are now in the German-speaking area of Belgium.

> The Treaty of Versailles (1919) transferred the territories around Eupen, Malmédy and Sankt-Vith from Germany to Belgium. These '**Eastern Cantons**' (Ostkantonen or Cantons de l'Est) have a distinctive place in Belgium's complex, multi-layered linguistic

On the plateau near Braunlauf

structure. Their German-speaking community is one of three linguistic communities in Belgium (along with the Flemish and French communities), with its own parliament and government, while the Eastern Cantons are part of the Walloon Region (the two other regions being Flanders and Brussels), which also has a parliament and government.

Continue straight ahead on the road, passing a picnic table at an intersection and then emerging from the forest. About 5km from Commanster, you reach **Braunlauf**. Turn left on a road beside a bus stop in the centre of the village, then left on a dead-end road. Soon, the tarmac yields to gravel, progressing generally east. Turn left at a T-junction to enjoy a pleasant walk across the fields, high up with vast views over the countryside. At the next T-Junction, another 750 metres further on, beside a table and shelter, turn right. ◄

There is a stone here that marked the boundary between two communes, Crombach and Thommen.

The GR5 goes generally south from here and eventually curves southeast to merge with a road. This road leads to a main road (**N62**): Walk a short distance to the left and cross the main road. The GR5 continues straight from here on a smaller road. Turn right at a T-junction and then left. (This turn is not marked, but there is a white-and-red X indicating that you should not continue straight on.) Next, follow a right

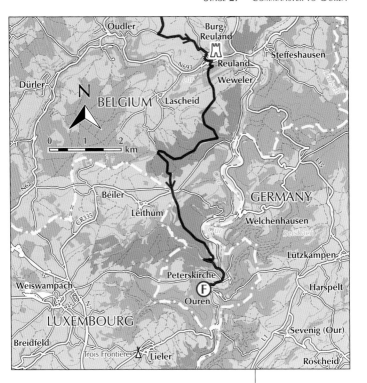

fork that runs east toward a forest. Reach the trees and soon turn right on a gravel road that descends between forest and fields. Cross another road and re-enter the forest.

The trail leads you (roughly southeast) through the forest for the next 1.2km. Emerge from the forest to cross some gently undulating fields. After a large mound (a water pumping station), the route reaches an intersection of several roads. Turn right here on a paved road. The road goes around a large dairy farm to a T-junction. Turn left here and walk downhill to **Burg-Reuland**.

The GR5 winds its way through Burg-Reuland, with a few navigational challenges. After passing a hotel/restaurant and turning right toward the castle, there is a point where another trail, the GR56 (the Sentier des Cantons de l'Est),

Reuland Castle

There is a café within the picturesque ruins of this medieval castle.

joins the GR5 from the opposite direction. The two GR trails cross the town together. At the top of a hill, turn left toward the **castle** again. ◄ Walk around the right side of the castle walls and then down to the street. Turn left toward the church, with its distinctive bulb steeple. Do not turn right where, confusingly, there is a GR mark on one side of the street and a white-and-red X on the other side of the street. Turn right at the church and then right again in front of a striking red building.

A poignant war memorial beside the church records the names of soldiers killed in World War I (when

Burg-Reuland was part of Germany) and World War II (when Burg-Reuland was part of Belgium).

Bear left where the street forks and then turn left to walk through an arched passage under a building. Cross a bridge over a small stream (the **Ulf**) and turn left on a RAVeL path.

> The RAVeL – **Réseau Autonome des Voies Lentes** – is a network of over 2000km of paths in Wallonia that follow old railway lines and towpaths, designed to be accessible to cyclists, horse riders and wheelchair users.

The GR56 and the GR5 separate 50 metres after the bridge. ▶ About 100 metres further on, the GR5 turns left and climbs up a steep slope. At the top of that slope, continue straight past three trees shading a bench and through a crossroads. At the next crossroads, where the road bottoms out, turn right on a dirt road.

The road leads to a good trail in a forest, descending gradually across a slope. At the bottom of the descent, make a hairpin right turn and continue on a level path through a narrow, wooded valley.

Be careful to follow the correct trail here. The GR56 continues straight, while the GR5 makes a hairpin right turn up a grassy path.

Ouren in the distance

About 700 metres along that path a GR mark signals another right turn and a trail branches off the trail to the right – but **beware** that is not the turn. The actual right turn is a few metres further where the trail forks in a clearing. The correct trail is obvious (with a good waymark) when you see it.

Take this turn and continue on a mostly level trail to a sharp turn to the left (southeast). The trail then climbs through open country. At the crest of that climb, the GR5 crosses a road and touches the **border** with Luxembourg but does not cross it.

The GR5 descends from here to Ouren (nearly 4km). Depending on the season, the fields beside the road may be filled with gorse in dazzling, golden bloom. Walk on the dirt road most of the way, but shortly before the road curves left, branch to the right on a trail into the forest. This trail descends to a road. Turn left here and walk 300m to the outskirts of **Ouren**. There is one hotel at the entrance to the village and a second one in the centre of Ouren after a bridge over the **Our** river.

4 LUXEMBOURG

Vianden, dominated by its castle (Stage 29)

173

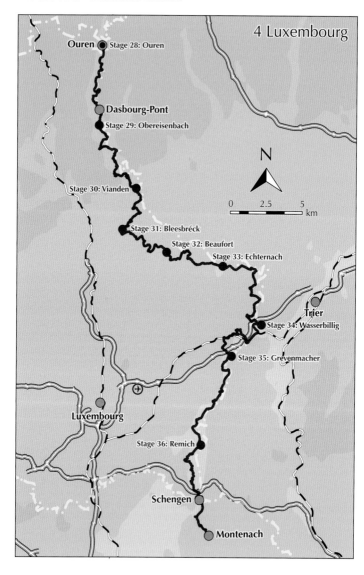

4 Luxembourg

Ouren — Stage 28: Ouren

Dasbourg-Pont

Stage 29: Obereisenbach

Stage 30: Vianden

N

0   2.5   5
km

Stage 31: Bleesbréck

Stage 32: Beaufort

Stage 33: Echternach

Trier

Stage 34: Wasserbillig

Stage 35: Grevenmacher

Luxembourg

Stage 36: Remich

Schengen

Montenach

If you think of Luxembourg as merely a small country with a large financial sector you will be pleasantly surprised by this section of the GR5 which follows its eastern border.

First, you walk through hilly forests beside the Our river and across high plateaus from Ouren to Vianden. The slopes of these forest trails are steeper than those of the Belgian Ardennes, not to mention the trails through Dutch polders and Flemish heathland. If you have been walking on the GR5 for a while, you will be ready to tackle those slopes – and enjoy every step along these magnificent trails.

Descending to the Sûre river you enter the Petite Suisse Luxembourgeoise between Beaufort and Echternach. Towering, eroded blocks of sandstone enclose the trail, sometimes leaving a passage only a few metres wide. Next you follow the Sûre south of Echternach to its confluence with the Moselle at Wasserbillig. From there to Schengen, your route traverses the steep slopes of vineyards on the Route du Vin (Wine Route) beside the Moselle, with occasional detours across the plateaus to the west. There is a lot of road-walking on the Wine Route, as the GR5 often follows routes used by grape growers, but it makes for easy walking.

Luxembourg has its own trail-marking system. The GR5 follows various trails that are marked with these waymarks, starting with yellow discs and followed by green triangles and yellow rectangles. There is often more than one waymark along a given trail. For example, the GR5 shares the trail in some places with St James' Way, marked with a scallop shell motif. Signposts give distances to various destinations with no mention of the GR5. It is helpful, therefore, to be aware of the towns and other places ahead of you on your route so that you can recognise where to go!

SECTION SUMMARY TABLE

Start	Ouren
Finish	Montenach (France)
Distance	184km
Ascent/Descent	6262m/6374m
Maps	Administration du Cadastre et de la Topographie: Carte Topographique Nord 1:50,000 and Carte Topographique Sud 1:50,000
Note	Although the Wine Route along the Moselle is a popular destination for tourists, there are relatively few hotels and B&Bs close to the GR5 here. As explained in the stage descriptions, this problem can be solved by taking buses to and from accommodation, without missing a step of the GR5.

STAGE 28
Ouren to Obereisenbach

Start	Ouren
Finish	Obereisenbach (Kohnenhof campground)
Distance	20km
Ascent/Descent	588m/637m
Time	6hr
Map	Carte Topographique Nord
Refreshments	Cafés at Tintesmühle campground and Dasbourg-Pont
Transport	Bus routes 663, 842 and 860 run along the N10 main road south of Dasbourg-Pont or Rodershausen
Accommodation	Hotel in Dasburg (500 metres from Dasbourg-Pont); Kohnenhof campground (with trekkershutten) 2km north of Obereisenbach
Waymarks	Standard GR to the Luxembourg border; then yellow discs

This is an excellent stage, although it does include a 2km walk beside a busy main road. The forest trail sometimes meanders close to the Our river and elsewhere climbs and descends away from it. Places where the trail traverses a steep slope high above the river, amid incredibly tall conifer trees, are particularly memorable.

In the centre of Ouren, walk toward the Dreiländerblick Hotel. Turn left to pass behind the hotel and walk up a small road, then down past a religious shrine to a road. Turn left where a road sign points to Luxembourg.

The road enters open country and passes a park beside the river. The road crosses the **Our** river and curves right beside a farmhouse. The GR5 branches off the road to the left here (south) to follow a grass path, marked by yellow discs.

A nearby monument commemorates the signing of the **Treaty of Rome** in 1957 establishing the European Economic Community. It was signed on 25 March by Belgium, France, Italy, Luxembourg, the Netherlands and West Germany and came into force on 1 January 1958.

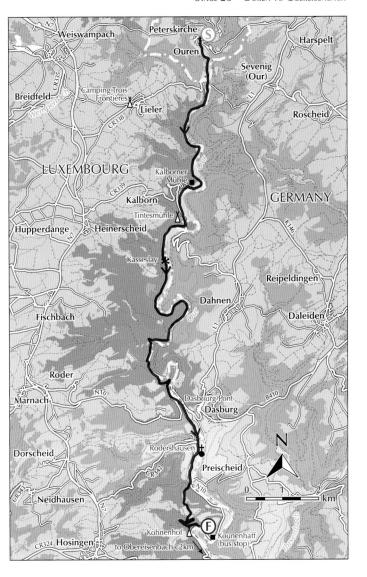

The Our

Next to this stream is footbridge across the river to Germany. The borders of the three countries meet in the middle of the river.

Here (as often in Luxembourg) there are benches beside the trail that offer of places to pause.

Walk along the path beside the Our and cross a small tributary stream that marks the Belgian-Luxembourg **border**. ◄

After the border, the GR5 soon re-joins the road. Turn left to walk close to the river, following the line of the border, and then pass a picnic area. Continue straight, past a shelter and across a small bridge, ignoring a road that climbs in the woods. Walk along a dirt trail above the river, surrounded by towering conifer trees and birdsong. ◄

The trail passes the site of **Kalborner Mühle** (an old mill) and then a modern water treatment plant. Follow a paved road for a short distance and then turn onto a trail that returns to the river. The GR5 soon leaves the river and rises to a paved road. Cross the road and climb up a shaly path on the opposite side, then descend the other side of this hill to meet the road again. Follow the road for just 50 metres and turn right on a grass path that leads to a small, dead-end road at the entrance to **Tintesmühle**. Turn right here and walk past the campground. The trail climbs into the woods and even offers steps built into the steep slope. The GR5 briefly follows a gravel road and then turns left back to a trail. At the entrance to an open field, take a right fork on a small trail, and then left on a dirt road.

The GR5 now traverses a steep slope high above the river. ▶ The trail descends to a stream and comes to a small concrete bridge with a bench on the other side. The main trail continues upstream (toward Heinerscheid), while the GR5 branches to the left and crosses the bridge. The trail climbs steeply here and then (after passing a short side-trail to the Kasseslay **viewing point**) descends steeply back down. Follow a small trail that branches to the left off the larger one and then climbs again to a place that offers a good view of Dasbourg-Pont and the valley. Descend from here to the road. Turn left on the road and then, after just a few metres, walk down wooden stairs to a trail that leads to **Dasbourg-Pont**, where there is a café and a service station with a small shop. ▶

The GR5 follows the **N10** from Dasbourg-Pont for about 2km. It's a busy road, and there is not a lot of room on its shoulder for pedestrians. ▶ About 600 metres after walking past the church in **Rodershausen** and in sight of a wooden footbridge below the road to the left, turn right off the main road and hike up a narrow, barely visible trail into the forest beside the road.

The trail leads to a quiet road, which the GR5 follows to the right as it winds through the forest and across the open fields of a plateau. Turn right on another road near the high point and then left on a trail at the entrance to the forest. Descend on a traverse across a steep slope in a narrowing valley. The descent continues after a hairpin turn to the left and finally ends at the main road (N10). The GR5 continues to the right, but to reach the Kohnenhof **campground**, a good place (with *trekkershutten* and a restaurant) to spend the night, cross the N10 and walk a short distance to the left (southeast).

Your position on this slope will help you appreciate how tall those pine trees can grow!

Most of the cars in the service station will have German number plates, attracted by Luxembourg's lower taxes on petrol and tobacco.

To avoid this walk, you could take Bus 842 from Dasbourg-Pont to Kounenhaff, near the Kohnenhof Campground, but this line has a limited timetable.

STAGE 29
Obereisenbach to Vianden

Start	Obereisenbach (Kohnenhof campground)
Finish	Vianden
Distance	23km
Ascent/Descent	1332m/1326m
Time	7hr
Map	Carte Topographique Nord
Refreshments	Cafés/restaurants in Obereisenbach, Untereisenbach, Wahlhausen, Pont de Gemünd, Stolzembourg and Mont Saint-Nicolas
Transport	Bus routes 663, 842 and 860 run along the N10 between Obereisenbach and Vianden; line 570 links Stolzembourg and Vianden.
Accommodation	Hotels and youth hostel in Vianden
Waymarks	Yellow discs

This is a relatively long stage and its 23km will require more time and energy that any similar distance on the Northern GR5 up to this point. The aspects that make this walk challenging, however, are also its positive elements. The route climbs and descends successive mountain trails in forests, with interludes of walking across high, broad plateaus. It's really a great stage (and it can easily be broken into two stages by using the bus service between Stolzembourg and Vianden).

The GR5, designated as European long-distance trail E2, joins the E3 (marked by green triangles) here. The E3 links the Atlantic to the Forest of Bohemia.

Starting from the campground, return to the trail at the N10 and turn left along the main road for 50 metres, then right on a small trail that climbs steeply into the forest. ◄ When the trail descends back to the main road, turn left and then right to walk beside the main road. After 600 metres, turn right on a smaller road (Bongertsweis) that climbs to **Obereisenbach**. The GR5 curves right beside a small, white chapel and then turns left on a broad path into the woods. Within a short distance, branch to the left on a narrow path that descends to a road. Turn left here to walk into **Untereisenbach**.

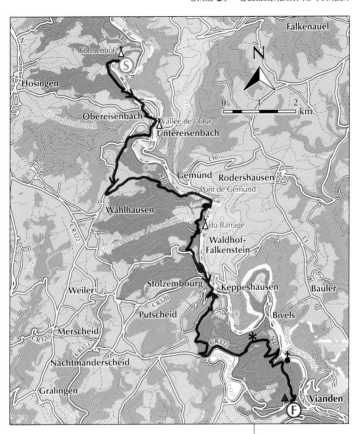

Turn right at a T-junction to cross a small bridge and walk briefly along the **N10**, passing a **campground** on the left. Just opposite the campground's café, turn right on Am Duerf. (There is another café a short distance beyond Am Duerf on the main road.) After the road crests, turn right on Wuelesser Wée. Leave the road where (after 500 metres) it makes a hairpin turn to the right and walk straight ahead onto a trail. There are waymarks at this turn, but they may be obscured by vegetation. Walk up this narrow, steep trail to a road (Am Duerf, again) and turn left.

A forest trail descends toward Gemünd on the Our

Continue straight for the restaurant in this village.

Walk from here up to a high plateau with good views in all directions. There is a picnic table beside the road with a striking, modern design inspired by the meandering **Our** river within its deep valley. At the entrance to **Wahlhausen**, turn left between farm buildings. ◄ Walk along the road as it gradually descends (northeast turning to east). The pavement ends where it enters the forest. A winding trail goes up and down along a narrow ridge. Finally, after a long descent, the GR5 arrives again on the N10 near **Pont de Gemünd** (and a bench).

Turn right and walk beside the N10 for 600 metres then turn right on a small paved road. Where the road makes a hairpin turn to the right, the GR5 turns just as sharply to the left on a trail that climbs in the forest, levels off and descends steeply. At the bottom of that descent, cross a small concrete bridge and turn right on a dirt road. Walk just a short distance on that road before turning left on a trail and left again on smaller trail that branches off to climb a steep hillside with a dozen switchbacks. Happily, there is a bench at the top of this climb!

From here, the GR5 follows a broad, level trail to a paved road that descends to the N10 near the Bei der Kiirch bus stop in **Stolzembourg**. Turn right and walk beside the main road, and then turn right on Rue du Faubourg (opposite a bridge across the Our). After passing the houses on this road and just before the road enters the forest, turn left to cross a small wooden bridge that leads to a narrow forest trail. ▶ Turn left on a paved road that winds upward and enters open country. After the road becomes a dirt trail, turn left on a small trail that continues to climb. It passes through an open, wind-swept area with small oak trees. Return to the forest on a broad, grassy path that bends off to the left, and then left again on a narrow trail. As the trail traverses a steep slope in the forest, watch for a left turn on a trail that descends with switchbacks – and then climbs back up. The GR5 crosses other trails here, so pay close attention to the waymarking.

There is a bench beside this trail with a beautiful view over Stolzembourg and the river.

The trail reaches a road and levels off beside a café. Turn left on the road and walk past the **upper reservoir** (basin supérieur) at the summit of Mont Saint-Nicolas.

The **hydroelectric plant** was commissioned in 1964 and is owned by the Société Electrique de l'Our. Water is pumped from the lower reservoir (c10 million cubic metres) to the upper reservoir (c7 million cubic metres) during periods of low demand. Water stored in the upper reservoir is then released to flow through the turbines and generate electricity when demand is high. The fall between the two reservoirs is about 280 metres. You can visit between Easter and September (www.seo.lu/fr/visite/visite).

Turn left on a side road posted 'Point de Vue Victor Hugo'. The road leads to that **observation point**, a pleasant place for a pause with a sheltered bench and information about Hugo's several visits to Vianden as a tourist and a political exile. ▶ Further on, leave the road on a forest trail to the right where the road turns sharply to the left. The trail traverses a steep slope and then turns left on a gravel road.

There is a museum devoted to Victor Hugo (Musée Littéraire Victor Hugo, **www.victor-hugo.lu**) in Vianden.

Follow the road down to the **lower reservoir** of the hydroelectric plant. Walk to the end of the reservoir and turn left on a trail that climbs in the forest. The trail goes around the plant and climbs steeply on the other side. At the top of that climb stands the **Bildchen Chapelle Notre Dame**, with a good view over the valley and surrounding countryside.

Walk past the chapel along a road with sculptures depicting the Stations of the Cross. At the fourth station, turn

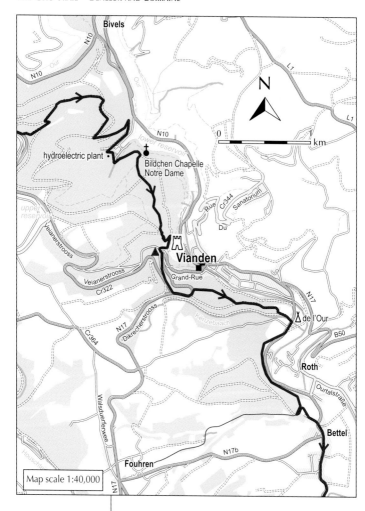

right on a trail that climbs with switchbacks up a steep slope. Pass a cabin at the top and then walk downhill on a dirt road through the woods. At a large crossroads in the woods, where there could be some doubt about the correct road to follow, go straight. Eventually, there are waymarks along this road that confirm the route. The road passes under a chair lift, and Vianden comes into view below. Follow a trail that descends in the woods and turn right on a paved road. Pass Vianden **castle** on the left and continue downhill. Curving left, the road leads directly to the **youth hostel**. The road, meanwhile, continues to the left and downhill to the lower part of Vianden. In addition to its youth hostel, Vianden has hotels, restaurants and other services, making it a convenient place to spend a night.

Vianden's **castle** looms above the town on a spur of rock. The Counts of Vianden built this formidable castle during the 11–14th centuries. The County of Vianden passed under the rule of the House of Orange-Nassau in 1477. The most famous Count of Vianden was William the Silent (1545–1584), the first leader of the Dutch revolt against Spanish rule. As the House of Orange-Nassau devoted their energies to the Netherlands – first as stadholders and later as kings – Vianden and its castle were neglected. King William I sold the castle in 1820 for 3200 florins. The buyer proceeded to sell the furnishings and masonry, producing such an outcry

Vianden Castle

that the king re-purchased what was left in 1827 for 1100 florins. The castle was a dilapidated ruin when the Grand Duke of Luxembourg ceded it to the State in 1977. Since then, it has been fully restored and is now open to visitors.

STAGE 30

Vianden to Bleesbréck

Start	Vianden
Finish	Bleesbréck
Distance	14km
Ascent/Descent	419m/497m
Time	4hr
Map	Carte Topographique Nord
Refreshments	There are restaurants at the campground de l'Our and in Bettel, but they are unlikely to be open in the morning.
Transport	Bus route 570 runs from Vianden to Bleesbréck (and Diekirch, which is on a railway line).
Accommodation	Campground (with trekkershutten) in Bleesbréck; hotels off the GR5 in Bettendorf and Diekirch.
Waymarks	Yellow discs

This transitional stage leaves the rough, mountainous terrain of the Our valley between the Belgian border and Vianden. It passes through forests and open, rolling countryside to finish in the valley of the Sûre (Sauer) River. Compared to the previous stages, this one is easier but less exciting.

From the youth hostel, the road climbs gently to a larger road, where there is a good viewpoint over the valley and Vianden Castle. Do not cross the road, but instead turn left and walk 100 metres to a main road (**N17**). Turn left on the main road, which descends and curves left.

Just before a sign welcoming people to Vianden and listing the city's twin cities there is a gravel road that branches off to the right. Cross the main road and walk along this road

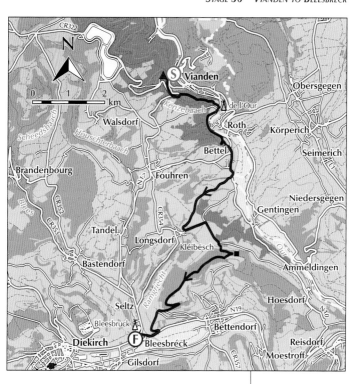

into the forest. It's a pleasant, easy walk. The GR5 turns left beside a bench and passes several houses. Now a dirt trail, it follows a wooded ridge and then narrows as it descends the slope. Follow the trail down to a dirt road, turn left here and descend to a main road (**N10**). There is a **campground** and a restaurant on the other side of the road.

Turn right and walk a short distance beside the main road, then bend to the right on a bicycle path (marked 'Piste Cyclable des Trois Rivières'). The path traverses a steep slope, climbing gently with views through trees over the valley to the hills on the opposite side, to reach a clearing with benches and a small brick building with a sign 'Bettel' on it. ▶ The trail takes a hairpin turn to the left on a road here. Follow the road, passing a cemetery on the right, down to

This is a former railway station on a line between Diekirch and Vianden, now the site of occasional special events and festivities.

the main road (N10 again). Turn right and walk along the main road into **Bettel**, passing a restaurant on the right and a church on the left. Continue through the village and, after leaving it, turn right on a small road (Op der Telleschbaach).

The road climbs gently through open country, passing a gazebo that offers a pleasant place to take a break and admire the view. At the high point (342m), there is a religious shrine and a bench. Continue straight, walking beside fields of wheat and maize, as the road descends to a village, **Longsdorf**. Walk through the village and turn left (east-south-east) at a T-junction on Um Sand. This road leads to another T-junction. Turn right here (southeast) and walk along a road rising to a forest. Along the way, there is a picnic table under a shelter, perfect for a hot, sunny day. Just after that shelter, turn right on a trail into the woods.

The trail turns left just after entering the woods and climbs to a point where there is a cabin and a bench. Turn right sharply, continue from here through a clearing and then curve right on a dirt path where the main path descends through a hairpin left turn.

A pleasant vantage point on the road between Bettel and Longsdorf

The GR5 now follows a pleasant trail through the woods. At one point, there is a fork without a waymark: the trail follows the right fork, but the left fork re-joins the main trail within a short distance. A bit further, the trail bends to

the right beside an open field on the left. Continue walking through the woods, with a steep slope falling away on your right and the fields on your left. The trail winds through the forest and descends. After turning right on a broader path, it merges to the right on a paved road. ▸ Diekirch and other towns are visible in the distance.

Where the road forks beside a picnic table, bear right on the smaller road that descends to the main road (**N19**). Turn right and walk beside the main road (or on the grassy verge where possible) 600 metres to a roundabout. The entrance to Bleesbruck **campground** lies on the other side of the roundabout. The campground has *trekkershutten* and a restaurant. **Diekirch** (with hotels and other services) is 2km west of this roundabout.

Following this road to the left leads to Bettendorf (1.5km), where there is a hotel. Re-join the GR5 from Bettendorf by walking west on the N19.

STAGE 31
Bleesbréck to Beaufort

Start	Bleesbréck
Finish	Beaufort
Distance	16.5km
Ascent/Descent	496m/347m
Time	4hr 30min
Map	Carte Topographique Nord
Refreshments	Cafés/restaurants in Gilsdorf
Transport	Numerous bus routes pass through Bleesbréck and Beaufort, as well as nearby Diekirch (which has railway service).
Accommodation	Hotels, youth hostel and campground (with trekkershutten) in Beaufort
Waymarks	Yellow discs

This stage includes two fine sections of forest walking – the first near the beginning and the second at the end (where the GR5 enters the Petite Suisse Luxembourgeoise). There is a 7km section in the middle of paved (mostly quiet) roads. Most trekkers prefer to avoid walking on roads, but you would not want to miss the magnificent forest trails of this stage.

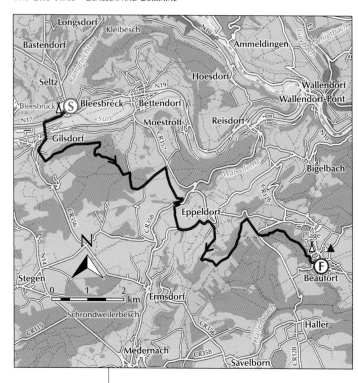

Starting at the roundabout beside the campground, walk west beside the main road (**N17**) to the bridge. Turn left to cross it and walk through **Gilsdorf**.

> The GR5 is joined here by the **GR57**, marked by green triangles. This is the GR5's second intersection with the GR57, the first being north of Liège (see Stage 22). An intrepid trekker could walk a big loop between Liège and Gilsdorf, following the GR5 in one direction and the GR57 in the other direction.

Follow the road past Gilsdorf's church as it climbs gently and curves right. Notice the houses neatly painted in various

Attractive homes in Gilsdorf

striking colours, characteristic of Luxembourg. Turn left on a small road beside house No 23 and then fork to the right on a grassy path that climbs to the wooded ridge directly ahead. Turn left at a T-junction with a paved road. Continue on a dirt road into the forest until it peters out. In a clearing, the trail continues on the left up stone steps that lead to a marvellous forest trail – broad and level, traversing a steep slope. On a perfect day, sunlight filters through the trees, dappling the ground, and birds sing lustily. ▸

The trail continues in the forest as the terrain flattens, with several well-marked turns. About 3.3km after leaving the dirt road, turn left at a T-junction with a dirt road. The road reaches another T-junction where an open field lies ahead. A well-placed bench offers a view over the country-side. Turn right here to stay in the forest. Then, 500 metres further, the road turns left beside another bench and leaves the forest. Walk northeast, first on the edge of the forest and then in the open. The road becomes paved and reaches a T-junction with another road.

Turn right here and follow the road as it descends between fields of grain and maize. After curves to the left and right, the road reaches a main road. Pass a large house painted bright orange, then turn left and walk a short

There are great blocks of stratified stone beside this trail, a foretaste of the Petite Suisse Luxembourgeoise further along the GR5.

191

distance on the main road. Watch for a small, stone bridge on the right. Cross that bridge, turn left after a short distance and walk up a dirt path that climbs steeply, becoming paved along the way.

At the crest, turn left at a T-junction with a main road and walk to **Eppeldorf**. ◀ Turn right as you reach the village and walk through the centre. There are no services here, but there is a shelter with benches. Continue on the road as it climbs and leaves the village, curving to the right. Stay on the road as it enters the forest (briefly) and then turns sharply left. There is an intersection where the road reaches its high point: turn left here and walk into the nearby forest.

There is a shaded picnic table at this T-junction – a good place for lunch.

Shortly after entering the forest, the GR5 forks to the left. Leave the forest but continue along its edge before turning left back into the forest. (These turns, like most others, are well-marked.) The trail descends abruptly in the forest and then traverses the steep slope. It crosses an open area and then follows the edge of the forest. At a T-junction with a road, turn right and briefly walk again in the open. The GR5 soon finds an excellent forest trail for the final approach to Beaufort. There are signposts at the entrance to this forest that point to several routes, in particular the Mullerthal Trail.

> The **Mullerthal Trail** is a network of trails in the beautiful area between Beaufort and Echternach. It is made up of three interconnected trails, totalling 112km, and four 'Extra Tours'. The route followed by the GR5 here coincides with sections of the Mullerthal Trail, marked by a stylised *M*.

Cross a road and continue briefly on a broad dirt path before branching to the left on a narrow trail. Follow this trail as it descends gently through the forest. It's a very pleasant walk, and soon great blocks of sandstone loom beside the trail.

Pass a pond and continue on a broad path to the right. With very little transition, the forest trail leads to a road, CR128, on the edge of **Beaufort**. ◀ The GR5 heads to the centre of Beaufort by turning right here and then left on a small road where the CR128 curves and descends to the right (toward the castle).

If your destination is the campground or other accommodation on the northern side of Beaufort, turn left on this road and follow it up to Grand-Rue.

There are two **Beaufort castles**: a medieval fortress and a Renaissance castle. The medieval fortress was built in the 11–17th centuries. In the mid-17th century, the owner built a new structure behind the medieval fortress, the Renaissance castle. The medieval fortress was unoccupied after the mid-18th century, fell into ruin and was latterly used as a quarry. It was restored in the 20th century and opened for visits by the public in 1932. The Renaissance castle suffered relatively little damage or deterioration over the years and was inhabited until 2012. It is now open to visitors, as well.

The medieval fortress at Beaufort

STAGE 32
Beaufort to Echternach

Start	Beaufort
Finish	Echternach
Distance	16.8km
Ascent/Descent	572m/750m
Time	5hr
Map	Carte Topographique Nord
Refreshments	Cafés/restaurants in Grundhof and Berdorf
Transport	Bus route 848 links Beaufort, Berdorf and Echternach.
Accommodation	Hotels, B&B and campground (with trekkershutten) in Berdorf; hotels, B&B and youth hostel in Echternach
Waymarks	Yellow discs and green triangles

This stage is one of the most dramatic and memorable of the Northern GR5, as it passes through the heart of the Petite Suisse Luxembourgeoise, an area of spectacular geology with trails winding within narrow gorges and beside towering blocks of sandstone. You could break this stage into two short days, with an overnight stay in Berdorf.

Walk from the centre of Beaufort along the main road that descends to the castle. Turn left into the parking lot opposite the entrance to the castle, where there is the first of several panels describing the geology, plants and animals of the Petite Suisse Luxembourgeoise. Follow the excellent trail that enters the forest from the far side of the parking lot. The trail winds its way around and over obstacles as it follows a small stream, the Haupeschbaach. Blocks of sandstone (*grès de Luxembourg*) tower over both sides of the trail. There are numerous benches beside the trail, where you can pause, listen to the birds and admire the surroundings. This section of the trail, in a deep, wooded gorge, is a humid environment, so moss and ferns are abundant.

After meeting a dirt road, the trail branches left and broadens briefly as it continues to follow the stream. Finally (3km from Beaufort Castle), the trail marked with yellow discs and green triangles branches to the left away from the stream. After a short, steep climb, the trail levels off beside the blocks of stone. It crosses a main road (**CR364**), where there is a shelter and picnic table. ▶ Steps behind the shelter lead up to a broad, level forest trail. It's a pleasant trail, but quite ordinary compared to what you have just walked through (and to what lies ahead). The trail crosses a plateau, and eventually the land to the left opens up, while you remain in the forest.

The rock face beside the shelter exhibits the distinctive honeycomb pattern of erosion that is common in this area.

The trail through this forest is, as usual, well marked. Nevertheless, there is one turn where the waymark is ambiguous. Watch for a right fork, where the trail descends from the plateau, 30 metres before a wooden bench. Going down from here, pass close to huge blocks of stratified stone, then bend right at another fork in the trail and continue straight through an intersection of trails beside a bench. The trail drops down to a road at **Grundhof**, a village where there is a restaurant nearby to the left.

This is a transition between two areas of the **Petite Suisse Luxembourgeoise**. Turn right on the road and walk a short distance to a trail on the left. The trail immediately climbs, first across open fields and then steeply in the forest. The trail passes between large blocks of stone and reaches a lookout point, the **Belvédère de Kasselt**. The trail descends slightly

The Petite Suisse Luxembourgeoise near Beaufort

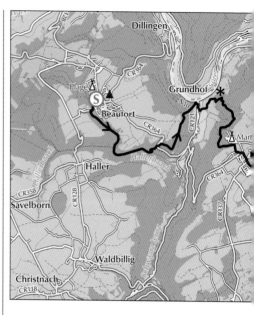

A signpost here gives distances to Berdorf, 1.1km, and Echternach, 10.1km.

here and then follows the base of the tall blocks of stone and slips through narrow passages between them. There is a popular rock-climbing area here, the 'Sept Gorges'. Finally, just after crossing a small wooden bridge, the trail turns left into a passage through the rock. ◄ On a hot day, the air here will feel deliciously cool.

The trail emerges into the open, on a plateau, and enters **Berdorf** (where there are restaurants, cafés and accommodation). Follow waymarks into the centre of the town. Turn right, between the church and the mairie, and then left on An der Kéier. The road curves right and descends slightly. Leave the village here and continue on a paved path that is reserved for bicycles and horses (and, of course, walkers). Walk straight on between fields of grain and maize to a forest.

Enter the forest, turn left and follow waymarks into another encounter with the extraordinary local geology. It's an easy trail – broad and flat, with steps and little wooden bridges.

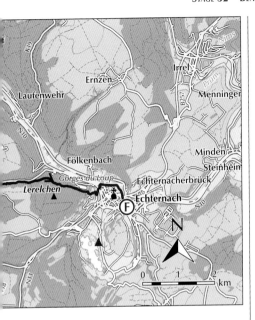

What you see first as the trail goes through caverns and passageways reflects considerable human intervention. This area served as a **quarry** at least as far back as the Middle Ages. Millstones were cut from this rock. There is even an **amphitheatre** carved out of the rock which would be a good venue for a rock concert!

The trail reaches the CR364 but does not cross it, instead running through the forest parallel to the road and above it for 1km. It passes through stone blocks that form a labyrinth (duly identified as such by a painted label). Then, after passing a shelter and crossing a wooden bridge over a stream, you take a right fork on a trail in the direction of the Gorges du Loup/Wolfsschlucht. This is one of the most dramatic rock formations of the area, and you get a close-up view of it. The trail slips between tall, stratified blocks of rock.

Here steep steps going upward offer the opportunity to explore the gorges further but the GR5 descends a set of

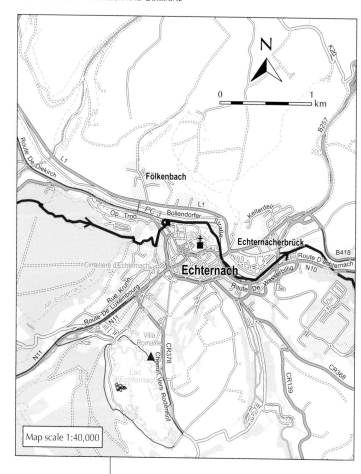

Map scale 1:40,000

There is a great view from here of Echternach, dominated by its abbey.

steps here. After passing a tall wall of yellowish stone, the trail levels off and becomes a smooth traverse above the valley. Soon, the trail reaches a gazebo constructed of logs and tree branches. ◄

Descend from the gazebo on a winding stone path to **Echternach**. After crossing a road and continuing straight between apartment buildings, you reach the bus station (*gare*

The GR5 slips through the Gorges of the Wolf

routière). The yellow disc waymarks end here. To reach the centre of Echternach, make a hairpin turn to the right and walk along Rue de la Gare.

In AD698, Willibrord of Northumberland (who had been trained at Rathmelsigi Abbey in Ireland) founded a **Benedictine abbey** in Echternach. The abbey became famous for its scriptorium, which produced fine illuminated manuscripts during the 9–11th centuries, drawing upon Irish calligraphic traditions. Facsimiles of these manuscripts are displayed at the Abbey Museum in Echternach. Willibrord died in 739 and was honoured as a saint.

His crypt in the basilica beside the abbey became a pilgrimage destination – the origin, perhaps, of the Dancing Procession that now takes place in Echternach every Whit Tuesday.

STAGE 33
Echternach to Wasserbillig

Start	Echternach
Finish	Wasserbillig
Distance	26.4km
Ascent/Descent	817m/843m
Time	7hr 30min
Map	Carte Topographique Sud
Refreshments	Rosport; near the GR5 in Born and Moersdorf
Transport	Bus route 485 (Echternach–Wasserbillig–Grevenmacher (Stage 34)); railway service at Wasserbillig
Accommodation	Hotel in Ralingen (across Sûre river from Rosport); campground (with trekkershutten) in Born; hotel in Oberbillig (across Moselle river from Wasserbillig).
Waymarks	Green triangles (briefly); then yellow rectangles
Note	Instead of struggling for accommodation, you could base yourself at Remich (Stage 35) and use the frequent buses along the N10 to pace your walking as you like between Echternach and Schengen (Stage 36).

This is another transitional stage. After leaving Echternach, you walk again, briefly, in a forest beside big blocks of sandstone. The trail runs roughly parallel to the Sûre, although often above it and out of sight. Finally, on the approach to Wasserbillig, the GR5 follows the Sûre to its confluence with the Moselle. Here, you enter a land of vineyards and fine wine.

As you face the Echternach bus station (gare routière) and the **Sûre** river, the GR5 (marked by green triangles) passes to the left of the station and then turns right to follow a pleasant path beside the river. After passing tennis courts, bend right and walk through a park. Just as you leave the park, with a

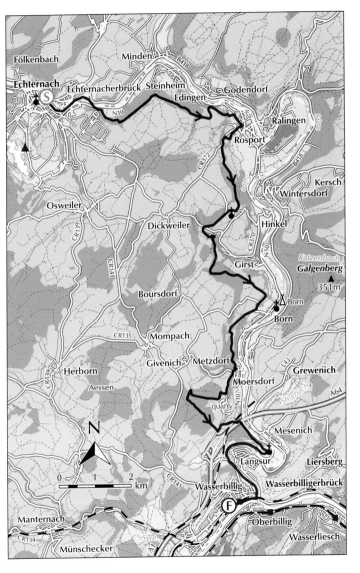

The dramatic rock formations continue south of Echternach

The green triangles mark the Ardennes-Eifel trail, which crosses the Sûre river here into Germany.

bridge ahead, the route marked by green triangles turns right, but the GR5 now follows yellow rectangles straight under the bridge. ◄ Continue along the riverside path, passing the large Archimedes screws of a pumping station.

The GR5 follows the river for 1.5km and then turns right across a road onto a trail that climbs in a forest. After a brief passage on a paved road beside the forest, turn right on a trail back into the forest. The trail winds beside and between great blocks of stone. There is a short section, following a right turn, where the trail follows a paved road. About 4km after leaving the river path, you fork to the left and then turn left on a trail into the woods. Still beside the blocks of stone, the trail is smooth and easy here.

Henri Tudor was an engineer, inventor and industrialist who developed the first practical lead-acid battery in 1886. He died of lead poisoning in 1928.

Finally, turn left on a dirt road and leave the forest. The road descends between fields and curves left. Upon reaching the woods ahead, turn right on a small trail (signposted 'Rosport'). The trail continues to descend through these woods to the outskirts of **Rosport** but turns right beforehand, when a café comes into view ahead on the left. Walk up a set of steps, past a church, and turn left into a park which houses the Musée Henri Tudor. ◄

Continue for 300m through the park and then turn right on a road that leads to a trail in a forest. Turn left on this trail and follow it for 2km through the forest, heading generally south. Emerging from the forest, the trail reaches a road. Turn right here and pass between a **church** on the left and a café on the right. Bear left on a dirt road beside a picnic table.

The trail returns to the forest, descending into a ravine and then climbing up the other side. Cross a road and continue in the forest. The trail follows the edge of the forest and then goes through another ravine. It leaves the forest and descends toward **Born** on a paved road. Before you get there, however, you turn right on a road that climbs again (passing a signpost for Moersdorf, 2.1km).

The GR5 now approaches **Moersdorf** through open fields and woods (passing between moss-covered stone walls) but, as with Born, turns away without entering the village. Upon reaching the first houses, turn right on a trail that climbs into the forest. **Navigate carefully here.** A short distance up the trail, there is a gazebo in a clearing to the left. Turn left here, walk behind the gazebo and find a set of descending stone steps that are somewhat overgrown with vegetation. Curiously (since trails in Luxembourg are normally well marked), there is no waymarking for this trail until the bottom of the slope. Cross a wooden bridge here and climb up the other side of the ravine.

Continue on this trail as it crosses a main road and climbs further. When the trail levels off, cross an open plateau and walk on a gravel road around a large **quarry**. The GR5 then goes straight into a forest on a broad path where the road curves left. The trail comes to a picnic table where a waymark indicates a left turn. This is a hairpin turn (do not follow the road that runs left from the picnic table and then curves right). The GR5 goes south and then curves left in the forest.

Emerging from the forest, you will see a spectacular motorway viaduct. At a fork, follow the dirt path to the left (not the right fork under the viaduct). ▶ After 100 metres, the path curves right and finally passes under the viaduct. The GR5 turns left on a road and descends into open country. At a T-junction near the base of the hillside, it turns right beside a small chapel. Turn left after passing a picnic table to cross a main road (**N10**) and then right on a bicycle path parallel to the main road. Walk 3km along that path to Wasserbillig. The path follows the Sûre to the point where it flows into the Moselle, a place that is home to a large population of geese and ducks. Turn right and continue beside the river

Until recently, the GR5 took the right fork and passed under the viaduct here. That route, shown in the topoguide (2009), has been superseded by the route described here.

The GR5 passes under a motorway viaduct near Wasserbillig

There is a landing here for the ferry between Wasserbillig and Oberbillig.

on the Esplanade de la Moselle, which becomes Rue de la Moselle. ◄ Side streets on the right lead to the centre of the town and the train and bus stations.

Wasserbillig's sole hotel closed recently. Assuming that no new hotel or B&B opens (check online for the current situation), there are several solutions to the problem of **accommodation** here. There is a hotel across the Moselle in Oberbillig, Germany (easily accessible by ferry), and there is a campground in Wasserbillig (for those with camping gear). Alternatively, you could take a bus from Wasserbillig to Ehnen (about 30min away) and return by bus the next day to continue the walk.

Another option would be to base yourself in **Remich** (where there are several hotels, restaurants and other services) and use the buses to tick off several stages of the GR5 from there. The 485 bus links Wasserbillig and Grevenmacher and the 450 Grevenmacher and Remich. Buses are reliable and frequent and a ticket valid for two hours costs €2.

STAGE 34
Wasserbillig to Grevenmacher

Start	Wasserbillig
Finish	Grevenmacher
Distance	14km
Ascent/Descent	453m/439m
Time	3hr 30min
Map	Carte Topographique Sud
Refreshments	Cafés/restaurants in Mertert, Manternach, Grevenmacher
Transport	Bus routes 485 (Wasserbillig–Grevenmacher) and 468 (Grevenmacher–Potaschberg); railway service at Wasserbillig and Manternach
Accommodation	Campground (with hikers' cabins, called 'pods') in Grevenmacher; hotel in Potaschberg (3km from Grevenmacher, by bus 468)
Waymarks	Yellow rectangles

This stage is interesting in its diversity. After a long, quiet walk on a bicycle path beside the Moselle, you turn inland and leave the vineyards behind. The GR5 crosses open countryside with expansive views and passes through dark forests where you might forget that you are anywhere near a place where grapes are grown.

From the ferry landing, follow the Esplanade de la Moselle (southwest). The paved path for cyclists and walkers soon leaves the built-up area of Wasserbillig and follows the river for nearly 2km. It's a pleasant, easy-going walk with trees and benches beside the path.

When the path reaches the industrial port of **Mertert**, it turns inland and follows a small stream, the **Syre**, into a municipal park. Pass a football pitch and a white kiosk on the right, then exit the park between two pillars surmounted by statues of lions. Turn left and walk past the Mertert campground (where there is a café/restaurant). After crossing a small **railway line**, turn right at a roundabout, walk under a

The path beside the Moselle

railway viaduct and turn left on Route de Manternach. Turn right at the first road (Rue de Mompach) and then immediately left on Rue Widderbierg, where the road forks beside a striking white and grey modern home.

The road enters the open countryside. Turn left on a road just after a bridge over a motorway (**A1**). The gentle rise of the road provides views in all directions over the fields and distant forests. The road then descends to a T-junction. Turn right here to walk a short distance through the forest. Leaving the forest, the road reaches an intersection beside a farm. Turn right here and walk up to the woods.

Where the road forks beside a panel describing the collection of oak bark for its tannin, turn left. The route levels off and then turns right at an intersection. Here, the metalled surface ends and the GR5 enters the forest on a narrow trail. Walk down to a **stream** (which may be dry) and cross it on a wooden bridge and turn left. The trail follows the stream for a short distance and then climbs to a road. Turn right on the road and then immediately right on a trail back into the forest that climbs beside a large home and its expansive grounds.

The GR5 follows a small trail to the left past a picnic table and bench, and then descends a steep slope with stone steps. It levels off and offers a pleasant walk through the forest. When the trail reaches a road, turn left and walk under

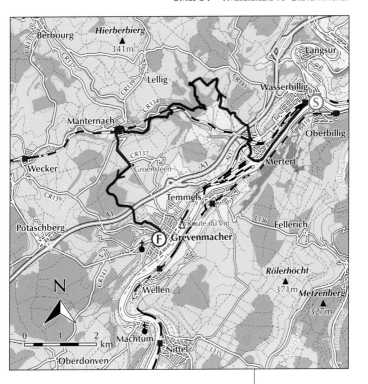

another railway viaduct. Just beyond the viaduct, turn right on a dirt path leading into the forest, cross a large wooden bridge and follow a trail to the right that leads to another good walk through the forest. A **railway line** runs parallel to the trail, mostly out of sight but you may hear trains passing and catch a glimpse of them. Along the way, there is a solidly-constructed bench mounted on a wooden structure – a good place for train-spotting.

Watch for a left turn shortly after that bench. The trail traverses a steep, wooded slope. When it leaves the forest, the trail passes through two wooden gates and then continues between two fences. **Manternach** comes into view in the distance to the right. At a T-junction beside the town's first houses, turn right, walk over a stream (the Syre again) and

207

cross the railway line. The waymarks lead into the town on a major road (CR134). The road curves left, opposite a church, and passes the **railway station** (where there is a café). Cross the tracks and, after 200 metres, bear left on a smaller road. Continue straight ahead on Om Groestän, which merges with a main road (**CR137**).

Walk uphill beside this main road and, near the crest, branch right on a smaller road marked for 'Groensteen'. After 100 metres, you reach the **Groensteen** in a cluster of trees on the left. ◄ Turn right here on a path that enters the woods. Turn left in a clearing. The path leads from here to a paved road out of the forest. Continue straight ahead on the road and cross a bridge over the motorway (A1), then fork right on a small road that is closed to motor traffic. Where that road forks, descend to the left through vineyards to Grevenmacher.

> The Groensteen is the remains of a dolmen that may have marked the grave of a Gallic warrior. The dolmen was probably broken up by treasure hunters.

A variety of **white wines** are produced in the Moselle Valley of south-eastern Luxembourg: Riesling, Pinot Blanc, Pinot Gris, Auxerrois, Rivaner, Elbling and Gewürztraminer, as well as sparking Crémant. According to the Luxembourg tourist office, 'the limestone soils of the area around Grevenmacher make for fine and vivacious wines, [while] the keuper and marl soils around Remich give the wines a more opulent character'. You walk through both areas on the GR5, so you can taste and judge for yourself.

After walking through a quiet residential area in the upper part of **Grevenmacher**, turn right at a T-junction. The GR5 curves right on Fossé des Tanneurs, turns left on Rue de Wecker and then reaches a main road (**N1**). From here you can catch a 468 bus west along the N1 to the hotel at **Potaschberg**, or turn left, right and left again with the N1 to reach the **campground**, about 1km away.

Grevenmacher to Remich

Start	Grevenmacher
Finish	Remich
Distance	26km
Ascent/Descent	755m/759m
Time	6hr 30min
Map	Carte Topographique Sud
Refreshments	Cafés/restaurants on or near the GR5 in Machtum, Ahn, Wormeldange, Ehnen, Greiveldange and Stadtbredimus
Transport	Bus route 450 (Grevenmacher–Remich)
Accommodation	Hotels in Ehnen, Stadtbredimus and Remich
Waymarks	Yellow rectangles

This is the Route du Vin par excellence. The GR5 follows small roads and offers iconic views of the winding Moselle river, bounded by the steep slopes of the vineyards. It passes occasionally through forests that provide welcome shade on a hot, sunny day, and it drops down to towns that lie beside the river – including one (Ehnen) with a wine museum.

Starting from where the GR5 meets the N1 on the northern edge of town, turn right along the road to a roundabout. Leave the road here and walk up the broad steps on the left, passing sculptures representing the Stations of the Cross to reach a small **chapel**. Continue on a road above the vineyards, following the waymarks.

The road enters a forest and the hard surface ends. The trail runs above the Moselle again and soon passes a shelter with benches offering a magnificent view over Machtum, vineyards and the winding river. When the trail emerges briefly from the woods, turn left on a gravel road and then immediately left at a fork beside a picnic table. The trail returns to the woods and descends, with a left turn, to a streambed and then climbs up the other side. At the top, there is another shelter with benches. Continue beside the woods, with a field on the right.

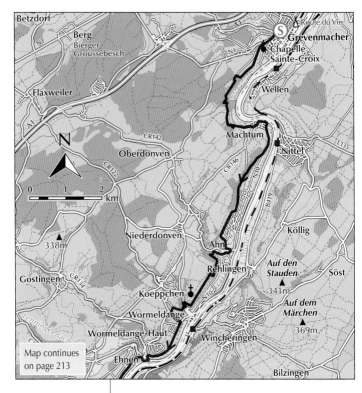

Map continues
on page 213

When the trail reaches a road, turn left and walk down
to **Machtum**, following the waymarks. The route descends
through vineyards to the **church** at the centre of Machtum.
There is a café beside the church, as well as a restaurant on
the main road (**N10**) near the bus stop for route 450.

Follow Rue de l'Eglise to your right (east) as you face
the church. This becomes Rue des Vignes as it curves right
and climbs to the vineyards. The GR5 now follows a route
through the network of small roads that are used by grape
growers, cyclists, runners – and walkers. The route, with
occasional changes of direction, is well-marked. The GR5
mostly stays on the upper side of the vineyards, thus offering
views over the countryside and the Moselle far below.

Vineyards around Machtum

As you walk, you may be struck by the extraordinary efforts and equipment that must be necessary to tend the vines and harvest the grapes on these steep slopes. The gradient on almost a quarter of the cultivated area of vineyards in Luxembourg's Moselle Valley exceeds 30% – and for 2.6% of the area, it is more than 45%!

About 1km after leaving Machtum, the GR5 enters the woods above the vineyards. Walk for 1.5km on a trail through the woods before returning to the vineyards. As the GR5 descends to **Ahn**, it passes a group of benches and a shelter with a splendid view over the village and the river. In Ahn, follow Rue de la Résistance past a restaurant and then back up to the vineyards. Fork left toward the woods on Rue des Roses. Continue straight ahead on the road as it climbs and then turn left near the crest of the hill. A hairpin left turn returns briefly to the forest. The GR5 then emerges in the open, above the vineyards.

Watch now for a right turn up a long, steep flight of steps. At the top of these steps, turn right and then immediately left at a hairpin turn. The route is now a considerable distance above the Moselle, with extensive views over the area. The route leads to the **Koeppchen**, where there is a

Chapel on the Koeppchen

small chapel and several benches – another excellent place for a break or a picnic.

The GR5 follows steps down from the chapel. Turn right on a road at the bottom of these steps and then left down another set of steps that lead to a main road (**CR122**). Turn left to walk a short distance beside the main road toward **Wormeldange**. Just before a children's play area, turn right on Gehaansdëmpel, a trail into the woods. Do not follow the broad trail beside a balustrade but instead the little dirt path to the left, beside a house, that climbs steeply into the woods and then descends on the other side of this ridge.

The GR5 emerges from the forest and returns to the vineyards. Continue straight and then turn left beside some industrial buildings. At a T-junction, turn left to enter a residential area (still part of Wormeldange). Walk past a brasserie and, where the road descends and curves left, turn right on Wéngertswee. Continue straight ahead on the road toward Ehnen. The marked route turns left to descend some steps, then left on a road beside a stream that leads to the **N10**.

Turn right and walk along the main road for 100 metres through **Ehnen** (passing a hotel, café and restaurant). Turn right on Frongass next to the wine museum (Musée du Vin, closed for renovation for about two years from October 2018), left on Am Stach and continue on Hohlgaass back

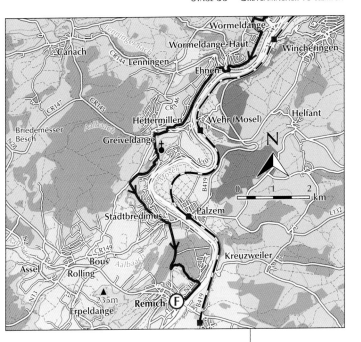

to the vineyards. Following waymarks (right at a fork, left at the next fork), after a further 2.5km enter **Greiveldange**. The route descends to a major road (**CR145**).

Turn right and then immediately left across the road to walk up the hill beside the imposing building of the Caves Coopératives des Vignerons Greiveldange. Turn right on Aséngen and right again at a T-junction beside a metal cut-out representing a bugling elk (painted an incongruous sky blue). Turn left at another T-junction and continue on a tree-lined path (south) beside a broad residential street. ▶

After leaving Greiveldange, branch left on a dirt road where the main road (**CR146**) curves right. Climbing toward the woods, turn right beside a finely constructed wooden bench and walk up steps that lead to a religious **shrine** in a clearing beside a main road. There are several picnic tables here with excellent views over the Moselle Valley. Turn right to walk beside the main road and then, after 50 metres, turn

A traditional wooden grape press stands beside the road, a common sight in villages along the Route du Vin.

Traditional grape press

right on a quiet road. When the road reaches a small wooden cabin, turn left and then right to walk in front of it. The road leads to a T-junction. Turn left here and left again at a second T-junction (beside an electrical transformer). The road passes agricultural buildings and then descends through woods to **Stadtbredimus**.

Cross a main road (**CR149**) and leave Stadtbredimus on Juddegaas. A right turn at a T-junction leads to a bridge over a small stream. The path climbs to enter a forest and reach a crossroads with a shrine and a bench. Continue straight to the edge of the forest where there is a barrier. Turn left at this barrier and re-enter the forest on a trail that follows a stream.

> This stream is the **Heedbaach** and this is a delicate environment. Most of the way, you walk on a boardwalk that follows its meanders. There are posters that describe the plants and animals of this unique habitat, for example the *salamandre tachetée* (fire salamander).

> As you leave the forest, turn left on a road, left at a T-junction beside a fire station and right to reach a path that runs through a park beside the river to **Remich**.

> Shortly before a bridge across the Moselle, note the arch of **Porte St Nicolas** on the right. A plaque

near the top of the arch records the high-water mark ('CRUE') on 31 December 1947. That flood was one of many recorded on posters around Remich.

Remich has numerous cafés, restaurants and hotels, making it a good place to stop.

Remich has an unusual historical link with **Metz**, which lies a few days further on the GR5: In AD882, Wala, Bishop of Metz, was killed in Remich during a battle with Vikings who were marauding in the Moselle Valley. It was not uncommon for clerics to lead armies into battle during this period but the practice was criticised. Archbishop Hincmar of Rheims disapproved: 'Wala was bearing arms and fighting, contrary to sacred authority and the episcopal office' (*Annals of St Bertin*).

STAGE 36
Remich to Montenach

Start	Remich
Finish	Montenach
Distance	27.3km
Ascent/Descent	888m/834m
Time	6hr 30min
Maps	Carte Topographique Sud; French IGN 1:25,000 series: 3411 E Sierck-les-Bains
Refreshments	Cafés/restaurants in Wellenstein, Wintrange, Remerschen, Schengen and Sierck-les-Bains
Transport	Luxembourg bus 185 between Remich and Schengen; in France: railway service at Apach and Sierck-les-Bains; TIM bus 112 links Apach, Sierck-les-Bains and Montenach (school term)
Accommodation	Youth hostel in Remerschen; chambre d'hôtes in Apach; hotel in Montenach
Waymarks	Yellow rectangles until crossing the Moselle River; thereafter standard GR white-and-red in France

This stage straddles Luxembourg and Lorraine: The final section of the walker's version of the Route du Vin follows paths that wind across steep vineyards above the Moselle. It's mostly paved but the views over the valley are excellent. The GR5 descends to Schengen and crosses the Moselle. After a few steps in Germany, it enters France, where familiar white-and-red GR marks greet the trekker like an old friend. The walk across Lorraine begins with a bicycle path to Sierck-les-Bains but becomes more interesting after as you follow an excellent trail through forests with some short but steep climbing.

With your back to Remich's Esplanade and the river, walk through the Porte St Nicolas. The road curves left and crosses a main road (**N2**). Go straight ahead on Rue de la Gare,

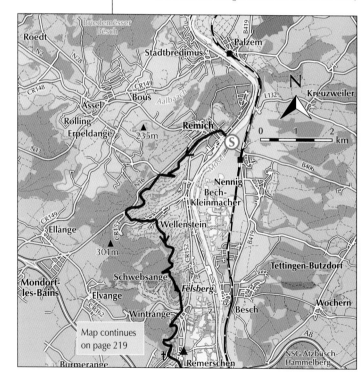

Map continues on page 219

passing a church on the right. Continue on Avenue Lamort-Velter a short distance and then branch right on the Chemin des Vignes, which – as its name indicates – crosses the vineyards. The road and its turns are generally well marked. Look out for a left turn beside a burgundy-coloured bench.

The GR5 briefly touches the N16 and there turns left to go past a picnic area and then branches diagonally left on a small road. Soon returning to the main road, this time it follows it for 150 metres to another picnic area with good views over the river and vineyards. Turn left here on a vineyard road that goes back downhill. After only 50 metres, turn left off the road to walk down steps between rows of grape vines. At the bottom of the steps, turn left on a road to enter **Wellenstein**. At an apartment building called (aptly enough) Résidence Dionysos, turn right on Plinnegässel and then left on Rue de la Source to walk to the centre. Turn right between the church and a café to walk up Borgeck.

The road returns to the vineyards. Turn right at a T-junction and fork left beside a bench. The road heads roughly south to follow rolling hills in mixed forest and vineyards and climb to the wooded crest of the **Fëlsberg** (270m), a truncated cone that looms over the surrounding countryside. After curving to the right, the trail reaches a statue of St Donat (patron saint of wine producers), standing protectively

Steps descending from the Fëlsberg to Wintrange

over vineyards. Turn left here and walk down a long series of steps (594 by my count) to **Wintrange**.

The GR5 curves to the right and then turns left in this village, passes a church and a café, and climbs on Rue Brékelter through a residential neighbourhood to a forest, where it turns left on a road. The route weaves its way through vineyards. At a fork in the trail near a large **cross**, bear left toward Schengen, joining a trail that is marked with yellow discs, along with yellow rectangles.

> Previously, the **GR5** turned right here and continued across southern Luxembourg to Rumelange. There, it turned south to enter France and follow a route west of the Moselle River to Metz. The GR5 now leaves Luxembourg at Schengen, crosses a small corner of Germany and enters France to follow a route east of the Moselle to Metz.

Descend another long series of steps to **Remerschen**. Turn right on the principal road, Waistrooss, pass a restaurant on the left and then turn right on a small road, Simengseck. Climb into the woods on Simengseck and continue straight through an intersection at the crest of the hill. Pass a telecommunications tower and walk down to a tunnel under a motorway (**A13**).

Turn left after the tunnel and continue down to a children's playground. Turn right here and immediately right again. (The trail marked by yellow discs does not make these turns.) The road makes a hairpin left turn toward Domaine Henri Ruppert, and when it reaches the Domaine (a large structure perched incongruously on the crest of the hill), the GR5 turns right. Turn right again at a tower and then left at a T-junction. The road leads from here down to a main road (**CR152**). ◄

There is a stop here (Schengen Um Haff) for the 185 bus from Remich.

Cross the main road and follow Konzewee on a diagonal to the left. A road sign announces the French border in 450 metres, but you do not enter France just yet. Instead, turn left at the first road and walk into open country. The road leads to a forest, but the GR5 turns left before entering it. Stay on the paved road, bearing right at two successive forks. The road offers a good view over the Moselle valley and the locks in the river near Schengen.

Through a series of turns in the vineyards, descend to a main road running beside the river. Turn left and walk

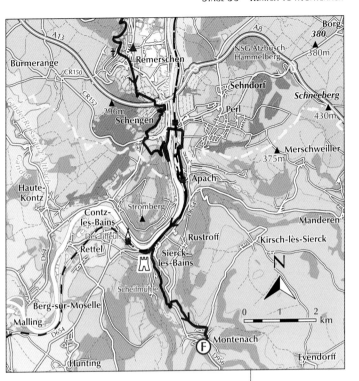

on the bicycle path beside the main road. At the entrance to **Schengen**, there are posters describing highlights in the history of the European Union (and its predecessor entities), with special attention of course to the Schengen Treaty (1985). There are cafés and a food shop near the bridge over the river.

Cross the bridge and enter Germany. Continue straight ahead a short distance to a roundabout. The trail marked by yellow rectangles goes through the roundabout and into the woods, but the GR5 turns right (south) on a bicycle path. ▶

Somewhere near here, the GR5 crosses the Franco-German border but it is unmarked. Voilà Lorraine!

This turn was **not well marked** in 2017. There is, however, a standard, white-and-red GR mark on the south side of a pylon beside the roundabout.

Finally, 250 metres down the path, there is a GR mark that faces those walking south.

At a T-junction, turn right and then, a short distance further, make a hairpin left turn onto a bicycle path, the Chemin de la Moselle.

There are signs at the T-junction that reflect the **modification of hiking routes**. One sign points the way to 'GR5.E2 Metz', another 'Vers [toward] GR5F Thionville'. The new route of the GR5 follows (with a few minor changes) what used to be the GR5F, and is marked as the GR5F on the current (2010) edition of IGN map 3411 E. What appears on that map as the 'GR5F Variante' is now the main GR5F.

The bicycle path enters **Apach**, passing the fire brigade (*pompiers*) and railway station. About 2km further on, reach **Sierck-les-Bains**, along the Quai des Ducs de Lorraine (**D654**). The GR5 tours this attractive town, dominated by the ruins of a medieval **castle**. At the western edge of town, the GR5 reverses direction in a left hairpin turn to return along Grand' Rue. ◄ After a few hundred metres, turn right (south) on Rue St George les Baillargeaux (which becomes Rue de Cardinal Billot) past the castle and out of the town.

At a fork in the road, bear left on Rue de Marienfloss. Where the road turns left and crosses a stone bridge, continue straight ahead through a clearing and enter the forest on a trail beside a stream, the Ruisseau de Montenach. Follow a left fork and pass the ruins of an old watermill, the **Scheifmühle**. ◄ The well-marked trail winds through the forest and then climbs steeply. It levels off briefly where it emerges from the forest and follows a road to the left for a short distance. The GR5 then turns right back into the forest to climb further. Where it levels off again, the trail passes through a 'green tunnel' of dense, second-growth vegetation.

Finally, the trail emerges from the forest, and **Montenach** comes into view. A road leads to the upper part of the village. Turn right at a T-junction to walk down to the centre of the village, where the mairie, the primary school and a hotel/restaurant stand together in a cluster of buildings beside the village square.

The GR5F separates and follows its own route to Thionville here.

There are panels beside the trail that explain the use of water power here (the last watermill ceased operations in 1957) and the quartzite industry.

5 LORRAINE

The GR5 climbs through the forest toward the
summit of Le Donon (Stage 48)

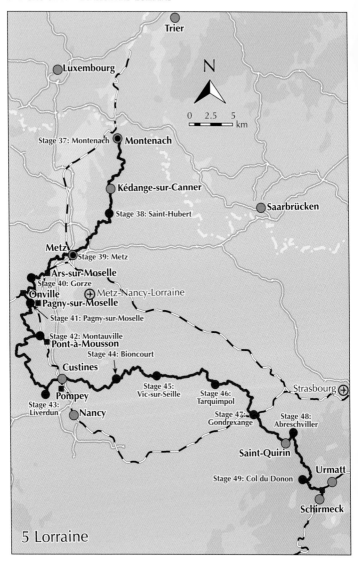

Trier

Luxembourg

N

0   2.5   5
km

Stage 37: Montenach   Montenach

Kédange-sur-Canner

Saarbrücken

Stage 38: Saint-Hubert

Metz

Stage 39: Metz

Ars-sur-Moselle

Stage 40: Gorze

Onville

Metz-Nancy-Lorraine

Pagny-sur-Moselle

Stage 41: Pagny-sur-Moselle

Stage 42: Montauville

Pont-à-Mousson

Stage 44: Bioncourt

Custines

Strasbourg

Stage 45:
Vic-sur-Seille

Stage 46:
Tarquimpol

Pompey

Stage 43:
Liverdun

Nancy

Stage 47:
Gondrexange

Stage 48:
Abreschviller

Saint-Quirin

Urmatt

Stage 49: Col du Donon

Schirmeck

5 Lorraine

Lorraine is a land of beautiful, rolling countryside, with long forest trails. The region suffered badly from the decline of its heavy industry, and the de-industrialisation and rural exodus have had an impact on accommodation for travellers. Hotels in villages and small towns have closed and chambres d'hôtes are less common here than elsewhere. But wherever you do stay, you will find that the local people's hospitality still glows with undiminished warmth.

The last stage in Luxembourg brought you into Lorraine, to end in Montenach. From Montenach to Metz is about 55km on the GR5, which can be walked in two or three stages. Metz, with a population of about 220,000 in its metropolitan area, is the largest city on the GR5 before Nice. It takes a while to walk across the city, but there are many attractions in Metz that make it a pleasant and interesting place to visit. The route then crosses the Moselle and continues south through forests and over the hilly terrain of the Côte de Moselle. When it crosses the Moselle again,

east of Liverdun, it returns to the gently rolling countryside of the Lorraine plateau. About one week of easy walking through this area brings you to the Vosges Mountains. You will feel a sense of achievement as you reach the summit of Le Donon (1008m) near the end of this section and savour the majestic view of the surrounding mountains.

Finally, for accuracy we should note that the Northern GR5 meanders through two French departments, Moselle and Meurthe-et-Moselle, and ends in the Bas Rhin Department in the Vosges Mountains, but it does not actually pass through the region of 'Lorraine' – because that region no longer exists. A recent administrative reform merged Lorraine, Alsace and Champagne-Ardenne into a new region called the Grand Est (Great East). So there is no longer a geographical entity officially called 'Lorraine'. However, the name lives on throughout the region, from the Parc Naturel Régional de Lorraine to the Université de Lorraine – and this guidebook!

SECTION SUMMARY TABLE

Start	Montenach
Finish	Schirmeck
Distance	299.1km
Ascent/Descent	6160m/6046m
Maps	French IGN 1:25,000
Note	There are stretches of this section where accommodation options are few and far between. The stage descriptions here suggest solutions to this problem. In addition, your host or hostess in a chambre d'hôtes will often be happy to provide a lift to your preferred starting point for the day.

STAGE 37
Montenach to Saint-Hubert

Start	Montenach
Finish	Saint-Hubert
Distance	30km
Ascent/Descent	508m/485m
Time	7hr 30min
Maps	3411 E Sierck-les-Bains; 3412 E Vigy
Refreshments	Café/restaurant and bakery in Kédange-sur-Canner
Transport	TIM bus route 112 passes through Montenach (school term); SNCF TER (bus) 03 passes through Kédange-sur-Canner
Accommodation	Chambres d'hôtes in Sainte-Marguerite; hotel in Kédange-sur-Canner; chambres d'hôtes in Saint-Hubert

This stage includes long sections of walking across the beautiful rolling countryside of Lorraine (some of it on quiet country roads), interspersed with pleasant forest trails. It all seems very peaceful and bucolic – until vestiges of the Maginot Line beside the trail remind you of the area's tormented history. With accommodation available in Sainte-Marguerite and Kédange-sur-Canner, it is not necessary to walk the full 30km between Montenach and Saint-Hubert in one day.

The GR5 diverges here for 1km from the former route of the GR5F as shown on IGN map 3411 E (2010). Follow the GR marks.

From the square in front of the town hall, follow a stream uphill (southeast) and leave the village on Rue de la Forêt. Enter the forest and continue to climb on a trail to the right (southwest). ◄ At the top of the hill, turn right to cross a main road (**D956**) and continue into open country on a small road. The road climbs gradually, and the pavement ends near the crest, where there are views in all directions. At an intersection, the GR5 continues straight ahead on a grass path. It descends, crosses a main road (**D855**), and follows a paved road to a village, **Haute Sierck**.

Pass through the village, turn right at a T-junction (main road D63) and then immediately left on a road that returns to the country. Soon, where the pavement ends, enter the **Forêt**

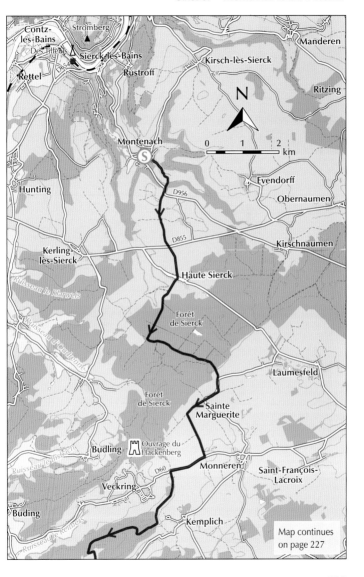

Map continues
on page 227

225

A monument marks the Saint James' Way in Lorraine

de Sierck on a dirt road. After 1km you reach a magnificent monument carved with symbols and images of the Way of St James, which follows the same route as the GR5 at this point. Turn left here and continue straight ahead on the Route Forestière de Haute Sierck for 2km.

The GR5 emerges from the forest beside a small cabin and follows a dirt road across open fields. Continue straight ahead on a paved road that joins from the left and soon curves right to enter **Sainte-Marguerite** (a village, with a chambre d'hôtes, that is part of Monneren Commune). About 500 metres after an intersection in the centre of the village, the GR5 turns left on a quiet road through grain fields. When you reach the **D60**, turn right and walk 1km beside it. Shortly before it enters **Veckring**, turn left on a dirt path.

There are several armoured **cupolas**, resting upon buried concrete bunkers, beside the path. These were small parts of the complex of fortifications that made up the Maginot Line. One of the major works of the Maginot Line, the Ouvrage du Hackenberg, can be visited from Veckring.

THE MAGINOT LINE

A Maginot Line bunker guards the GR5

France suffered enormously in World War I, with 1.4 million dead and missing and more than 3 million wounded. The demographic impact of these losses had strategic implications, as French generals and politicians could see that the manpower available for military service would drop significantly in the late 1930s. Defence against a resurgent Germany and avoidance of the slaughter epitomised by the Battle of Verdun naturally preoccupied them. They could not count on much assistance from other countries in the event of a war with Germany. One solution to these strategic problems was to fortify France's eastern border with Germany with the Maginot Line (Ligne Maginot), built in the 1930s. This was not in itself a bad idea, but the Maginot

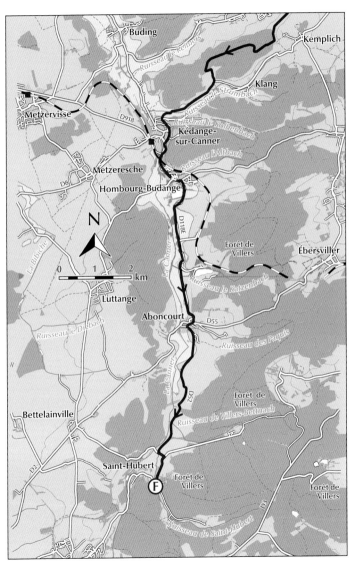

Line, alone, could not protect France. The Maginot Line gave it a strong shield, but France did not develop a sword that could exploit the shield's protection.

Recognising the defensive strength of the Maginot Line, the Germans attacked elsewhere in May 1940. Their armoured forces drove through the Ardennes and seized bridgeheads over the Meuse River within days. This breakthrough opened the way to cut off and surround the principal French and British forces in the north. The garrisons of the Maginot Line were spectators to this debacle.

Your path bends left to skirt a clearing. Opposite a church in the distance, turn right and enter the forest. The trail climbs gently and then levels off after a left fork. A right turn onto a different trail leads to a long, pleasant walk along a wooded ridge. Finally, where the trail enters a clearing, turn left to descend from the ridge. As you leave the woods at the bottom, turn right on a road at two successive T-junctions. Follow a left fork on a trail that rises gently in the woods beside a river. The trail merges with a gravel road that leads (after a left turn on Rue du Buding) to Kédange-sur-Canner.

Follow the waymarks to arrive at the square at the centre of the town, with its fountain and post office, on Rue de l'Eglise. (The town's hotel is nearby.) Cross the square on a diagonal and walk on Rue de l'Ancienne Mairie past the fire brigade (*sapeurs pompiers*) on the left. The street merges with Rue du Collège and passes a bakery on the right. Continue out of the town beside a main road (**D918**). After passing under a **railway bridge**, the main road enters **Hombourg-Budange**. In the town centre, turn right on the **D118E**, between a church and the mairie.

The GR5 sets off from here on a walk south along this quiet road with little traffic. After 4km you reach Aboncourt and carry straight on where the main road curves right and follows its own route to the centre of the village. After passing the church and the mairie, turn left on Rue de Neudelange. Follow this road as it curves left and then right to leave the village.

The pavement ends after the road passes a large farm on the right. It is a pleasant 3km walk from here to **Saint-Hubert**, across fields and with forests nearby. When the path reaches a T-junction with a road, turn left and then, 100 metres later, turn right and walk the last few hundred metres to Saint-Hubert on the **D52**. There are two chambres d'hôtes on Rue Principale: one (with a spa) on the left where you enter the village and the second on the right near the other end of the village.

STAGE 38
Saint-Hubert to Metz

Start	Saint-Hubert
Finish	Metz
Distance	24.6km
Ascent/Descent	374m/415m
Time	6hr
Maps	3412 E Vigy; 3412 O Woippy/Uckange; 3413 O Metz
Refreshments	Café, bakery and restaurant in Vigy; café/restaurant in Sanry-lès-Vigy; café after Villers l'Orme on the D3
Transport	Metz is a hub for railway service and numerous bus routes, including TIM route 6 from Vigy and Le MET' route C13 from Mey
Accommodation	Chambre d'hôtes in Vigy; hotels, chambres d'hôtes and youth hostel in Metz

The highlight of this stage is its destination – Metz, the largest city on the GR5 (apart from Nice at the end of the trail), with a history that stretches back to the Roman Empire and a vibrant present. The walk to Metz includes easy forest trails and pleasant roads across the open countryside. There is also road-walking, especially as you walk through the suburbs of Metz into the centre of the city.

The GR5 leaves Saint-Hubert on Rue Principale and turns left (southeast) where the road forks. A short distance after leaving the village, bend left into the forest to follow a trail that runs parallel to the road. When the trail leaves the forest, after 600 metres, cross the road to the right and continue straight ahead on a small road past the **Chapelle Notre Dame de Rabas**. The road crosses an open field and curves left to enter the forest.

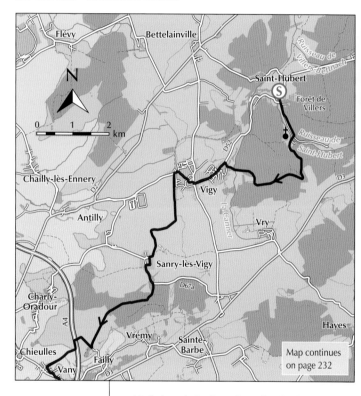

Map continues on page 232

Walk through this forest for 2.5km, heading southeast and south at first and then turning west. The route is generally well marked, although there is one intersection with no GR mark until 50 metres further on the trail. It's a pleasant trail with some variety, ranging from a narrow path through high grass to a wide, smooth trail but some sections can be quite muddy and slippery.

The GR5 leaves the forest and turns left at a T-junction with a main road (**D52**). Pass a football pitch on the right and tennis courts on the left to enter **Vigy**. Turn right beside a restaurant with a pizza vending machine (offering hot pizza within four minutes, 24/7!) and, after 50 metres, turn left to walk through the centre of the village (mairie, church, café).

Still on the D52, turn left beside the Centre des Finances Publiques.

As you leave the village, turn left on Rue du Val de Metz. Cross some tracks (used for a pedal-powered tourist train) and turn left on a small dirt road that runs parallel to the tracks, with woods on the left and open fields of grain on the right. Bear right on a narrow wooded trail when the road curves left through a gap in a tree-covered concrete barrier. The trail soon emerges from the trees and crosses open country, curving left. Turn right at a T-junction, where a signpost offers encouragement – Metz 14.6km – and walk into Sanry-lès-Vigy.

In the village, turn left onto Rue de l'Eglise (with a café/restaurant beside the church). A right turn on Rue des Cherbons and a left on Rue de la Gare soon take you out of the village again. Walk a short distance beside a main road (**D67a**) and then turn right to follow a broad, smooth trail in a forest. ▸ This is your last walk among trees for a while, so enjoy it! After 1.5km, the GR5 follows a path bounded by trees on the right and rolling fields on the left. It's a pastoral scene, apart from the motorway visible (and increasingly audible) in the distance.

At a junction with a paved road, make a hairpin right turn and walk under an old railway viaduct. Follow the road

A signpost here identifies the trail as the 'GR5F', its designation prior to the modification in 2016.

Bucolic approach to Sanry-lès-Vigy

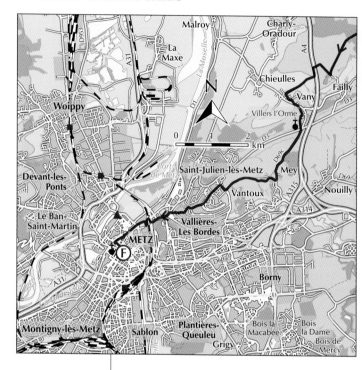

300 metres northwest, then turn left to cross the motorway (**A4**) on a bridge. Turn left immediately after the bridge and walk down a grassy path parallel to the motorway. Near the bottom of the slope, turn right and walk into Vany.

The GR5 winds its way through the village – left on Rue Principale (passing the mairie), curving first to the left and then to the right. Turn left and walk a short distance beside a main road (**D69c**), then turn right at the first road to enter **Villers l'Orme**. Walking through a residential neighbourhood, turn right at an intersection. The road curves right beside a shaded bench and then left to ascend a hill. Near the crest of the hill, pass Chapelle Notre Dame de la Salette on the left and a large **oratory** dedicated to Notre Dame de Fátima on the right. Cross the main road (**D3**) beside a café and continue at an angle to the right on a smaller road (D69c).

Walk beside the D69c for 1.4km to **Mey**. Along the way, there is a monument (erected in 1908, when this part of Lorraine was part of Germany) dedicated to soldiers who were killed during the Franco-Prussian War. Turn right at the Place de l'Eglise in Mey and continue on Rue de l'Ecole. ▶ The road descends past several shaded benches and the mairie. Fork left on Chemin du Praillon (posted as a cul de sac) and continue past a barrier on a dirt road into open fields. Follow the path for 1km through these fields to a road, Rue des Marronniers, in a residential area.

This is the final approach to **Metz** – the centre of the city is 4km away. The route of the GR5 through this urban area is reasonably well marked, but there are a few places where one or two additional waymarks would be helpful.

Turn right on the bicycle path beside Rue des Marronniers and then left to walk straight through a series of parks. Turn left beside a tennis court and right on a road (**Rue des Carrières**) that descends (southwest) to enter St-Julien-lès-Metz. Turn right at a roundabout on **Rue des Mélèzes**, which descends and curves left, then right on Rue des Terres Rouges. At the bottom of the hill, turn left on Rue Jean Burger and right (still on Rue Jean Burger) at a large intersection 100 metres further.

After crossing **Avenue de Lyon**, the GR5 reaches a T-junction with Rue du Fort. Cross this street and enter a park to follow a path around a section of the city's medieval fortifications, **Le Circuit des Remparts**. ▶ Leaving the ramparts, walk along quays beside a **canalised branch** of the Moselle, home to many aquatic birds. Along the way, steps on the left lead up to city streets. The **Pont des Roches** is a convenient place to leave the quays and walk into the centre of the city. The spectacular **cathedral** is just a few blocks away.

The Mey-les-Vignes bus stop is 250 metres further on Rue Emile Knoepfler. The C13 bus goes from here to the centre of Metz.

The towers bear the names of the medieval guilds that were responsible for their maintenance – for example, the Tour des Chauldronniers (coppersmiths, in an archaic spelling).

METZ

Metz is an excellent place for a pause during a trek on the GR5. There are interesting areas to explore, such as the Place St Louis in the old city centre. The gothic Saint-Etienne Cathedral is famous for its towering nave (41.77m) and its stained-glass windows (incorporating works by medieval and renaissance artists, as well as modern ones such as Chagall). Near the Cathedral, the Musée de la Cour d'Or (http://musee.metzmetropole.fr) presents Gallo-Roman, medieval

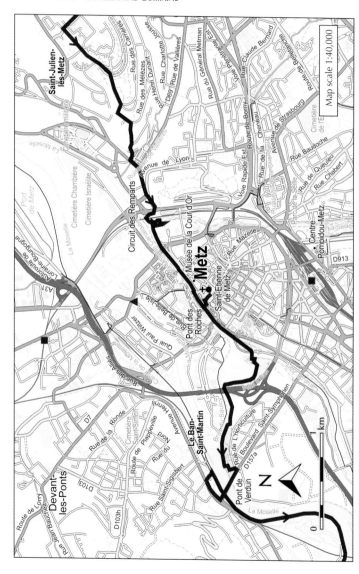

Map scale 1:40,000

Saint-Etienne Cathedral of Metz soars upward

and fine art collections. The Centre Pompidou-Metz (www.centrepompidou-metz.fr, opened in 2010) is one of those museums where the building itself is as much a breathtaking work of art as the modern and contemporary art displayed within it.

German rule over this area (1871–1918) left architectural souvenirs in Metz, such as the neo-Romanesque train station (1908) and the Temple Neuf (1904). The Arsenal, built in 1864 and extensively renovated in the 1980s, is now a highly-regarded venue for concerts and special exhibitions. Consider timing a sojourn to coincide with the Fêtes de la Mirabelle, a week-long festival of music, dramatic performances, traditional cuisine and crafts, a parade and fireworks that occurs in late August.

STAGE 39
Metz to Gorze

Start	Metz
Finish	Gorze
Distance	24.2km
Ascent/Descent	601m/568m
Time	6hr 30min
Maps	3413 O Metz; 3313 E Ars-sur-Moselle
Refreshments	Cafés/restaurants in Longeville-lès-Metz, Scy-Chazelles, Moulins-lès-Metz, Vaux and Ars-sur-Moselle
Transport	Metz is a hub for railway service and bus routes, including TIM route 78 to Gorze, and Le MET' routes to places along this stage: L5 (Pont de Verdun), N89 (Scy-Chazelles), P103 and C14 (Moulins-lès-Metz), N90 (Vaux), P103 (Ars-sur-Moselle).
Accommodation	Chambres d'hôtes in Scy-Chazelles, Jussy, Vaux, Ancy-sur-Moselle and Gorze

The first 14km of this stage, from Metz to Ars-sur-Moselle, pass through an urban area. Most of the route here is on roads and pavement but there is little vehicular traffic (and you could skip this part by taking a train to Ars-sur-Moselle). There is good forest walking after Ars-sur-Moselle. One of the highlights of this section of the walk, apart from great views over the Moselle Valley, is the mysterious 'pierre qui tourne'…

The GR5 continues along the quay from the Pont des Roches. Bend left after 500 metres near a pleasure boat harbour to walk down a tree-lined path. At the end of that path, signs point to two GR trails, both turning to the right. The GR5 crosses the first bridge here, turns left after the bridge and then immediately right to go through a large park. There are few GR marks here, but the route is easy to follow. Walk around what appears to be a lake (but is actually the Moselle **canal**) on the right, with a motorway (**A31**) on your left. The path curves left to pass under the motorway. It's a pleasant path beside the water with the sound of the motorway diminishing as you progress.

Just before a café-restaurant with an inviting terrace, turn left. Walk up to the **Pont de Verdun** and cross the Moselle to Longeville-lès-Metz. ◀ Descend from the bridge and turn right. Just after a traffic light, turn right toward the river. A GR mark here points to Scy-Chazelles. Go through a pedestrian tunnel and turn right to walk southwest beside the Moselle on a bicycle path. The GR5 follows this path for 2.6km. Watch for an unmarked right turn into woods 500 metres after a railway viaduct. (If you come to a pleasure boat harbour, you have walked 175 metres past this turn.) A GR mark confirming that you are headed in the right direction appears 30 metres after the turn.

Leave the woods and turn left on Rue de l'Etang. Continue on that road as it curves right and then turns right near a supermarket. Turn left on Rue du Stade, cross a major road (**D603**) and continue straight on. Turn right beside the Espace Liberté Bibliothèque, then left to walk through a small park (Parc de l'Archyre). The GR5 leaves the park, crosses a road and climbs up a path through woods to the centre of **Scy-Chazelles**, with its mairie, church – and, more importantly, a shady bench. Continue straight along

If you wish to skip the first 3km of this stage, you could take the L5 bus from the centre of Metz to the Pont de Verdun.

Statues of Alcide de Gasperi, Robert Schuman, Jean Monnet and Conrad Adenauer in Scy-Chazelles

the left side of the square. Turn left beside a fountain on a narrow path that goes back down the hill, then right on Chemin des Noques and left on a path that leads to Rue Robert Schuman. Turn right here to reach the former home of Robert Schuman. ▶

The GR5 turns left on a narrow path beside Schuman's house and continues its descent to Moulins-lès-Metz, turning right on Rue du Baoeton and then left at a T-junction. Cross the D603 and turn right after the *hôtel de ville* (city hall), left on a road beside a church and right on Rue des Moulins (opposite the Château Fabert). The road climbs to a village, Sainte-Ruffine, and continues straight past a church on Grand' Rue and a *lavoir* (communal washing basin), the first of several along this route.

The GR5 traces a route down to Vaux from here – left at the Place de la Hall, left on the main road through **Jussy** and right on Rue de la Fontaine. After a brief walk past vineyards and through woods, turn right at a T-junction and continue down a narrow country road. Fork right on a level road and then turn left on a paved path into **Vaux**. Turn right in the centre of this village beside its mairie, and then immediately left on a paved path that climbs through the woods. Pass a sign that describes the GR5 in Lorraine, cross a road and enter the forest. Turn left (south) where the trail forks (a

A group of statues honours four 'fathers of Europe': Alcide de Gasperi, Robert Schuman, Jean Monnet and Conrad Adenauer. Schuman's home now houses a museum.

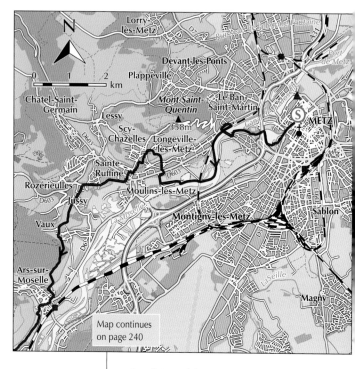

Map continues
on page 240

weathered GR mark here is barely visible). The trail traverses
a slope and, after leaving the forest, turns left to descend on
a road into **Ars-sur-Moselle**. After another left turn, the tall
steeple of the church stands before you. Turn right to enter
the centre of the town.

Continue straight to a roundabout and then turn right on
the **D11**. Walk 100 metres on this main road and then turn
left on small road. Continue straight where the road leads to
a broad, grassy path that soon narrows in thick undergrowth.
The trail passes two reminders of the area's history: a monument marking a small cemetery for French and Prussian soldiers killed during the 1870 war (erected in 1898, some of its
German text is now effaced), and the recently-restored ruins
of a Roman aqueduct that carried water from a spring near
Gorze to Metz, a distance of 22km. ◀

Another portion of
this aqueduct stands
at Jouy-aux-Arches,
on the right bank
of the Moselle.

238

At a small road, the GR5 turns right and then curves left in front of a group of houses. After 250 metres, just before a fork in the road, turn right and walk up a narrow, dirt path. There is a good view from here back over **Ancy-sur-Moselle**. Turn right at the top of the trail on a dirt road, which soon curves left. The route becomes a narrow forest trail that traverses upward. The trail passes a large, flat **stone** resting upon a larger rock: It's 'la pierre qui tourne' (the rock that turns). Pause here to see whether its magic works for you (or vice versa).

Continuing through the forest, follow a left fork where a sign for the right fork warns: 'ZONE DANGEREUSE ACCÈS INTERDIT PENDANT LES TIRS' (Danger Zone: Entry forbidden during shooting). A short distance further, a sign indicates a trail to the **Belvédère des Varieux**, where there is a great view over the Moselle valley (and a picnic table).

The trail reaches a broad gravel road. Turn left here and walk to the **Croix Saint-Clément**, then turn right on a path in the woods. Turn left at an intersection in the woods and descend to the edge of the forest, where there is a beautiful view over grain fields, undulating hills and Gorze. The GR5 does not go straight to Gorze, but instead turns right to follow three sides of a large, open field. Finally, leaving the forest and fields, it enters **Gorze** on a path beside Rue

La pierre qui tourne

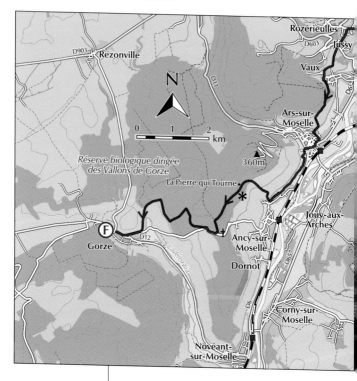

Raymond Mondon, which merges into Rue du Commerce close to the chambre d'hôtes. To reach the centre of Gorze, walk 250 metres further to Rue de la Meuse, where there is a war memorial.

Saint Chrodegang, Bishop of Metz and a counsellor of Pepin the Short (Charlemagne's father), founded a **Benedictine abbey** in Gorze in AD749. The abbey became a centre for the reform of monastic practice, promoting a more rigorous observation of the Rule of Benedict. Gorze was also a centre of 'chant messin', from which Gregorian Chant developed. The abbey was dissolved in 1572 during the Reformation.

STAGE 40
Gorze to Pagny-sur-Moselle

Start	Gorze
Finish	Pagny-sur-Moselle
Distance	15.6km
Ascent/Descent	502m/482m
Time	4hr 15min
Maps	3313 E Ars-sur-Moselle
Refreshments	None, apart from a café in Onville that might be open
Transport	TIM bus route 78 (Gorze to Metz); railway service at Onville and Pagny-sur-Moselle
Accommodation	Gîte in Pagny-sur-Moselle, hotels and chambres d'hôtes in Pont-à-Mousson (6min away by train)

Most of this stage follows forest trails – generally broad and level, but narrow and steep in a few places. It's a fine stage for a sunny, hot day, when you will appreciate the shade of the trees.

From the war memorial, turn left (west) on Rue de la Meuse (**D12**) and walk 100 metres to the Place du Château. Turn left here and walk past the Palais Abbatial. Continue on Rue du Général de Gaulle. After 600 metres, where the road turns left and a dirt road continues straight, make a diagonal right turn on a dirt road that climbs into the forest. In a clearing, fork left and then fork right upon re-entering the forest. At yet another fork, bend left as the trail continues to climb (there is GR mark after this turn). Then turn left on a dirt road where the trail emerges from the forest and levels off.

The road turns right beside a special tree (Cèdre de l'Atlas) and a small hunting cabin (*baraque de chasse*), but the GR5 continues straight here on a grass path into the forest, following a signpost toward the Col de Rudemont. The trail, turning south, is broad, smooth and level. You pass several old boundary stones (*bornes frontalières*) that marked the border between France and Germany from 1871 to 1918. An F (for France) is carved into the western side of

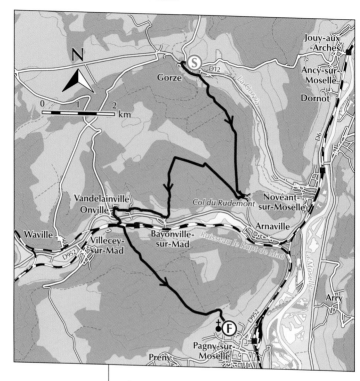

each stone. Each D (for Deutschland) that once marked the eastern side has been chiselled out. The old border is now the boundary between the departments of the Moselle and Meurthe-et-Moselle.

'LOCAL LAW'

In 1918, France recovered the territories that it had lost to Germany in 1871: northern Lorraine (today's Moselle) and most of Alsace. Important domestic legislation had been enacted in France and Germany between 1871 and 1918. For example, France had adopted a law separating church and state (1905), thereby abrogating the Concordat of 1801. Germany had introduced a system of state health insurance (1911). The question arose whether to align the law in Alsace and Moselle with the rest of France. Should they give up their health insurance system? Should church and state be separated?

It was decided to retain the elements of German law that were considered more favourable than the existing law in France. Hence, 'local law' in Alsace and Moselle today, a century later, includes a health insurance system that is more generous than the general French system, the Concordat and related legislation still apply here, and these territories enjoy two additional public holidays (Good Friday and December 26).

The GR5 descends in open country to the **Col du Rudemont**, where (without reaching the lowest point of this pass) it makes a hairpin right turn, followed immediately by a fork to the left. The trail climbs again, northwest, along the edge of a forest. A left fork leads into the forest on a broad path, followed by left and right turns on a narrow trail. Later, a left turn is signalled only by a small sign marked both 'GR5' (red background) and 'E2' (green background). ▸

In the Department of Meurthe-et-Moselle, waymarks often include this European designation of the GR5.

Continuing through the forest in a generally southerly direction, the GR5 descends towards **Bayonville-sur-Mad** but turns right before entering the centre of the village. Pass a *lavoir* with a drinking water tap and return to the open country. The trail crosses fields, westward, for 1km and then descends on a dirt path between walls to enter **Onville**. Meander through this village, following GR marks past the church and down Grand' Rue to a main road (**D952**). Turn left here and immediately right to cross a bridge over the **Rupt de Mad** (a small stream). Follow the road to the right and then walk under a **railway viaduct**. Turn left at a T-junction on a dirt road and then right at a fork to enter the forest.

The French side of a *borne frontalière (boundary stone)* on the old Franco-German border

The trail climbs quite steeply in the forest for 500 metres. It then levels off, crosses a dirt road and begins a gradual descent. Along the way, there is a bench with a good view over Pagny-sur-Moselle. Continue straight ahead on this road (passing other roads on the right), which curves and passes an old stone water fountain. The GR5 reaches a large oratory, Notre-Dame-de-Bonsecours. The GR5 turns right here, as indicated by a sign pointing to Prény and the Gîte de Serre.

Pagny-sur-Moselle would be a logical place to end a stage, but it's complicated. The nearby Gîte de Serre may

A broad, forest trail over the Côte de Moselle between Onville and Pagny-sur-Moselle

be reluctant to accept one-night stays, and there is currently (2017) no hotel or chambre d'hôtes there. (Check online.) A convenient solution is to walk 1km to the centre of Pagny-sur-Moselle and take a train to a town that does have accommodation, such as Pont-à-Mousson. It's easy to return to Pagny-sur-Moselle the next morning and resume your walk on the GR5.

STAGE 41
Pagny-sur-Moselle to Montauville

Start	Pagny-sur-Moselle
Finish	Montauville
Distance	19.5km
Ascent/Descent	538m/545m
Time	5hr
Maps	3313 E Ars-sur-Moselle; 3314 E Pont-à-Mousson
Refreshments	None
Transport	Railway service in Pagny-sur-Moselle and Pont-à-Mousson; bus route 3 from Montauville to Pont-à-Mousson
Accommodation	Hotels and chambres d'hôtes in Pont-à-Mousson (by bus)

This stage follows a wide arc west of the Moselle, starting and finishing close to the river. You walk in forest most of the way, climbing and descending some steep hills of the Côte de Moselle. The trail passes reminders of history that are interesting and moving – in particular, the World War I battlefield in Bois-le-Prêtre and a nearby military cemetery. To avoid an extra 2.5km to your accommodation in Pont-à-Mousson at the end of the day, take the No 3 bus from Montauville.

From the centre of Pagny-sur-Moselle, walk out of the town on Rue Gambetta (northwest) to the **oratory** and turn left on Chemin des Andelins. A GR5 signpost points the way: Prény 2.8km.

Walk southwest on a dirt road traversing open country, with views of villages and vineyards. The road turns left after 650 metres and then right after another 150 metres. Enter a forest beside a bench, turn left on a road beside another bench and then, after just 50 metres, follow a trail on the left into the woods. The trail climbs the slope to a road. Turn right here, walk a short distance on the road and then turn sharply left on a smaller road that leads to **Prény**. Having climbed up the hill to Prény and admired the view, you can easily understand why a castle was built here during the Middle Ages.

> **Prény Château** was a coveted strongpoint in conflicts between the Dukes of Lorraine, the Bishops of Metz and the Counts of Bar, among others. In 1636, after French troops had taken it, Cardinal Richelieu ordered that the castle be demolished. The castle suffered further damage in later years (for example, during combat between American and German armies in 1918), producing the current state of picturesque ruins.

Enter Prény on Rue des Remparts and, before reaching the church, turn right to walk up steps to the **castle**. Turn left at the top of the steps to walk through its ruins. The GR5 continues a short distance beyond the castle and then descends on a trail through the forest back to the road, below the church. Turn left on the road and then immediately right to walk down a paved path. Continue on a road to a T-junction.

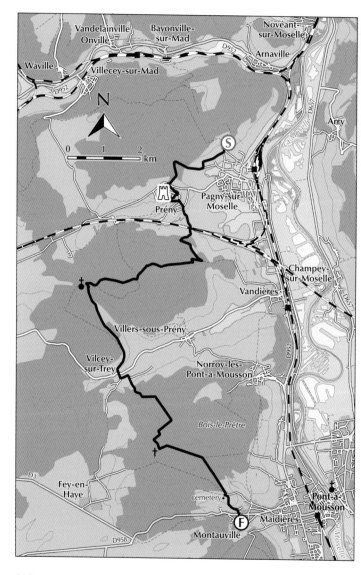

Turn right here and walk past a chapel (with lavender plants in full blossom at the right time of year) and a pond, then across fields. The calm of this scene is periodically shaken by the passage of a fast train (TGV). You may get a close look at one as you cross over the **railway line**.

Turn right on a road just after the bridge and then left on a trail into the forest. (You will see a GR mark only after making this turn.) Turn left after a short distance on a smaller trail through dense vegetation. The trail broadens and makes a hairpin turn to the right on a road. ▶ Watch for a left turn on a grassy path within 150 metres. The GR mark for this turn, high on a tree, is easy to miss.

The road leads in the other direction to Vandières, 2.5km, where there is a train stop.

The GR5 continues on a broad, level path through dense vegetation. After about 2km the trail narrows and reaches a T-junction, turn left and then immediately right at a crossroads called Les Quatre Chemins. The trail leads to a dirt road, where you turn right. Then, after 250 metres, two left turns lead to the site of the **Abbaye Sainte-Marie**. Turn right on a road here which then climbs to the left and levels off in open country with grain fields beside the road.

The GR5 descends to **Vilcey-sur-Trey**, a small village. Turn left on Rue de l'Eglise and then right to cross a stream. The trail goes straight uphill in the woods here and then levels off to become a broad dirt road. At a large crossroads, turn right and enter **Bois-le-Prêtre**. The GR5 makes several turns in these woods, so watch for waymarks at each crossing of a road or path.

Bois-le-Prêtre was the scene of intense fighting between French and German soldiers in 1915, with inconclusive results. French casualties amounted to 7000 killed and 22,000 wounded and the Germans suffered similar losses. A large monument, the Croix-des-Carmes, stands near one of the focal points of the fighting.

Continuing on the road after the **Croix-des-Carmes**, bend right at a fork. Pause and reflect as you pass the French military **cemetery**, Cimetière Nationale du Pétant, in its beautiful setting on a hill.

Walk down the road to Montauville itself and cross a main road (**D958**). The GR5 turns right (west) on this main road, but Pont-à-Mousson, with hotels, chambres d'hôtes,

Montauville military cemetery

*The Musée au Fil du Papier in Pont-à-Mousson (**www.ville-pont-a-mousson.fr**) is interesting and unusual: it is devoted to objects made of papier mâché.*

restaurants and railway service, is a good place to end this stage. ◄ To go there, turn left (east) on the main road. It's 2.5km from here to the centre of the city. Local bus route 3 runs between Montauville and Pont-à-Mousson along this main road (except on Sundays).

Cardinal Charles of Lorraine, acting under the authority of Pope Gregory XIII, established a **Jesuit university** in Pont-à-Mousson in 1572 that would be a beacon of the Counter-Reformation. With faculties of theology, philosophy, law and medicine, the university flourished in the 17th century and attracted students from Western and Central Europe. In 1768, two years after France annexed Lorraine, King Louis XV ordered the expulsion of Jesuits from Lorraine (as he had done in France in 1764) and the transfer of the university from Pont-à-Mousson to Nancy.

Pont-à-Mousson declined after the departure of its prestigious university, but it became an important **industrial centre** following the establishment in 1856 of the Société Anonyme des Hauts Fourneaux et Fonderies de Pont-à-Mousson (now Saint-Gobain PAM), which specialised in the manufacture of pipeline materials. Pause to look at a cast-iron manhole cover next time you are walking along a pavement in France. It will probably bear the words 'Pont-à-Mousson' or 'PAM', often accompanied by a stylised bridge logo.

STAGE 42
Montauville to Liverdun

Start	Montauville
Finish	Liverdun
Distance	33.2km
Ascent/Descent	567m/579m
Time	8hr 30min
Maps	3314 E Pont-à-Mousson; 3315 ET Nancy/Toul/Forêt de Haye
Refreshments	Café in Rogéville
Transport	Bassin de Pont-à-Mousson Le Bus route 3 from centre of Pont-à-Mousson to Montauville; railway service in Liverdun
Accommodation	Chambres d'hôtes in Liverdun
Note	For a shorter stage, follow the GR5F from Pont-à-Mousson via Jezainville, Dieulouard and Saiserais to its junction with the GR5 at the Carrefour de la Grande-Tranchée (Stage 43, northeast of Liverdun), and then continue to Custines. The total distance for this alternative (including 1.5km from the centre of Custines to a hotel) is 27.5km. Additionally, you would need map 3414 O (Custines/Nomeny).

This is a long stage, albeit mostly easy, agreeable walking. The route follows tranquil roads and trails through open fields and verdant forests. Vast fields of cheerful sunflowers will put a bounce in your step no matter how many kilometres you've covered. There are currently (2017) no hotels or chambres d'hôtes along the route and only one place to stop for refreshments, which may not be open when you pass through so be prepared. The best part of this stage is the trail through the forest between Mamey and Saint-Jean. However, there could be hunting in this forest on Saturdays or Mondays between 8:30 and 14:00, so avoid walking through this area then.

From where the GR5, coming from the northwest, intersects the **D958** in Montauville walk west along the road. After 300 metres, bend left on a diagonal road, pass a **war memorial**

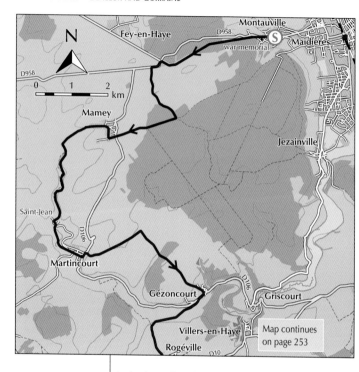

in the form of an obelisk (also the Monument bus stop on route 3 from Pont-à-Mousson) and continue straight ahead on a dirt road.

> Like many war memorials in small towns and villages, Montauville's **monument** lists the names of soldiers killed during World War I. The repetition of surnames on these monuments offers searing insight into the horrible impact of the war upon people's lives. This monument includes one group of three men with the same surname and five pairs with the same surname.

The dirt road passes through woods and meets the D958 again at a junction with the **D3**. Turn left and walk beside the main road. After a few hundred metres, the GR5 leaves the main road on a narrow path to the left. Walk beside an open field and enter a 'green tunnel' of dense vegetation. The forest, quiet and peaceful, then opens up.

Turn right at a crossroads with a broad gravel road (popular with cyclists) and follow the road out of the forest. The church steeple of Mamey appears on the horizon. Walk through **Mamey** on Rue de Puvenelle, turn right beside the church and left at the end of the road to leave the village. Bear left at a fork in the road and pass a sign that warns: 'Chasse le Samedi ou Lundi de 8h30 à 14h00' (Hunting Saturday or Monday from 8:30 to 14:00). ▶ Walk down an easy trail in the forest from here and turn left beside another sign about hunting. The trail follows the course of a stream on the right and then traces the periphery of several large, fenced fields. Turn left on a road and walk past a small building with a sign: Syndicat des Eaux du Trey/Saint Jean.

The GR5 passes through **Saint-Jean**, turns right and then left over a small bridge into the woods. The trail goes over a small hill, emerges to cross a field between two fences and crosses another bridge to continue in the open country a short distance to **Martincourt**. Go straight ahead on Rue St Jean, cross a main road (**D106**) and continue on Rue de l'Eglise past a play area with a bench. A sign at a T-junction

Hunting is seasonal but varies from place to place. It would be unwise to walk this trail at these times.

Sunflowers beside the road descending to Gézoncourt

The roundabout route from Martincourt to Rogéville, via Gézoncourt, is now 7.5km, instead of 5km along the former, more direct route.

then announces a change in the route ('TRACÉ MODIFIÉ'). Instead of turning right here for Rogéville (as shown on the IGN map), the GR5 turns left toward Gézoncourt. ◄

The GR5 branches right 200 metres after the new left turn on a road that climbs to a plateau. Walk through fields on a straight dirt road for 1.5km to a farm. Turn right at the farm, descend into a small, wooded area and then climb briefly before a final descent into **Gézoncourt**. If it's a sunny day during the summer, vast numbers of sunflowers in fields beside the road seem to stare at you as you walk by.

Bear right entering Gézoncourt, pass the church and turn right on Rue de la Petite Suisse. After 200 metres, bend left on Rue de Villevaux, which descends and enters a forest. Cross a stream over a bridge to the left and pass the ruins of a small lock and watermill. The trail climbs gently, straight up the slope. Emerging from the forest, the GR5 curves left, joins a road and passes through **Rogéville**.

Just beyond this village, fork left and begin a long walk across open country. Cross the **D10** to continue on a dirt road that rises gradually and then descends. About 2km after Rogéville, turn left at a T-junction and immediately right to follow the road into **Rosières-en-Haye**. Cross the main road (**D907**) here, turn left (direction: Salle des Fêtes) and then right to walk past the church, a war memorial and the mairie. As you leave the village, curve left past a **crucifix** and continue across a main road (**D611**).

The GR5F joins the GR5 from the left at this point. The two trails go downhill together for 500 metres and then the GR5F turns off to the right.

The road now leads to a trail that enters a forest. Turn left at the first major crossing in the forest (2km from the D611) to walk on a broad dirt road, then turn right after a few hundred metres on a trail. Turn left at an intersection and climb gently. The GR5 leaves the forest to approach **Liverdun**, passing an exercise area and sports fields. Continue on Rue des Miternes through a residential neighbourhood. Walk past the *gendarmerie* and merge with **Route de Saizerais** (the **D90B**) beside a large **crucifix**. ◄

Soon after passing a chambre d'hôtes, the GR5 branches off the main road to the right on a smaller road (Avenue de la Libération) and passes through the medieval **Porte Haute**. The GR5 meanders through Liverdun's picturesque old city. The route is mostly well marked, but there are gaps. The railway station in the lower part of the city is the destination.

In the Place d'Armes (where the tourist office is located), turn left beside the church and then right on Grande Rue (in

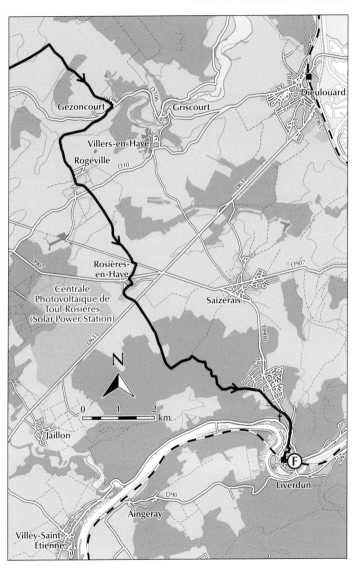

Porte Haute at the entrance to Liverdun

a small square with a fountain). Another right turn takes you past a *lavoir*. Turn left on the next road and then immediately left down a long series of steps that lead to the **railway station**. There is a chambre d'hôtes 350 metres east from here on Rue de la Gare.

STAGE 43

Liverdun to Bioncourt

Start	Liverdun
Finish	Bioncourt
Distance	32km
Ascent/Descent	646m/654m
Time	7hr
Maps	3315 ET Nancy/Toul/Forêt de Haye; 3414 O Custines/Nomeny; 3415 E Saint-Nicolas-de-Port; 3414 E Delme
Refreshments	Cafés/restaurants and shops in Custines
Transport	Railway service in Liverdun; Bassin de Pompey Bus 1 between Liverdun and Pompey; Ted Bus R370 between Pompey and Custines; Ted Bus R350 links Brin-sur-Seille and Bioncourt
Accommodation	Hotel 1.5km from Custines; chambre d'hôte in Bioncourt

This is another long stage, but the route itself is pleasant: easy forest trails and quiet roads in the open countryside. If you need a short rest near the end of this walk, you will enjoy sitting beside the placid waters of the Etang de Brin. The comfort and hospitality of the chambre d'hôtes in Bioncourt will amply reward your exertions.

Facing the railway station turn left (east) and walk 350 metres on Rue de la Gare. Continue straight through a large intersection, cross a bridge and turn left on Rue du Tir. The route becomes a dirt road that climbs gently in woods beside a narrow, deep ravine. ▶ The GR5 emerges from the woods and turns northeast to cross the open country in a long, straight line. At a large crossroads, **Carrefour de la Grande-Tranchée**, the GR5 re-enters the forest. The road curves in a more easterly direction and enters the woods as a narrow trail. Near the end, it descends steeply and emerges from the woods beside apartment buildings.

The GR5F joins this road from the left and runs beside the GR5 for 2.5km as far as Carrefour de la Grande-Tranchée, where it turns to the northwest.

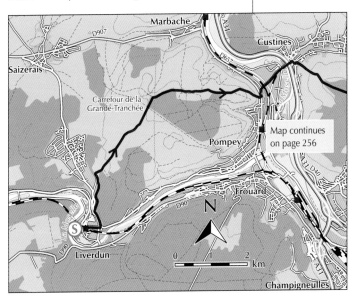

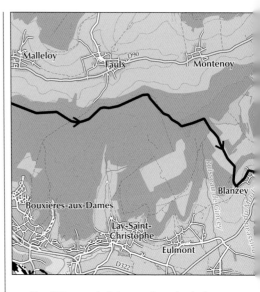

The GR5 now winds its way through a built-up, commercial area in order to cross the Moselle and reach the countryside and forests on the other side of Custines. Walk past the apartment buildings to a main road (**D657**). Turn left on the path beside the main road and walk 100 metres to a pedestrian crossing. Cross the main road here and walk through a park past a cemetery. Continue straight from here over bridges that cross two branches of the **river**, a **railway line** and a **motorway** (A31). This is the GR5's third and final crossing of the Moselle, after Schengen and Metz. Turn right at a roundabout at the entrance to **Custines**. ◀

To reach the nearby hotel, turn left (northwest) at the roundabout and walk 1.5km beside the D40 main road.

Turn left on Rue du Général Custine 100 metres after the roundabout and then right on Chemin de Biarre. This road leads directly into open country, climbing to provide good views back over Custines. After 1km, the GR5 forks to the left and enters a forest. It climbs a bit further and then levels off.

Follow a broad, direct gravel road through the forest for 4.5km. Then, after a curve to the right, turn right off the road to follow a trail southeast into the forest. Continue straight ahead on this trail for 1.3km and then turn left on a broad path. When you reach a high-voltage transmission

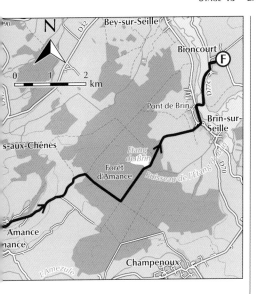

line pylon, turn right. The GR5 follows a route southeast from here out of the forest and across open country. This is relatively high ground, so the countryside is spread out in a great tableau before you.

After a final, brief passage through the woods, walk down to **Blanzey**. Turn left at the first houses and traverse the slope on a path between them and the fields. At the end of that path, turn right on a road that descends to another road where you turn left. ▶ Walk 100 metres up that road and turn right on a grass path. Follow GR marks to descend to a main road (**D913**). Traffic is fast on this main road so cross it carefully and continue straight ahead on the dirt path that climbs up the hill. The trail levels off when it reaches a wooded area and then traverses the hill, merging with a road (D37) and entering the attractive village of **Amance**.

The GR5 proceeds straight through Amance, passing its church and war memorial (and benches). After following the road downhill for 1km, branch left on a dirt road beside four old, rusty silos. Fork right toward the **Forêt d'Amance** and then turn right (southeast) to enter the forest on a road. Turn left on another road after 1.2km. The GR5 passes a beautiful

If you are lucky, you will encounter Antoine, who lives in a house right on the GR5, here. He has been greeting GR hikers with a smile and inviting them to sign his book for almost 20 years.

Farm work in a field beside Brin-sur-Seille

pond, **Etang de Brin**, and emerges from the forest. Curve right through fields to approach **Brin-sur-Seille**.

At the entrance to Brin-sur-Seille, turn left and then follow a right fork on Rue de l'Etang. This brings you to the centre of the village, where there is a café, a small food shop and the mairie. Turn left and follow the D70c main road to the bridge over the **Seille** river (**Pont de Brin**). After the bridge, turn left (off the GR5) and walk along the road to **Bioncourt**, 1km away.

SALT COUNTRY

Place names in the valley of the Seille River – such as Salonnes, Château-Salins, Marsal – remind us that this is salt country, the Pays du Sel (or 'Saulnois'). From prehistoric times, people have produced salt from subterranean deposits of brine in this area. An early technique, 'briquetage', involved heating brine in earthenware vessels. When the water had evaporated, the vessels were broken to obtain the salt that had been left as a deposit. Enormous piles of broken earthenware accumulated, in some places 10 metres deep, forming foundations for settlements in the marshlands. The production of salt using more efficient techniques and its transport and sale became a major commercial activity in the Middle Ages, avidly controlled and taxed by religious and secular rulers.

STAGE 44

Bioncourt to Vic-sur-Seille

Start	Bioncourt
Finish	Vic-sur-Seille
Distance	21km
Ascent/Descent	387m/363m
Time	4hr 45min
Maps	3414 E Delme; 3514 O Château-Salins
Refreshments	None
Transport	TIM bus route 30 stops in Bioncourt, Attilloncourt, Grémecey, Salonnes and Château Salins (limited, on-request service); bus routes 27 and 33 link Château Salins with Vic-sur-Seille.
Accommodation	Chambre d'hôtes in Vic-sur-Seille

This stage begins and ends beside a small river, the Seille, that you will cross again at Marsal during the next stage. The GR5 mostly crosses open plateaus on quiet roads and paths during this stage, but it also includes a good forest walk.

Retrace the previous day's final steps by walking south from Bioncourt along the **D77c** to join the GR5, turning left where the road curves right to cross the bridge. After a short climb, the trail levels off. It's a pleasant walk, with views of surrounding villages, each with a church steeple marking the horizon. Finally, the trail merges with a small main road (**D77**) and descends to **Attilloncourt**.

Walk straight into Attilloncourt past the church to the mairie and then turn left on Rue des Meix, which climbs out of the village. The route levels off to cross fields. Walk 2km (generally northeast) to an intersection at the entrance to a forest. The GR5 does not enter the forest here but instead turns right. It briefly follows the edge of the woods and then descends to **Grémecey**.

The pattern of walking through little villages continues in Grémecey. Pass the mairie and turn left beside the church. Cross a bridge over a small stream and then walk back up to

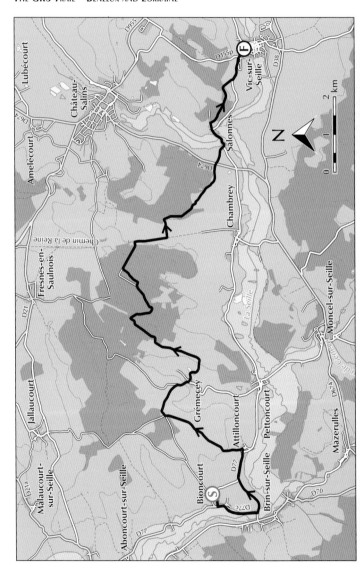

the plateau. Turn left on a dirt road where the tarmac ends. The road crosses level ground and, after 1km, enters a forest. Turn left on a dirt road within the forest and then, after 800 metres, right on the Route Forestière de Merlinsol.

This is a pleasant forest for walking, but the waymarking here is uneven and inadequate. Watch for GR marks and you will sometimes have to continue a certain distance after a turn without the reassurance of a mark. At one point, the narrow trail crosses a broad, muddy path and continues straight (northeast) through overgrown vegetation. It is easy to doubt that you are still following the GR5 (there are a few yellow rings on trees, marking another trail). Finally, 270 metres from that broad, muddy path, there is a GR mark indicating a right turn at a T-junction with another broad path. The trail descends gradually southeast from here, leaves the forest and turns right at a T-junction on a road that goes south through fields.

> This is the **Chemin de la Reine** (queen's road). Maria Leszczyńska, daughter of Stanislaus, King of Poland and later the last Duke of Lorraine, travelled along this road during her journey to Paris to marry King Louis XV in 1725.

After several hundred metres on this road, turn left on a path that leads to a forest. Turn right here and follow a

A beautiful view over Salonnes

narrow trail along the edge of the forest. The trail leaves the forest and turns left to pass through large bushes to a field that it crosses in a straight line southeast. After crossing a small stream (or ditch), the GR5 follows a path that climbs in the woods. The trail forks, but the two branches soon come back together. The trail leads to a road (**D674**): cross here and continue to **Salonnes**, a picturesque village.

> Here and in many other villages in this area, you will observe large doors, often with a graceful arch, in the façades of houses. These **portes de grange** (barn doors) are characteristic of Lorraine and date back to the time when the houses were farm buildings. The large doors provided convenient access for carts carrying hay, grains and other bulky agricultural produce.

On the far side of the village, across a small stream, a sharp right turn is posted for Vic-sur-Seilles, your destination, but that is for vehicular traffic. Continue straight a short distance and then follow a right fork on a small road uphill. After 150 metres, turn right to walk across a field and along the edge of a forest, with a good view to the right over the valley of the Seille.

The trail enters the forest, emerges briefly beside vineyards and enters the trees again. Descend to the right toward Vic-sur-Seille, turn left at a T-junction and walk to a main road (**D155p**) just outside Vic-sur-Seille. The GR5 turns left here, while the road to the right leads to the centre of **Vic-sur-Seille**.

> The Baroque painter **Georges de La Tour** was born in Vic-sur-Seille in 1593. His work reflected the influence of Caravaggio, and he is known for his religious paintings lit by candlelight. One such painting, *St John the Baptist in the Desert,* is exhibited at the Georges de La Tour Museum in Vic-sur-Seille, alongside works by other artists.

STAGE 45

Vic-sur-Seille to Tarquimpol

Start	Vic-sur-Seille
Finish	Tarquimpol (Château d'Alteville)
Distance	23.7km
Ascent/Descent	290m/289m
Time	5hr
Map	3514 O Château-Salins; 3514 E Dieuze; 3515 E Avricourt
Refreshments	Cafés/restaurants in Marsal and Dieuze
Transport	TIM bus 27 (Metz–Dieuze) stops in Vic-sur-Seille.
Accommodation	Gîtes d'étape in Blanche Eglise and nearby Mulcey; chambres d'hôtes in Dieuze and Tarquimpol

This stage starts well. A 2km section at the beginning has recently been taken off the road and into a forest. There is a considerable amount of road walking after that, but the roads are quiet. A highlight of the stage is the Etang de Lindre and the nearby stork sanctuary.

From the intersection of the D155P and the Route de Salonnes, just north of town, walk about 200 metres north and then turn right onto a quiet dirt road. ▶ The road climbs gently in the woods, continuing straight past roads on the left, and levels off beside open fields. There are few GR marks here, but there is one at the key point where the GR5 turns right to descend. The road emerges from the woods and meets the **D155Z**.

The current (2006) IGN map shows the GR5 running east from this intersection on the Rue des Hosties but this has been changed.

Turn left here and walk 600 metres beside the road to a busier main road (**D955**). Cross that main road, turn right and then immediately left on a path through fields. Follow the trail to woods that it skirts along their southern side. Parts of the trail here are a vague track through high grass, but you soon reach a paved path that passes a house and leads to a main road (D38). Turn left and walk 400 metres beside this main road, then turn right on a road to **Marsal**.

Enter Marsal through its imposing Porte de France.

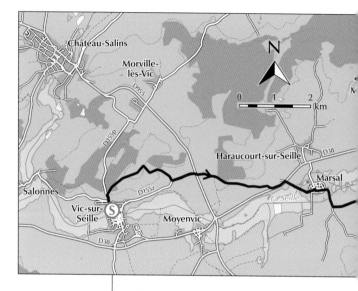

The **Porte de France** is a vestige of the fortifications built under the supervision of Louis XIV's great military engineer, Vauban. The fact that such fortifications were built here reflects the strategic and economic importance of salt in those days. The structure now houses a museum devoted to that vital commodity: the Musée du Sel (www.moselle. fr and search for Musée du Sel). Elsewhere in and near Marsal, there are more remnants of Vauban's fortifications.

THE GABELLE

The gabelle was a tax on salt instituted by French kings during the Middle Ages. Louis XIV's Finance Minister, Jean-Baptiste Colbert, codified the gabelle in an *ordonnance* (1680) that divided France into six very different and unequal regions: Grande Gabelle, Petite Gabelle, Pays de Salines, Pays Rédimés, Pays Exempts and Pays de Quart-Bouillon. The rules governing the sale and taxation of salt differed from one region to another. For example, the gabelle was high in the Grande Gabelle (a large territory that included Paris), and everyone there over the

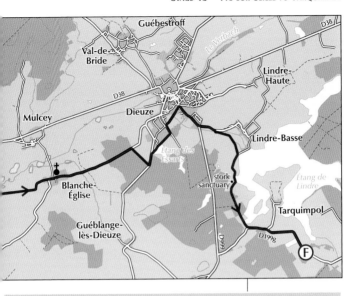

age of 8 was obliged to purchase a minimum amount of salt annually. Brittany, a Pays Exempt, paid no gabelle at all, a privilege that was granted when the Duchy of Brittany became part of the Kingdom of France in the 16th century. The gabelle was relatively low in Lorraine, a salt-producing region (Pays de Salines), since the State received revenue directly from the sale of salt there.

Large variances in the price of salt naturally led to widespread smuggling – countered by the State's zealous efforts to prevent and punish it. Corruption and exemptions for privileged social classes exacerbated the anger of those who paid exorbitant prices for salt. The gabelle was abolished during the French Revolution (1790), but restored by Napoleon in 1806. It still existed in the 20th century (albeit in a more rational form) until the gabelle was definitively abrogated in 1945 – shortly before India rescinded the notorious salt tax of the British Raj that Mahatma Ghandi had dramatically challenged with his Salt March in 1930.

Walk through the centre of the village – right on Rue des Cadets, right on Rue des Capucins and left through the Place d'Armes (where there is a restaurant) – and out on a road that curves right past a football pitch. Cross a bridge over the Seille River and turn left at a T-junction beside farm

The Seille near Marsal

buildings. From here, follow a quiet country road 4.5km to **Blanche Eglise**. This village has a gîte d'étape, many distinctive *portes de grange* (often smartly painted) – and a (surprisingly) grey church.

The GR5 continues on the road beyond Blanche Eglise for another 2km, the latter part through a forest. Finally, the GR5 turns off the road to the right on a trail into this forest. It's a beautiful forest, too. However, after just 700 metres, the trail confronts a sign announcing 'ZONE DANGEREUSE'. Entry is forbidden 'pendant les tirs' (during the shooting), and the times for such shooting are listed. The message concludes with a statement of the obvious: 'DANGER DE MORT' (Danger of death). You could venture into this forest during the days when, according to the sign, there is no shooting (Friday, Saturday, Sunday), but the GR5 prudently turns away.

Follow a road to the left for several hundred metres and then bend on a diagonal to the right on a gravel path. There are shaded benches beside the trail – a good place for a pause – and a peaceful pond, **Etang des Essarts**.

The GR5 continues straight where the path curves to the right around the pond. Walk beside a fence with signs proclaiming 'Zone Protégée' (it's a military facility) and then turn left to walk through a parking lot and onto a residential street in **Dieuze**. Turn right at the first intersection on Chemin du Pont Moreau, which leads to a roundabout. The marked route goes from this roundabout left into the centre of Dieuze and then back to the roundabout.

The Salines Royales would be worth a visit, but if you prefer to omit that, turn right at the roundabout and walk up the **D999** (Chemin Royal). ▶ At the next roundabout (featuring a sculpture called 'La vague des cristaux de sel'), turn left toward Lindre-Basse. Within 200 metres, where the road curves left, turn right on a gravel road. Watch for storks flying around here!

The road reaches a paved path. Before turning right on this path to follow the GR5, walk a short distance to the left to admire the vast **Etang de Lindre**, with its many aquatic birds. Most of all, pause to admire the **stork sanctuary**, a large cage with several nests for white storks (*cigognes blanches*) mounted above it. When you return to the path, walking generally south beside the Etang de Lindre, you may see the Vosges Mountains on the distant horizon (southeast). In a few days, you will be there!

The GR5 enters an area of large ponds, the Pays des Etangs.

These **ponds** – such as the Etang de Lindre here and the Etang du Stock in the next stage – were created in the Middle Ages. They were an important source

Dieuze was a leading centre of salt production over the centuries. Its Salines Royales are a group of 18th century buildings where salt was produced on a grand scale.

Protected nests for white storks beside the Etang de Lindre

of fish. In addition, they were periodically drained and used for arable farming for a limited period of time (generally one year), a practice called 'l'assec'.

The path enters the woods and becomes a dirt trail, passing a stand for bird watching (with illustrated panels about the local birds). The trail broadens and leaves the forest, leading to a main road (**D199g**). Turn left and walk along this main road. After 600 metres, there is a road on the left to **Tarquimpol**. Ignore this and continue straight along the main road a further 1km to the Château d'Alteville, where there is a comfortable and very hospitable chambre d'hôtes (with table d'hôte).

STAGE 46
Tarquimpol to Gondrexange

Start	Tarquimpol (Château d'Alteville)
Finish	Gondrexange
Distance	22.8km
Ascent/Descent	237m/192m
Time	5hr
Maps	3515 E Avricourt; 3615 O Lorquin
Refreshments	Cafés/restaurants at Assenoncourt and Rhodes
Transport	None
Accommodation	Chambres d'hôtes in Assenoncourt and Rhodes; campground (with hikers' cabins) in Gondrexange; gîte d'étape in Landange (4km beyond Gondrexange on the GR5)

This stage includes a substantial amount of walking on hard surfaces, but most of it is rather pleasant, in particular the 4km walk along a bicycle path beside the Canal des Houillères. You also walk through forests and beside beautiful ponds – this is, indeed, Le Pays des Etangs.

Set off southeast beside the D199g. Less than 1km from the Château d'Alteville, the GR5 reaches the Maison Forestière

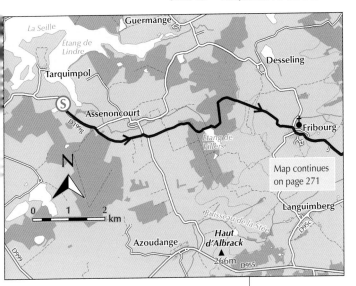

du Bois de l'Evêque. Turn right here on a small road that leads to a grass path. Continue southeast and then, after 600 metres, curve left (northeast) on a dirt road that leads to **Assenoncourt**. Turn right on a road and walk past a chambre d'hôtes. ▶ Turn left on a small road where the main road curves right and walk east into the woods. Follow a pleasant trail in the woods, passing the **Etang de Villers**.

The path broadens and becomes a gravel road, still in the woods. Follow this road when it turns left (north) and next curves right. Then, just 100 metres further where the road curves left, the GR5 branches off to the right (southeast) on a trail. There is a GR mark for this turn, but it is not prominent. The trail is rough and faint in places but easy to follow, as it is bounded by trees. Continue straight when the trail emerges from the forest. A telecommunications tower is visible straight ahead on the horizon. It is 3.5km away, and you will eventually walk past it.

The path becomes a dirt road, but where the road turns left, the GR5 continues straight down a grass path that becomes a dirt road leading to **Fribourg**. Turn right after entering Fribourg, pass a school and then turn left on a

Turn left here for the centre of Assenoncourt, where there is a small restaurant.

*The church in Fribourg
with children's
gardening projects*

The Canal des
Houillères was built in
the 1860s to transport
coal from mines
near Saarbrücken.
It connects the
Marne-Rhine Canal
to the Sarre River
in Sarreguemines.

road (**D95**) toward the **church**. Continue on the D95 1.5km
beyond Fribourg. Just before the telecoms **tower**, turn right
on a gravel road through fields of maize and other crops and
then left on the **D95c** main road toward **Rhodes**. After 200
metres, turn right toward **Les Bachats**, where there is a chambre d'hôtes and a restaurant.

Walk past a small arm of the **Etang du Stock**. Follow
the road as it curves left and then turn left again to follow a
tree-lined path, at the end of which it turns right and crosses
a dyke beside another arm of the Etang du Stock. Follow that
road straight into the forest. One kilometre after the dyke,
turn right at an intersection and then, 800 metres further, left
on the Route Forestière de Diane Capelle. The road leaves
the forest and becomes paved. Continue straight to a bridge
that crosses the **Canal des Houillères**. ◄

On the other side of the bridge, descend steps on the left
and then turn left to walk southwest along the path (formerly
a tow-path, now for bicycles) beside the canal. After 4km,
there is a footbridge near the point where this canal meets
the **Marne-Rhine Canal** (a sign indicates Nancy to the right,
Strasbourg to the left). Cross the footbridge and continue on

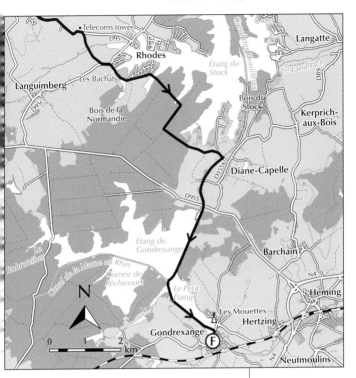

the other side of the canal southeast, but now on dirt path beside the pavement. After a further 2km (now beside the Marne-Rhine Canal), the path arrives in **Gondrexange**. A campground with hikers' cabins (and a restaurant) is to the left, across a bridge before entering Gondrexange.

STAGE 47
Gondrexange to Abreschviller

Start	Gondrexange
Finish	Abreschviller
Distance	22.4km
Ascent/Descent	457m/437m
Time	5hr
Maps	3615 O Lorquin; 3715 OT Saverne/Sarrebourg
Refreshments	Café in Niderhoff; cafés/restaurants and shops in Saint-Quirin
Transport	TIM bus routes serve towns along this stage: 84 (Landange), 142 (Niderhoff and Saint-Quirin, limited service on request), 155 (Saint-Quirin and Abreschviller)
Accommodation	Gîtes d'étape in Landange and Abreschviller; hotels in Saint-Quirin and Abreschviller; chambre d'hôtes in Saint-Quirin

Much of this stage crosses familiar terrain of the Lorraine plateau: rolling, open country with scattered forests offering varied perspectives at different distances. But those mountains on the horizon – the Vosges – are getting perceptibly closer. Indeed, this stage concludes with a foretaste of mountain walking that may whet your appetite for more…

From the southeast corner of the **Petit Etang**, where your incoming path along the Marne-Rhine Canal met Rue de l'Étang, cross the main road, turn left and walk a few metres to Rue de la Pêche. Turn right on Rue de la Pêche and immediately left into a small parking lot. Walk through the lot and turn right on the path beside the canal.

After 500 metres, cross a bridge over the canal to the left and continue walking along the path on the other side of the canal. ◀ The canal and its path curve gradually to the left, arriving at a bridge 2km after the previous one. Leave the canal path, cross this bridge and walk straight ahead on a small road that approaches the **N4**. The road curves right and then left to pass under the main road. Turn right on the

A sign here states that the route has been modified ('Itinéraire Modifié'). The old route crossed the busy N4 main road but the new route passes safely underneath.

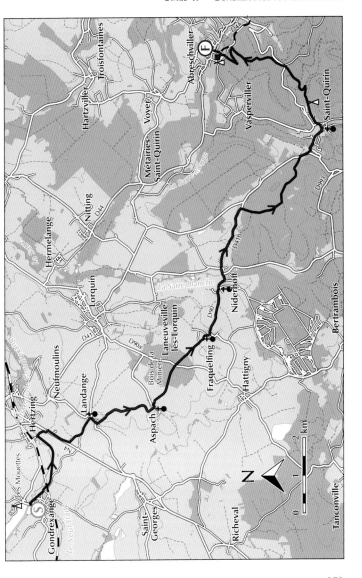

273

other side and walk on a gravel road parallel to the main road (southwest). This road leads to a paved road. Turn left here to walk into **Landange**.

Turn right on Rue du Savé in the centre of Landange, just before the church. Walk past a gîte d'étape on the right and continue on the road as it climbs gently and curves left to leave the village. Follow the road roughly south through open country 2km to another small village, **Aspach**. The GR5 passes quickly through Aspach. Go left after the **church** (where there is a pleasant, shaded picnic table), right opposite the mairie, and then it is back in the open country.

The road enters woods, the **Bois de la Minière**, and continues straight across a main road (**D90a**). When you emerge from these woods, there is a good view of the Vosges Mountains.

You can appreciate from here how French patriots around the turn of the 20th century spoke of '**la ligne bleue des Vosges**', expressing a sense of loss after Germany's annexation of Alsace and part of Lorraine in 1871 and their determination to recover those territories. The phrase was taken from the will of Jules Ferry, a French politician from the Vosges.

Descend from here to another small village, **Fraquelfing**. Turn right beside the mairie of Fraquelfing and walk towards the **church**. Follow the road as it curves left, then turn left at a T-junction and right to leave the village. It is not much more than a kilometre on the road from there to **Niderhoff**.

Walk through Niderhoff, passing a **church** and a café, and turn left beside the mairie on Grand' Rue. Continue southeast on Grand' Rue, which becomes the **D41b**. Walk beside this main road for 2km. Then, after passing the Maison Forestière de Heille on the left, turn right to walk up a dirt road into a forest, the Route Forestière de la Neuve Grange. The GR5 follows trails through this forest toward Saint-Quirin, among other trails and destinations.

The priory church of Saint-Quirin is notable for its beautiful baroque design and its restored 18th century Silberman organ.

When the trail emerges briefly from the forest, turn right on a road and then, after 200 metres, left on a trail that descends in the forest to **Saint-Quirin**. Turn left on a road that leads into the centre of this attractive town. ◄ After passing Saint-Quirin's mairie and tourist office, curve to the left and then turn right on Rue d'Alsace. Waymarks for the GR5 and other trails appear on signs at these turns. Follow a left fork and walk past the municipal campground into the forest.

This is the domain of the **Club Vosgien**, a walking association established in Alsace in 1872. You will see a great number and variety of the Club's waymarks along the trails. Standard white-and-red rectangles continue to mark the GR5, but that will change at the Col de l'Engin during the next stage.

The Club Vosgien marks many trails in this area

Within this forest, the GR5 follows a series of *routes forestières*, starting with a hairpin turn left on Route Forestière Basse Jordy. The trail climbs steeply, follows a right fork and comes to an intersection, the Lieu Dit les Deux Croix. Turn left here on a gravel road, Route Forestière de Vasperviller, then right on Route Forestière du Réémetteur, which descends to a telecommunications tower. ▸ The trail continues its descent to Abreschviller. Walk past a pond and a campground on the left and cross the **railway line** of a tourist train. The gîte communal is on the right and, a short distance further in the centre of the village, there is a hotel.

There is a good viewing point with benches here, looking over Abreschviller.

Abreschviller

STAGE 48
Abreschviller to Col du Donon

Start	Abreschviller
Finish	Col du Donon
Distance	21.8km
Ascent/Descent	939m/505m
Time	6hr 30 min
Maps	3715 OT Saverne/Sarrebourg; 3616 OT Le Donon
Refreshments	None after Lettenbach
Transport	None
Accommodation	Hotels at Col du Donon
Waymarks	Standard white-and-red GR marks until Col de l'Engin; red rectangles from there

The Northern GR5 leaves Lorraine and enters Alsace during this stage. The steep, rocky trail to the summit of Le Donon is a good introduction to the Vosges. If you have been walking on the GR5 since Hoek van Holland – in one go or a series of sections – you will appreciate the spectacular view from the 1008m summit all the more. It may inspire you to tackle the challenges that lie between you and Nice.

Standing in the centre of Abreschviller, you will be presented with a dozen trails marked with different symbols. Set off southeast along the main road (**D44**) out of town and notice some the other trails heading off in different directions. The GR5 turns right after about 1.5km on the road (**D96**) to Lettenbach. Pass a restaurant (closed in the morning) and you soon arrive in this attractive village.

Walk straight through a small park (with the mairie and school on the right), and then, before reaching the **church**, turn left on a path that cuts discreetly through hedges. The path leads to an open field where the route to follow may be obscured by tall grass. Walk uphill along the edge of the field (southeast) and then turn right to walk along the upper side of the field (southwest) to a point where the trail enters the forest.

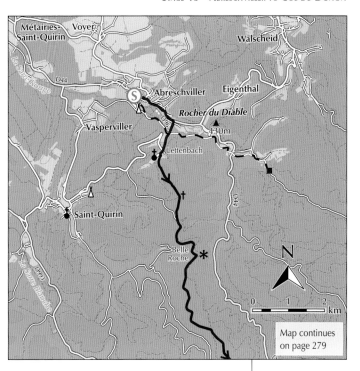

Follow the broad trail that climbs in the forest. The trail continues straight after crossing a clearing at **Croix Guillaume**.

> Shortly after that clearing, there is a side-trail to the excavated ruins of a **Gallo-Roman settlement** that was occupied during the 1st–3rd centuries AD. It's worth the short detour to visit.

The trail descends in the forest. At a crossroads (Quatre Chemins) continue straight ahead on Route Forestière de la Belle Roche and then follow a right fork on the Route Forestière de Lendenstein. The dirt road climbs and forks left on a trail. ▸ Follow a pleasant, level traverse across a wooded slope before descending to the left on a broad path.

A short side trail to the left leads to Belle Roche, a small clearing with a magnificent view over the Vosges Mountains (picnic table and bench).

View over the Vosges Mountains from Belle Roche

The trail levels off on a dirt road, forks to the left and climbs gently in the direction of the Abri Paul Bechler. Follow a narrow forest trail and pass a large rock called the 'Pierre ou Fauteuil de Saint-Quirin' (Saint Quirin's stone or chair), which is, indeed, a comfortable place to sit for a moment. A bit further, the trail reaches the **Abri Paul Bechler**, a shelter 11km from Abreschviller that is a good place for lunch if the weather is bad. Continue straight beyond the shelter through a large, open crossroads (La Main de Fer).

The trail next forks to the left and climbs. The ascent continues on a narrow, winding path after turning left at the **Borne Brignon**.

There are ancient **bornes militaires** along this trail. These are milestones placed by Roman soldiers to mark certain distances and crossroads on the roads that they built and maintained.

The GR5 curves right (west) around the **Croix Simon** in a large clearing. It then climbs steeply for nearly 1km before merging with a gravel road.

The gravel road leads to a main road (**D44**) 1.2km further on. Turn right here and walk 100 metres to the **Col de l'Engin**.

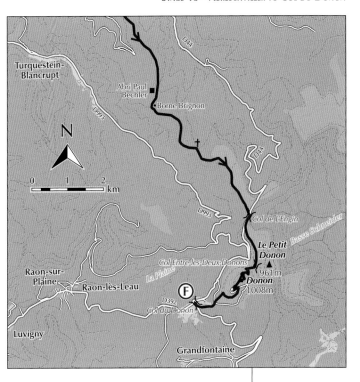

This is the border between the Departments of the Moselle and Bas-Rhin and thus between Lorraine and Alsace. More importantly, for the hiker at least, the **waymarking** changes here. From the Col de l'Engin through the Vosges Mountains to the southern slopes of the Ballon d'Alsace, the GR5 is marked by the Club Vosgien's red rectangles.

Red rectangles lead to a broad, smooth path that climbs gently in the woods from the Col de l'Engin to the next pass, the **Col Entre-les-Deux-Donons**. There are several trails from this pass to the summit of Le Donon. The GR5 opts for the direct route on a straight, uphill trail (west). After 250 metres on this trail, turn sharply left and follow switchbacks up a

279

A mock Gallo-Roman temple on the summit of Le Donon

rocky trail to the summit of **Le Donon** (1008m) and breath-taking views.

> **Le Donon** was a sanctuary dedicated to the worship of Mercury by Gallo-Roman peoples. The temple on the summit, however, built in 1869, reflects 19th century romanticism and imagination, not an actual ancient structure.

Pass the temple going over the summit and descend stone steps on the other side. Walk to the left of a large telecom tower and continue down the trail. The path is initially rough and rocky but eventually becomes smooth. The trail emerges from the forest and follows a gravel road a short distance to the main road that crosses the **Col du Donon** (**D392**). Turn right here to walk to the hotels at the Col du Donon.

STAGE 49

Col du Donon to Schirmeck

Start	Col du Donon
Finish	Schirmeck
Distance	8.3km
Ascent/Descent	114m/532m
Time	2hr 15min
Maps	3616 OT Le Donon; 3716 ET Mont Ste.-Odile
Refreshments	None
Transport	Railway service in Schirmeck
Accommodation	Chambres d'hôtes in Wackenbach; hotels in La Claquette (2.5km from Schirmeck) and Urmatt (12 minutes from Schirmeck by train)
Waymarks	Red rectangles

This stage offers a pleasant, easy conclusion to the Northern GR5. It is especially enjoyable on a clear day in the morning, with shafts of sunlight passing through the tall pine trees as the trail descends through the forest. It's a short walk, so you can fit it within your plans – either ending the trek in Schirmeck and departing by train from there or continuing on the GR5 in the Vosges.

From the Col du Donon walk southeast along the main road (D392) to a point where a narrow forest trail branches off to the right, 300 metres from the pass. There is a GR mark for this turn, pointing to Schirmeck, but it helps to be watching for it!

The broad, smooth trail crosses a road and continues gently downhill. Curve around a stream crossing and fork left on a smaller path that traverses the slope. Follow a gravel road for 150 metres before shifting back to a forest trail on the right that runs parallel to the road. The trail turns down a short, steep slope that is quite slippery when wet.

At the bottom of this slope, cross a road and a small metal bridge to reach a trail that leads up to a main road (D392 again) after its curve. Turn right and walk outside the main road's guard rail on a grass path for 225 metres. Cross

281

Wackenbach

the main road where a large tree stump assists scrambling over the guard rail and follow a trail that returns to the forest.

The GR5 descends to cross a road and continues in the forest. After crossing another road, traverse a steep slope on a narrow trail, gradually downhill – a very enjoyable walk. Turn left where the trail reaches a road and walk into **Wackenbach**, an attractive village where there are chambres d'hôtes.

Make a hairpin right turn near a bench and fountain and walk up the road. Continue through the village, following GR marks to a gravel road that enters the forest, the Route Forestière de la Basse Scierie. Walk just 50 metres on that road and then bend left on a trail that climbs into the forest. The trail crosses a road and then descends in the forest to a main road (**D392**). Continue in the same direction along that main road, which leads to **Schirmeck**.

Within a short distance, as you will see, the GR5 exits Schirmeck, enters **La Broque** and then re-enters Schirmeck. Cross a small bridge and then turn left to walk past a restaurant and the parking lot of a supermarket. Cross the **railway tracks** ahead on a concrete footbridge. On the other side, turn left to walk to the **train station**. To reach the centre of the village, turn right here and walk a short distance on Rue de la Gare to the **church** and tourist office.

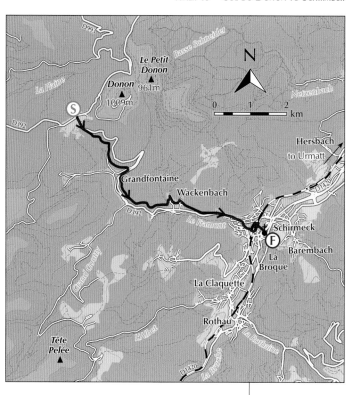

You've arrived at the end of the Northern GR5, but the rest of the trail leads on beyond the church into the Vosges… and on to Nice!

APPENDIX A

Route planner

This planner is included to help you plan your own itinerary along the northern GR5. Note that your pace is likely to slow a little once you reach the mountains in Luxembourg!

Places with facilities on the GR5	Distance (km)	Cumulative distance (km)	Facilities
Hoek van Holland	0.0	0.0	Hotels, cafés/restaurants, shops
Maasland	18.5	18.5	B&B, restaurant, shops
Maassluis	2.8	21.3	B&B, cafés/restaurants, shops
Brielle	10.0	31.3	Hotels, B&Bs, cafés/restaurants, shops
Oostvoorne	8.0	39.3	Hotel, café/restaurant
Tenellaplas	3.5	42.8	Café/restaurant
Rockanje	6.5	49.3	Hotels, café/restaurant
Havenhoofd	11.2	60.5	B&B
Goedereede	2.0	62.5	B&Bs, café/restaurant, shop
Herkingen	18.5	81.0	B&B, restaurant, shop
Nieuw-Vossemeer	24.0	105.0	B&B, cafés/restaurants, shops
Lepelstraat	7.5	112.5	B&B
Bergen op Zoom	11.2	123.7	Hotels, B&B, youth hostel, cafés/restaurants, shops
Trail to Wouwse Plantage	10.4	134.1	B&B (2km off GR5)
Kalmthout	16.6	150.7	B&Bs, cafés/restaurants, shops
Wuustwezel	12.0	162.7	Cafés/restaurants, shops
Brecht	10.8	173.5	Hotels, cafés/restaurants, shops
Brug 11	3.5	177	Café
Westmalle Abbey	7.0	184	Café/restaurant
Zoersel	3.0	187	Youth hostel, hotels
Herentals	21.5	208.5	Hotels, cafés/restaurants, shops
Olen	7.6	216.1	Cafés/restaurants, shops
Westerlo	8.9	225	B&B, youth hostel, café/restaurant
Averbode	15.0	240	Café/restaurant
Scherpenheuvel	9.0	249	B&B, cafés/restaurants, shops
Diest	10.0	259	Hotels, B&B, campground with trekkershutten, cafés/restaurants, shops
Lummen	15.5	274.5	Hotels, B&B, cafés/restaurants, shops
Viversel	7.5	282	Hotel, café/restaurant, shops

Places with facilities on the GR5	Distance (km)	Cumulative distance (km)	Facilities
Bolderberg	6.5	288.5	Hotels, café/restaurant, shops
Stokrooie	4.5	293	B&Bs
Herkenrode Abbey	2.0	295	Café/restaurant
Kiewit Domain	10.3	305.3	Café/restaurant
Hasselt variant trail	2.3	307.6	B&B (2km off GR5)
Bokrijk Provincial Domain	1.4	309	Cafés/restaurants; youth hostel (2.7km off GR5)
Termien	11.0	320	Café/restaurant
Kattevenia	4.5	324.5	Café/restaurant
Wiemesmeer	2.5	327	Café/restaurant
Zutendaal	2.6	329.6	Hotels, cafés/restaurants, shops
Lanaken	18.0	347.6	Hotels, cafés/restaurants, shops
Maastricht	11.0	358.6	Hotels, B&Bs, cafés/restaurants, shops
Kanne	9.0	367.6	Hotels, cafés/restaurants, shops
Eben-Emael	3.0	370.6	B&B, restaurant
Visé	19.0	389.6	Hotel, cafés/restaurants, shops
Dalhem	4.0	393.6	Shops
Saint-Remy	3.8	397.4	Café
Evegnée-Tignée	9.0	406.4	Chambre d'hôtes
Soumagne	6.2	412.6	Chambre d'hôtes (1.5km off GR5)
Olne	4.5	417.1	Café/restaurant, shops
Nessonvaux	3.5	420.6	Hotels, café/restaurant, shops
Banneux	6.0	426.6	Hotels, cafés/restaurants, shops
La Reid	7.0	433.6	Chambres d'hôtes, café/restaurant, shops
Spa	10.0	443.6	Hotels, chambres d'hôtes, cafés/restaurants, shops
Stavelot	16.0	459.6	Hotels, chambres d'hôtes, cafés/restaurants, shops
Vielsalm	15.5	475.1	Hotels, chambres d'hôtes, cafés/restaurants, shops
Commanster	9.5	484.6	Chambre d'hôtes
Braunlauf	5.0	489.6	Chambre d'hôtes
Burg-Reuland	10.8	500.4	Hotels, café/restaurant, shops
Ouren	10.2	510.6	Hotels, cafés/restaurants, shops
Tintesmühle campground	8.0	518.6	Café
Dasbourg-Pont	7.4	526	Café; hotel in Dasbourg, Germany (500m off GR5)
2km before Obereisenbach	4.6	530.6	Campground with trekkershutten, café/restaurant
Untereisenbach	3.3	533.9	Cafés/restaurants
Wahlhausen	2.4	536.3	Café/restaurant

Places with facilities on the GR5	Distance (km)	Cumulative distance (km)	Facilities
Pont de Gemünd	3.2	539.5	Café/restaurant
Stolzembourg	4.6	544.1	Café/restaurant
Mont Saint-Nicolas	3.8	547.9	Café/restaurant
Vianden	5.7	553.6	Hotels, youth hostel, cafés/restaurants, shops
Bleesbréck	14.0	567.6	Campground with trekkershutten, café/restaurant
Gilsdorf	1.0	568.6	Cafés/restaurants
Beaufort	15.5	584.1	Hotels, youth hostel, campground with trekkershutten, cafés/restaurants, shops
Grundhof	5.4	589.5	Café/restaurant
Berdorf	4.2	593.7	Hotels, B&B, campground with trekkershutten, cafés/restaurants, shops
Echternach	7.2	600.9	Hotels, B&Bs, youth hostel, cafés/restaurants, shops
Rosport	8.4	609.3	Café/restaurant; hotel in Ralingen, Germany (500m off GR5)
Born	8.1	617.4	Café/restaurant, campground with trekkershutten
Moersdorf	2.4	619.8	Café/restaurant
Wasserbillig	7.5	627.3	Cafés/restaurants, shops; hotel off GR5 in Oberbillig (Germany)
Mertert	2.8	630.1	Café/restaurant
Manternach	6.7	636.8	Café/restaurant
Grevenmacher	4.5	641.3	Cafés/restaurants, campground with cabins; hotel 3km off GR5
Machtum	6.0	647.3	Café, restaurant
Ahn	4.4	651.7	Café/restaurant
Wormeldange	3.0	654.7	Café/restaurant
Ehnen	2.8	657.5	Hotel, café/restaurant
Greiveldange	3.1	660.6	Café/restaurant
Stadtbredimus	3.5	664.1	Hotels, café/restaurant
Remich	3.2	667.3	Hotels, cafés/restaurants, shops
Wellenstein	5.9	673.2	Café/restaurant
Wintrange	3.7	676.9	Café/restaurant
Remerschen	2.0	678.9	Café/restaurant, youth hostel
Schengen	6.4	685.3	Café/restaurant, shop
Apach	2.0	687.3	Chambre d'hôtes
Sierck-les-Bains	2.5	689.8	Cafés/restaurants, shops
Montenach	4.8	694.6	Hotel, café/restaurant
Sainte-Marguerite	9.0	703.6	Chambre d'hôtes
Kédange-sur-Canner	10.0	713.6	Hotel, café/restaurant, shops
Saint-Hubert	11.0	724.6	Chambres d'hôtes

Places with facilities on the GR5	Distance (km)	Cumulative distance (km)	Facilities
Vigy	6.0	730.6	Chambre d'hôtes, café/resturant, shops
Sanry-lès-Vigy	4.0	734.6	Café/restaurant
Villers l'Orne	7.0	741.6	Café/restaurant
Metz	7.6	749.2	Hotels, chambres d'hôtes, youth hostel, cafés/restaurants, shops
Scy-Chazelles	8.0	757.2	Chambre d'hôtes, café/restaurant, shops
Moulins-lès-Metz	1.5	758.7	Café/restaurant
Vaux	2.5	761.2	Chambre d'hôtes, café/restaurant
Ars-sur-Moselle	2.0	763.2	Café/restaurant, shops
Rongeueville	2.5	765.7	Chambres d'hôtes in Ancy-sur-Moselle (500m off GR5)
Gorze	7.7	773.4	Chambre d'hôtes, café/restaurant
Pagny-sur-Moselle	15.6	789	Gîte; cafés/restaurants, shops (1km off GR5)
Montauville	19.5	808.5	Hotels, chambres d'hôtes, cafés/restaurants, shops in Pont-à-Mousson (3km off GR5)
Liverdun	33.2	841.7	Chambres d'hôtes, café/restaurant, shops
Custines	9.4	851.1	Cafés/restaurants, shops; hotel (1.5km off GR5)
Brin-sur-Seille	21.6	872.7	Café, shop; chambre d'hôtes in Bioncourt (1km off GR5)
Vic-sur-Seille	20.0	892.7	Chambre d'hôtes, café/restaurant, shops
Marsal	6.8	899.5	Café/restaurant
Blanche-Eglise	5.5	905	Gîte d'étape
Dieuze	4.7	909.7	Chambres d'hôtes, cafés/restaurants, shops
Tarquimpol	6.7	916.4	Chambre d'hôtes (Château d'Alteville)
Assenoncourt	2.5	918.9	Chambre d'hôtes, café/restaurant
Rhodes	8.0	926.9	Chambre d'hôtes, café/restaurant
Gondrexange	12.3	939.2	Campground with cabins, café/restaurant
Landange	4.0	943.2	Gîte d'étape
Niderhoff	6.0	949.2	Café/restaurant
Saint-Quirin	6.0	955.2	Hotel, chambre d'hôtes, cafés/restaurants, shops
Abreschviller	6.4	961.6	Hotel, gîte d'étape, café/restaurant, shop
Col du Donon	21.8	983.4	Hotels, café/restaurant
Wackenbach	5.3	988.7	Chambres d'hôtes
Schirmeck	3.0	991.7	Cafés/restaurants, shops, hotels in La Claquette (2.5km from Schirmeck) and Urmatt (12 minutes by train)

APPENDIX B

Four 5-day itineraries on the GR5

The following short treks along the Northern GR5 will fit the bill perfectly if you have about a week's holiday to take (including travel time from home to the starting point and back from the end point). As well as having convenient access (usually by train), they showcase some of the highlights of the Northern GR5.

The Dutch Delta

This trek includes dykes, dunes and polder lands, as well as major works of the Delta Project: the Haringvlietsluizen and two linked dams, Grevelingendam and Philipsdam. The walk through Voornes Duin (on the first day) is delightful. Two historic cities bookend the route: Brielle and Bergen op Zoom. See Stages 3–7.

- Brielle to Rockanje (18.0km)
- Rockanje to Goedereede (13.2km)
- Goedereede to Herkingen (18.5km)
- Herkingen to Nieuw-Vossemeer (24km)
- Nieuw-Vossemeer to Bergen op Zoom (16.5km)

Travel notes

- From Rotterdam, take RET Metro D to Spijkenisse and Connexion Bus 103 from there to Brielle.
- Trains run from Bergen op Zoom via Roosendaal to main lines.

Flemish Abbeys

This itinerary passes three of the great abbeys of Flanders: Westmalle (not open for visits, but they sell their excellent beer at a café across the street), Tongerlo (with a museum displaying a near-contemporary copy of Da Vinci's 'Last Supper') and Averbode (with a beautiful reflecting pool beside its baroque church). Scherpenheuvel is a popular pilgrimage destination. You might time your walk to join the annual Abdijentocht between Tongerlo and Averbode on Ascension Day. You pass through forests and across heathlands, with a particularly pleasant section beside a quiet stream, the Kleine Nete, leading to Herentals. The short fifth day leaves time to visit Diest. See Stages 10–14.

- Brecht to Zoersel (13.5km)
- Zoersel to Herentals (21.5km)
- Herentals to Westerlo (16.5km)
- Westerlo to Scherpenheuvel (24m)
- Scherpenheuvel to Diest (10km)

Travel notes

Brecht is linked by rail to Antwerp.
Diest is on a railway line linking Leuven and Hasselt.

The Ardennes

This testing trek covers the entire Ardennes section of the GR5 in five days of vigorous, glorious trekking in Wallonia and Luxembourg. The landscape is varied, with trails across high plateaus cut by narrow river valleys and peatland, along with the steep trails in the densely forested mountains that you would expect in the Ardennes. The stages are relatively long, and those distances naturally require more time and effort than similar distances in the Netherlands and Flanders. There is a full range of accommodation on this itinerary: hotels, chambres d'hôtes and trekkershutten in a campground. See Stages 24–29.

- Fraipont to Spa (21.3km)
- Spa to Vielsalm (32.6km)
- Vielsalm to Burg-Reuland (25.3km)
- Burg-Reuland to Obereisenbach (30.2km)
- Obereisenbach to Vianden (23km)

Travel notes

- Travel by train from Liège to Fraipont (about 15 minutes).
- In Luxembourg, bus routes 663 and 842 run from Obereisenbach to Vianden, and the 842 continues on to Diekirch and Ettelbruck, which are linked to Luxembourg City by rail. Another useful bus is route 570, running from Stolzembourg to Vianden, which can be taken to shorten the final stage by 10km.

The Côte de Moselle

For this one, you walk 'across the grain' of the Côte de Moselle south of Metz. This long ridge, running north-south, is cut by rivers and streams flowing roughly east into the Moselle river. The GR5 descends and climbs across the little valleys formed by these rivers. There are magnificent views over the Moselle valley from high points along this trail, such as Prény, the site of a medieval castle. Rather than returning to Metz after completing this itinerary, you could take a train to Nancy and return home from there. That way you could include visits to two great, historic cities: Metz and Nancy. See Stages 39–43.

- Metz to Gorze (24.4km)
- Gorze to Pagny-sur-Moselle (15.6km)
- Pagny-sur-Moselle to Montauville (19.5km)
- Montauville to Liverdun (33.2km)
- Liverdun to D657 main road (7.7km), then 900m to Pompey railway station.

Travel notes

- Abundant rail service (including TGV) in Metz and Nancy; flight connections through Lorraine Airport (located between Metz and Nancy).
- Travel by train from Pompey to Nancy (about 10 minutes).

APPENDIX C
Accommodation along the route

Note: The campgrounds included in this list have hikers' cabins (trekkershutten).

Netherlands

Hoek van Holland
Hotel Noordzee
tel +31 174 382 273
www.hotel-noordzee.com

Maasland
Bed & Breakfast Maasland
tel +31 6 53 72 35 50
www.bbmaasland.nl

Maassluis
Studio Kruisstraat
tel +31 6 47 23 63 16
http://studiokruisstraatmaassluis.
myfreesites.net

Brielle
See www.beleefbrielle.nl

Oostvoorne
Bed en Breakfast van Marion
tel +31 181 48 93 99
www.benbvanmarion.nl

Rockanje
Hotel Olaertsduyn
tel +31 181 40 23 50
www.olaertsduyn.nl

Badhotel Rockanje
tel +31 181 40 17 55
www.badhotel.nl

Beachhouse Rockanje
tel +31 6 158 93 659
www.beachhouserockanje.nl

Havenhoofd
Bed & Breakfast Haveneind
tel +31 187 750 772
www.haveneind.nl

Goedereede
B&B Goeree
tel +31 6 29 73 08 13

Het Oude Bakhuys
tel +31 6 23 58 87 95

Herkingen
Bed & Breakfast Herkingen
tel +31 6 10 30 56 66
www.bedandbreakfast.nl

Oude-Tonge
Hotel-restaurant 'Lely' (3.5km off GR5)
tel +31 187 645 909
www.hotellely.nl

Lepelstraat
Bed & Breakfast 't Koetshuys
tel +31 164 74 51 00
www.benbtkoetshuys.nl

Bergen op Zoom
See 'Geniet & Enjoy!' at:
http://onlinetouch.nl/vvvbrabantsewal

Wouwse Plantage
Bed & Breakfast Ouwerveldezicht
(2km off the GR5)
tel +31 165 37 92 04
www.ouwerveldezicht.nl

Flanders

Essen

Moerkantheide
(2.5km off the GR5)
tel +32 3 667 32 53
www.moerkantheide.be

Kalmthout

Huize de Roover
tel +32 3 666 48 64
www.huizederoover.be

Gastenkamers Christianne Kips
tel +32 3 666 76 68
Moniek Van Loon
Groene Weg 5
tel +32 3 666 71 92

Brecht

De Steenen Molen
tel +32 3 430 57 54
www.desteenenmolen.be

Die Statie
tel +32 3 315 10 05
www.destatiebrecht.be

Zoersel

Jeugdherberg Gagelhof
tel +32 3 385 16 42
www.jeugdherbergen.be

Lindehof Serviced Flats
tel +32 33 12 93 40
www.lindehof.org

De Heidebloem
tel +32 3 384 04 74
www.deheidebloem.net

Herentals

Hotel de Zalm
tel +32 14 28 60 00
www.dezalm.be

Hotel de Swaen
tel +32 14 22 56 39
www.hoteldeswaen.be

Tongerlo

Tongerlo Abbey
tel +32 14 53 99 17
www.tongerlo.org

Westerlo

Jeugdherberg Boswachtershuis
tel +32 14 54 79 38
www.jeugdherbergen.be

Jebola Bed & Breakfast
tel +32 475 37 22 61
tel +32 477 82 86 56
www.jebola.be

Testelt

Hotel Hoevebeemden
tel +32 13 77 29 20
www.hoevebeemden.be

Scherpenheuvel-Zichem

Mon Dieu B&B
tel +32 13 30 69 43
www.mon-dieu.be

Diest

See www.toerismediest.be
('Eten drinken & slapen in Diest')

Halve Maan Provincial Domain
tel +32 13 31 15 28
www.vlaamsbrabant.be/en/visit-us/
halve-maan-provincial-domain

Hotel de Modern
tel +32 13 31 10 66
www.hoteldemodern.be

B&B De Mansarde
tel +32 494 81 63 99
www.bbdiest.be

Hotel De Franse Kroon
tel +32 13 31 45 40
www.defransekroon.be

Lummen

Hove St-Paul
tel +32 13 556 490
www.hovestpaul.be

'T Buskruid Hotel
tel +32 13 53 22 94
www.tbuskruid.be

Viversel

Hotel De Pits Zolder
tel +32 11 85 82 82
www.lodge-hotels.be

Bolderberg

Hostellerie Soete-Wey
tel +32 11 25 20 66
www.soete-wey.be

Hotel-Brasserie Savarin
tel +32 11 25 23 50
www.hotel-savarin.be

Stokrooie

Het Zummerheem
tel +32 475 76 16 28
www.zummerheem.be

't Goed Leven
tel +32 494 864 804
www.tgoedleven.be

Hasselt

B&B Bij Liev en Jos
(2km off GR5)
tel +32 11 22 10 85
www.bijlieveenjos.be

Bokrijk

Auberge de jeunesse De Roerdomp
(2.7km off GR5)
tel +32 89 35 62 20
www.jeugdherbergen.be

Zutendaal

Hotel De Klok
tel +32 89 61 11 31
www.hoteldeklokzutendaal.be

Lanaken

See www.lanaken.be
('Bezoeken' then 'Slapen')

Maastricht

See www.visitmaastricht.com

For GR5 south of Maastricht,
see www.degr5telijf.nl
('Slapen langs de GR5')

Kanne

Hotel Limburgia
tel +32 12 45 46 00
www.hotellimburgia.be

Kanne & Kruike
tel +32 12 45 25 75
www.in-kanne-en-kruike.com

Wallonia

Eben-Emael

B&B Rue Haute
tel +32 43 55 80 47
www.ruehaute.nl

Visé

Hôtel de la Gare
tel +32 4 379 39 00
www.restodelagare.be

Argenteau (Sarolay)

L'élémen' terre chambre d'hôtes
tel +32 4 379 53 58
www.lelementerre.be

Evegnée-Tignée

Carnet de Voyage chambre d'hôtes
tel +32 475 590 757
www.carnet-de-voyage.be

Soumagne

Aux Cosmos chambre d'hôtes
(1.5km off the GR5)
tel +32 485 57 53 17
www.auxcosmos.be

Olne

Le Jardin d'Epicure chambre d'hôtes
tel +32 4 358 67 08
http://lejardindepicure.be

Aux Quatre Bonniers chambre d'hôtes
tel +32 498 45 71 48
www.quatrebonniers.be

Fraipont

A l'Orée des Bois chambre d'hôtes
tel +32 4 368 71 66
www.aloreedesbois.be

Banneux

Hôtel Maison Halleux
tel +32 43 60 81 25
www.hotelhalleux.be

Grand Hôtel Beco
tel +32 4 388 27 37
www.grandhotelbeco.be

La Reid

Gîte La Gervava
tel +32 486 86 99 38
http://lagervava.e-monsite.com

Chambre d'hôtes Escapades
tel +32 87 23 23 58
www.escapades-spa.be

Spa

See www.spatourisme.be

Stavelot

See http://tourismestavelot.be

Vielsalm

See www.vielsalm-tourisme.be

Commanster

B&B Le Tapis Rouge
tel +32 80 34 00 97
www.letapisrouge.be

Braunlauf

B&B Oase
tel +32 80 57 09 23
www.oasebraunlauf.be

Burg-Reuland

See https://www.eastbelgium.com

Ouren

Hotel Dreiländerblick
tel +32 80 32 90 71
www.hoteldreilaenderblick.be

Hotel Rittersprung
tel +32 80 32 91 35
www.rittersprung.be

Luxembourg

Lieler

Camping Trois Frontières (1.5km off
GR5)
tel +352 99 86 08
http://fr.troisfrontieres.lu

Dasburg (Germany)

Hotel Daytona (500m off GR5)
tel +49 6550 1530
www.daytonadasburg.com

Obereisenbach

Camping Kohnenhof
(2km north of Obereisenbach)
tel +352 929 464
www.campingkohnenhof.lu

Vianden

See www.vianden-info.lu

Vianden youth hostel
tel +352 26 27 66 800
http://youthhostels.lu

Bleesbréck

Camping Bleesbruck
tel +352 80 31 34
www.camping-bleesbruck.lu

Bettendorf

Hotel Terrace
(1.5km off GR5)
tel +352 26 80 13
www.terrace.lu

Beaufort

See www.visitbeaufort.lu

Camping Plage Beaufort
tel +352 83 60 99 300
www.campingplage.lu

Beaufort youth hostel
tel +352 26 27 66 300
http://youthhostels.lu

Berdorf

See www.visitberdorf.lu

Camping Martbusch
tel +352 79 05 45
http://camping-martbusch.lu

Echternach

See www.visitechternach.lu

Echternach youth hostel
tel +352 26 27 66 400
http://youthhostels.lu

Ralingen (Germany)

Landgasthof Ralinger Hof
tel +49 6585 537
www.ralinger-hof.de

Born

Camping Born
tel +352 73 01 44

Oberbillig (Germany)

Reza's Bistro, Restaurant & Gästehaus
tel +49 6501 96963 0
www.rezas-online.de

Grevenmacher

Camping de la Route du Vin
tel +352 75 02 34
http://grevenmacher-tourist.lu

Hotel Simon's Plaza
(3.2km from Grevenmacher)
tel +352 26 744 4
www.simons-plaza.com

Ehnen

Hotel Bamberg
tel +352 76 00 22

Stadtbredimus

Auberge du Château
tel +352 26 66 41 49
www.auberge-chateau.lu

Hotel Ecluse
tel +352 23 61 91 91
www.hotel-ecluse.lu

Remich

See http://visitremich.lu

Remerschen

Remerschen/Schengen youth hostel
tel +352 26 27 66 700
http://youthhostels.lu

Lorraine

See www.otsierck.com

See www.moselle-tourisme.com

See www.tourisme-meurtheetmoselle.fr

Apach

Le Moulin d'Apach chambre d'hôtes
tel +33 3 82 83 70 07
www.moulinapach.com

Montenach

Hôtel-Restaurant au Val Sierckois
tel +33 3 82 83 85 20
www.restaurant-val-sierckois.com

Sainte-Marguerite

Chez Monique 'Aux 3 Hirondelles'
tel +33 3 82 82 30 80

Kédange-sur-Canner

Hôtel de la Canner
tel +33 3 82 83 00 25
www.hotel-canner.com

Saint-Hubert

La Campagne
tel +33 3 87 77 96 08
www.lacampagnechambresdhotes.fr

Chambre d'hôtes Saint-Hubert
Godchure
tel +33 3 87 77 03 96
www.godchure.com

Vigy

Chambre d'hôtes Intemporelle
tel +33 3 87 77 00 18
http://fpetitmangin.pagesperso-orange.fr

Metz

See www.tourisme-metz.com

Auberge de Jeunesse de Metz
tel +33 3 87 30 44 02
www.ajmetz.fr

Scy-Chazelles

Chambre d'hôtes Saint-Quentin
tel +33 3 87 60 09 62
www.scy-chazelles.com/site/index.
php/fr/

Jussy

Chalet Marival
tel +33 3 87 60 10 48

Vaux

Par Monts et par Vaux chambre d'hôtes
tel +33 6 89 08 41 95
http://chambres-hotes-vaux.fr

Ancy-sur-Moselle

La Bergerie chambre d'hôtes
tel +33 3 87 31 30 49
http://labergeriechambresdhotes.e-
monsite.com

Cabanes en Lorraine
tel +33 6 68 59 83 54
www.cabanes-lorraine.com

Gorze

La Renaissance chambre d'hôtes
tel +33 3 87 64 73 41

Pagny-sur-Moselle

Gîte de Serre (may not be available for
one night)
tel +33 3 83 23 49 50

Pont-à-Mousson

Le Cottage chambre d'hôtes
(2.5km off GR5)
tel +33 3 83 81 20 38
www.lecottage-lorraine54.com

Le Relais de Poste
tel +33 3 83 82 27 21
www.lerelaisdeposte54.com

Abbaye des Prémontrés
tel +33 3 83 81 10 32
www.abbaye-premontres.com

Hôtel Restaurant Bagatelle
tel +33 3 83 81 03 64
www.bagatelle-hotel.com

Liverdun

Les Chambres de Coco chambre d'hôtes
tel +33 6 68 36 09 80
Les Vannes chambre d'hôtes
tel +33 6 09 02 05 25

Bioncourt

Le Clos des Pommes chambre d'hôtes
(1km off GR5)
tel +33 3 87 05 43 07
http://clos-des-pommes.com

Vic-sur-Seille

Château Mesny chambre d'hôtes
tel +33 6 88 29 24 95
www.chambres-hotes.fr

Mulcey

Mulcey chambre d'hôtes
(1.5km off GR5)
tel +33 3 87 05 24 76

Blanche Eglise

Gîte communal
tel +33 3 87 01 10 97

Dieuze

Chez Régine chambre d'hôtes
(1.5km off GR5)
tel +33 6 86 14 55 37
www.chezregine.fr
See www.salinesroyales.fr

Tarquimpol

Château d'Alteville chambre d'hôtes
tel +33 3 87 05 46 63
www.chateaudalteville.com

Assenoncourt

La Foly chambre d'hôtes
tel +33 3 87 03 93 02

Rhodes

Domaine Les Bachats
tel +33 3 87 03 92 03
http://domainelesbachats.com

Gondrexange

Le Camping Les Mouettes
tel +33 3 87 25 06 01
http://otsi-gondrexange.pagesperso-orange.fr/camping.htm

Landage

Gîte du Sâve
tel +33 3 87 25 07 15
www.gitedusave.com

Saint-Quirin

See www.saintquirin.fr

Abreschviller

Gîte communal
tel +33 3 87 03 75 73
www.moselle-tourisme.com

Hôtel Les Cigognes
tel +33 3 87 03 70 09
www.les-cigognes.eu

Col du Donon

Complexe Hôtelier du Donon
tel +33 3 88 97 20 32
www.donon.fr

Wackenbach

Chambre d'hôtes de Mme Catherine
Diniz-Monteiro
tel +33 6 77 29 90 68

Chambres d'hôtes chez Besnard
tel +33 3 88 97 11 08

La Claquette

La Rubanerie
(2.5km from Schirmeck)
tel +33 3 88 97 01 95
www.larubanerie-hotel.com

Urmatt

Hôtel-restaurant de la Poste(12min by
train from Schirmeck)
tel +33 3 88 97 40 55
www.hotel-rest-laposte.fr

Tourist information

General

Netherlands
www.netherlands-tourism.com

Flanders
www.vlaanderen.be

Wallonia
www.walloniabelgiumtourism.co.uk

Luxembourg
www.visitluxembourg.com

Lorraine
www.tourisme-lorraine.fr
www.moselle-tourism.com
www.tourisme-meurtheetmoselle.fr

Local

Netherlands
Hoek van Holland
tel +31 174 519 570
http://hoekvanholland.nl

Maassluis
www.ervaarmaassluis.nl

Brielle
www.beleefbrielle.nl

Rockanje
https://rockanje.org

Goeree-Overflakkee
www.vvvgoeree-overflakkee.nl

Bergen op Zoom
tel +31 164 277 482
www.vvvbrabantsewal.nl/
Click on Tourist Information

Maastricht
tel +31 43 325 21 21
www.visitmaastricht.com

Flanders
Zoom-Kalmthout Heath Border Park
tel +32 3 667 64 98
http://www2.grensparkzk.nl

Kalmthout
tel +32 3 666 61 01
www.toerismekalmthout.be

Herentals
tel +32 14 21 90 88
www.herentals.be

Scherpenheuvel-Zichem
tel +32 13 77 20 81
www.scherpenheuvel-zichem.be

Diest
tel +32 13 35 32 74
www.toerismediest.be

Hasselt
tel +32 11 23 95 40
http://visithasselt.be

Genk
www.visitgenk.be

Lanaken
tel +32 89 722 467
www.lanaken.be

Wallonia
Visé
tel +32 4 374 85 75
www.vise.be

Pays de Herve
tel +32 87 69 31 70
www.paysdeherve.be

Banneux
www.banneux-nd.be

Spa
tel +32 87 79 53 53
www.spatourisme.be

Stavelot
tel +32 80 86 27 06
http://tourismestavelot.be

Vielsalm
tel +32 80 21 50 52
www.haute-ardenne.be

Luxembourg

Vianden
tel +352 83 42 57
www.vianden-info.lu

Beaufort
tel +352 83 60 99 300
www.visitbeaufort.lu

Berdorf
tel +352 79 05 45
www.visitberdorf.lu

Echternach
tel +352 72 02 30
www.visitechternach.lu

Moselle Region
tel +352 26 74 78 74
www.visitmoselle.lu

Grevenmacher
tel +352 75 82 75
http://grevenmacher-tourist.lu

Remich
tel +352 27 07 54 16
http://visitremich.lu

Lorraine

Sierck-les-Bains
tel +33 3 82 83 74 14
www.otsierck.com

Metz
tel +33 3 87 39 00 00
www.tourisme-metz.com

Parc naturel régional de Lorraine
tel +33 83 81 67 67
www.pnr-lorraine.com

Gorze
tel +33 3 87 52 04 57
www.ot-gorze.fr

Pont-à-Mousson
tel +33 3 83 81 06 90
www.tourisme-pontamousson.fr

Liverdun
tel +33 3 83 24 40 40
http://tourisme.bassinpompey.fr

Pays du Saulnois
tel +33 3 87 05 11 11
www.tourisme-saulnois.com

Gondrexange
http://otsi-gondrexange.pages
perso-orange.fr/accueil.htm

Saint-Quirin
tel +33 3 87 08 60 34
www.saintquirin.fr

Abreschwiller
tel +33 3 87 03 77 26
www.abreschviller.fr

Schirmeck (Vallée de la Bruche)
tel +33 3 88 47 18 51
www.bruchevalley.com/en

Public transport

Netherlands
Rail
www.ns.nl/en

All public transport
http://9292.nl

Flanders
Rail
www.belgianrail.be
De Lijn buses
www.delijn.be

Wallonia
Rail
www.belgianrail.be
TEC buses
www.infotec.be

Luxembourg
Rail
www.cfl.lu
All public transport
www.mobiliteit.lu

Lorraine
Rail
www.ter.sncf.com/lorraine
Tim buses (Moselle)
www.simplicim-lorraine.eu
(click on Réseaux and choose Tim)
Ted' buses (Meurthe-et-Moselle)
www.simplicim-lorraine.eu
(click on Réseaux and choose Ted')
LE MET buses (Metz metropolitan area)
http://lemet.fr

Maps and information about routes

Public entities

Netherlands
Kadaster
www.kadaster.nl

Belgium
Nationaal Geografisch Instituut (Institut
Géographique National)
www.ngi.be

Luxembourg
Administration du cadastre et de la
topographie
https://act.public.lu

France
Institut Géographique National
www.ign.fr

Walking associations

Netherlands
Wandelnet
www.wandelnet.nl

Flanders
Grote Routepaden
www.groteroutepaden.be

Wallonia and Luxembourg
GR Sentiers
www.grsentiers.org

France
Fédération Française de la Randonnée
Pédestre
www.ffrandonnee.fr

Retail map sellers
Stanfords
www.stanfords.co.uk
The Map Shop
www.themapshop.co.uk
Pied à Terre
www.piedaterre.nl/reisboekhandel
de Zwerver
www.dezwerver.nl
Alta Via
www.altaviatravelbooks.be
Alpi sport
http://liege.alpisport.be

National Geoportal of the Grand-Duchy
of Luxembourg
www.geoportail.lu

Au Vieux Campeur
www.auvieuxcampeur.fr

Omni Resources
www.omnimap.com

ViewRanger
www.viewranger.com

Postal services

Netherlands
www.postnl.com

Belgium
www.bpost.be

Luxembourg
www.post.lu

France
www.laposte.fr

Museums

Listed in route order

National Towage Museum Maassluis
tel +31 10 59 12 474
www.nationaalsleepvaartmuseum.nl

Brielle Historical Museum
tel +31 181 475 475
http://historischmuseumdenbriel.nl

Markiezenhof Bergen op Zoom
tel +31 164 277 077
www.markiezenhof.nl

Tongerlo Abbey Da Vinci Museum
tel +32 14 53 99 17
www.tongerlo.org

Bokrijk Open Air Museum
tel +32 11 265 300
www.bokrijk.be/en

Maastricht
tel +31 6 106 271 95
www.visitmaastricht.com/things-to-do/
museums

Flint Museum Bassenge
tel +32 4 286 92 79
www.musee-du-silex.be

Stavelot Abbey Museums: Museum of
the Principality of Stavelot-Malmédy;
Guillaume Apollinaire Museum; Spa-
Francorchamps Racetrack Museum
tel +32 80 88 08 78
www.abbayedestavelot.be
(click on Musées)

Musée Littéraire Victor Hugo Vianden
tel +352 26 87 40 88
www.victor-hugo.lu

Wine Museum Ehnen
tel +352 76 00 26
www.entente-moselle.lu/fr/musee-du-
vin/presentation
Closed for refurbishment at the time of
going to print.

Centre Pompidou-Metz
tel 33 3 87 15 39 39
www.centrepompidou-metz.fr

Musée de la Cour d'Or Metz
tel +33 3 87 20 13 20
http://musee.metzmetropole.fr

Musée au Fil du Papier Pont-à-Mousson
tel +33 3 83 87 80 14
www.ville-pont-a-mousson.fr
(click on Culture)

Musée Georges de la Tour Vic-sur-Seille
33 (0)3 87 78 05 30
www.mosellepassion.fr
(Click on Les sites Passion Moselle then
Musée Georges de La Tour)

Musée du Sel Marsal
tel +33 3 87 35 01 50
www.moselle.fr
(search for Musée du Sel)

Mémorial Alsace Moselle Schirmeck
tel +33 3 88 47 45 50
www.memorial-alsace-moselle.com

APPENDIX E

A little Dutch and French for hikers

English	Dutch	French
Basics		
English	Dutch	French
morning	ochtend	matin
noon	twaalf uur	midi
afternoon	middag	après-midi
evening	avond	soir
night	nacht	nuit
welcome	welkom	bienvenu(e)
open	open	ouvert
closed	gesloten	fermé
none, no	geen	aucun
forbidden	verboden	interdit
entrance	ingang	entrée
exit	uitgang	sortie
no entry	verboden toegang	entrée interdite
free entry	vrije toegang	entrée libre
warning	waarschuwing	avertissement
men	heren	hommes
women	dames	femmes
child, children	kind, kinderen	enfant(s)
toilet	toilet	toilette
tourist office	VVV	office de tourisme, syndicat d'initiative
information	informatie	information(s), renseignement(s)

English	Dutch	French
Hello, Hi	hallo	bonjour
See you later, Goodbye	Tot ziens, Dag	Au revoir, A bientôt
Please	Alstublieft (AUB)	S'il vous plait (SVP)
Thank you	Dank U, Dank je	Merci
Good morning	Goedemorgen	Bonjour
Good afternoon	Goedemiddag	Bon après-midi
Good evening	Goedenavond	Bonsoir, bonne soirée
Good night	Goedenacht	Bonne nuit
My name is…	Ik heet…	Je m'appelle…
Have a good day	Goedendag	Bonne journée
Do you speak English/ French/German?	Spreekt U Engels/Frans/ Duits?	Parlez-vous anglais/ français/allemand?
I don't understand	Ik begrijp het niet	Je ne comprends pas
Look out! Beware!	Let op! Pas op!	Attention!

On the trail

right	rechts	droit
left	links	gauche
straight ahead	rechtdoor	tout droit
direction	richting	direction
north	noord	nord
south	zuid	sud
east	oost	est
west	west	ouest
walker, hiker	wandelaar	randonneur
pedestrian	voetganger	piéton
to follow	volgen	suivre
to walk	lopen	marcher, se promener
to turn	draaien, keren	tourner

English	Dutch	French
to cross	oversteken	franchir
to climb	beklimmen	grimper, monter
above	boven	au-dessus
under	onder	en dessous
to continue, go straight	blijven doorgaan	continuer, aller tout droit
turn	bocht	virage
to go around	langslopen	contourner
to descend, go down	neerdalen	descendre
beside, next to	naast	à côté de
distance	afstand	distance
near	nabij	proche
far, distant	ver	loin
along, past	langs	le long de
crossing	kruising	croisement
crossroads	kruispunt	carrefour
junction	knooppunt	croisement
detour	omweg, omleiding	déviation
trail	pad	sentier
footpath	voetpad	sentier pédestre
hiking trail	wandelpad	sentier de randonnée
long-distance walking/ hiking trail	lange afstand wandelpad	sentier de grande randonnée
variant	alternatieve route	variante
map	kaart	carte
compass	kompas	boussole
bicycle	fiets	vélo
bicycle path	fietspad	piste cyclable
horse path	ruiterpad	piste cavalière

English	Dutch	French
street	straat	rue
road	weg	chemin
paved road	geasfalteerde weg	route goudronnée
trail marking	bewegwijzering	balisage
corner	hoek	angle
canal	kanaal	canal
dyke	dijk	digue
dune	duin	dune
tree	boom	arbre
woods, forest	bos	bois, forêt
heath, moor	heide	bruyère
field	veld	champ
lake, pond	meer	lac, étang
river	rivier	rivière
stream	beekje	ruisseau
beach	strand	plage
sandy	zanderig	sablonneux
bridge	brug	pont
lock, sluice	sluis	écluse
fence	hek, versperring	clôture, barrière
fork (path)	(af)splitsen	bifurcation
hill	heuvel	colline
mountain	berg	montagne
observation, lookout point	uitzichtpunt	belvédère
post, pillar	paal	borne
rain	regen	pluie
storm	storm	orage
lightning	bliksem	foudre

English	Dutch	French
thunder	donder	tonnerre
wind	wind	vent
sun	zon	soleil
sunshine	zonneschijn	ensoleillement
(good, fine) weather	(mooi) weer	(beau) temps
Where is...?	Waar is...?	Où est...? Où se trouve...?
I'm lost	Ik ben verdwaald	Je me suis perdu
It will rain	Het gaat regenen	Il va pleuvoir
Be careful...	Doe voorzichtig!	Soyez prudent...
In town		
village	dorp	village, hameau
city	stad	ville
town/city hall	gemeentehuis, stadhuis	mairie, hôtel de ville
bus stop	bushalte	arrêt de bus
bus station	busstation	gare routière
train stop	treinhalte	arrêt de train
train station	station	gare
church	kerk	église
abbey	abdij	abbaye
windmill	molen	moulin à vent
watermill	watermolen	moulin à eau
bakery	bakker	boulangerie
food shop, grocer's	winkel	épicerie
chemist (drug store)	apotheek	pharmacie
restaurant	restaurant	restaurant, brasserie
café, bar, coffee house	café	café
snack bar	frituur, frietkot	friterie

English	Dutch	French
Accommodation		
hotel	hotel	hôtel
B&B	B&B	chambre d'hôtes
meal	maaltijd	repas
breakfast	ontbijt	petit déjeuner
lunch	lunch	déjeuner
dinner, supper	avondeten	dîner
I would like a room (with bath/shower)	Ik wil graag een kamer (met bad/douche)	Je voudrais une chambre (avec bain/douche)
How much...?	Hoe veel...?	Combien...?
Eating and drinking out		
to eat	eten	manger
to drink	drinken	boire
bill, check	rekening	addition
VAT	BTW	TVA
service included	inclusief bediening	service compris
milk	melk	lait
(drinking) water	(drinkbaar) water	eau (potable)
orange juice	sinaasappelsap	jus d'orange
beer	bier, pils	bière
wine	wijn	vin
coffee	koffie	café
tea	thee	thé
hot chocolate, cocoa	warme chocolademelk	chocolat chaud
yoghurt	yoghurt	yaourt
bread	brood	pain
butter	boter	beurre
jam	jam	confiture
cheese	kaas	fromage

English	Dutch	French
soup	soep	potage, soupe
sandwich	broodje	sandwich
chicken	kip	poulet
beef	rundvlees	bœuf
steak	biefstuk	steak
pork	varkensvlees	porc
ham	ham	jambon
fish	vis	poisson
potato	aardappel	pomme de terre
vegetables	groenten	légumes
lettuce, salad	sla	salade
chips, French fries	friet	frites
baked	gebakken	au four
cooked	gekookt	cuit
roasted	geroosterd	rôti
fried	gefrituurd, gebraden	poêlé, frit
steamed	gestoomde	à la vapeur
ice, ice cream	ijs	glace
I'm hungry	Ik heb honger	J'ai faim
I'm thirsty	Ik heb dorst	J'ai soif
I'd like...	Ik wil graag...	Je voudrais...
Enjoy your meal!	Eet smakelijk!	Bon appétit!
Cheers!	Prost!	À la vôtre! Tchin!

DOWNLOAD THE ROUTES
IN GPX FORMAT

All the routes in this guide are available for download from:

www.cicerone.co.uk/959/GPX

as GPX files. You should be able to load them into most formats of mobile device, whether GPS or smartphone.

When you go to this link, you will be asked for your email address and where you purchased the guide, and have the option to subscribe to the Cicerone e-newsletter.

www.cicerone.co.uk

LISTING OF CICERONE GUIDES

SCOTLAND

Backpacker's Britain: Northern Scotland
Ben Nevis and Glen Coe
Cycling in the Hebrides
Great Mountain Days in Scotland
Mountain Biking in Southern and Central Scotland
Mountain Biking in West and North West Scotland
Not the West Highland Way Scotland
Scotland's Best Small Mountains
Scotland's Far West
Scotland's Mountain Ridges
Scrambles in Lochaber
The Ayrshire and Arran Coastal Paths
The Border Country
The Cape Wrath Trail
The Great Glen Way
The Great Glen Way Map Booklet
The Hebridean Way
The Hebrides
The Isle of Mull
The Isle of Skye
The Skye Trail
The Southern Upland Way
The Speyside Way
The Speyside Way Map Booklet
The West Highland Way
Walking Highland Perthshire
Walking in Scotland's Far North
Walking in the Angus Glens
Walking in the Cairngorms
Walking in the Ochils, Campsie Fells and Lomond Hills
Walking in the Pentland Hills
Walking in the Southern Uplands
Walking in Torridon
Walking Loch Lomond and the Trossachs
Walking on Arran
Walking on Harris and Lewis
Walking on Jura, Islay and Colonsay
Walking on Rum and the Small Isles
Walking on the Orkney and Shetland Isles
Walking on Uist and Barra
Walking the Corbetts
Vol 1 South of the Great Glen
Walking the Corbetts
Vol 2 North of the Great Glen
Walking the Galloway Hills
Walking the Munros
Vol 1 – Southern, Central and

Western Highlands
Walking the Munros
Vol 2 – Northern Highlands and the Cairngorms
West Highland Way Map Booklet
Winter Climbs Ben Nevis and Glen Coe
Winter Climbs in the Cairngorms

NORTHERN ENGLAND TRAILS

Hadrian's Wall Path
Hadrian's Wall Path Map Booklet
Pennine Way Map Booklet
The Coast to Coast Map Booklet
The Coast to Coast Walk
The Dales Way
The Dales Way Map Booklet
The Pennine Way

LAKE DISTRICT

Cycling in the Lake District
Great Mountain Days in the Lake District
Lake District Winter Climbs
Lake District: High Level and Fell Walks
Lake District: Low Level and Lake Walks
Lakeland Fellranger
Mountain Biking in the Lake District
Scrambles in the Lake District – North and South
Short Walks in Lakeland Book 1: South Lakeland
Short Walks in Lakeland Book 2: North Lakeland
Short Walks in Lakeland Book 3: West Lakeland
Tour of the Lake District
Trail and Fell Running in the Lake District

NORTH WEST ENGLAND AND THE ISLE OF MAN

Cycling the Pennine Bridleway
Cycling the Way of the Roses
Isle of Man Coastal Path
The Lancashire Cycleway
The Lune Valley and Howgills
The Ribble Way
Walking in Cumbria's Eden Valley
Walking in Lancashire
Walking in the Forest of Bowland and Pendle
Walking on the Isle of Man
Walking on the West Pennine Moors
Walks in Lancashire Witch Country
Walks in Ribble Country

Walks in Silverdale and Arnside

NORTH EAST ENGLAND, YORKSHIRE DALES AND PENNINES

Cycling in the Yorkshire Dales
Great Mountain Days in the Pennines
Mountain Biking in the Yorkshire Dales
South Pennine Walks
St Oswald's Way and St Cuthbert's Way
The Cleveland Way and the Yorkshire Wolds Way
The Cleveland Way Map Booklet
The North York Moors
The Reivers Way
The Teesdale Way
Walking in County Durham
Walking in Northumberland
Walking in the North Pennines
Walking in the Yorkshire Dales: North and East
Walking in the Yorkshire Dales: South and West
Walks in Dales Country
Walks in the Yorkshire Dales

WALES AND WELSH BORDERS

Glyndwr's Way
Great Mountain Days in Snowdonia
Hillwalking in Shropshire
Hillwalking in Wales – Vol 1
Hillwalking in Wales – Vol 2
Mountain Walking in Snowdonia
Offa's Dyke Path
Offa's Dyke Map Booklet
Pembrokeshire Coast Path Map Booklet
Ridges of Snowdonia
Scrambles in Snowdonia
The Ascent of Snowdon
The Ceredigion and Snowdonia Coast Paths
The Pembrokeshire Coast Path
The Severn Way
The Snowdonia Way
The Wales Coast Path
The Wye Valley Walk
Walking in Carmarthenshire
Walking in Pembrokeshire
Walking in the Forest of Dean
Walking in the South Wales Valleys
Walking in the Wye Valley
Walking on the Brecon Beacons
Walking on the Gower
Welsh Winter Climbs

DERBYSHIRE, PEAK DISTRICT AND MIDLANDS

Cycling in the Peak District
Dark Peak Walks
Scrambles in the Dark Peak
Walking in Derbyshire
White Peak Walks: The Northern Dales
White Peak Walks: The Southern Dales

SOUTHERN ENGLAND

20 Classic Sportive Rides in South East England
20 Classic Sportive Rides in South West England
Cycling in the Cotswolds
Mountain Biking on the North Downs
Mountain Biking on the South Downs
North Downs Way Map Booklet
South West Coast Path Map Booklet – Minehead to St Ives
South West Coast Path Map Booklet – Plymouth to Poole
South West Coast Path Map Booklet – St Ives to Plymouth
Suffolk Coast and Heath Walks
The Cotswold Way
The Cotswold Way Map Booklet
The Great Stones Way
The Kennet and Avon Canal
The Lea Valley Walk
The North Downs Way
The Peddars Way and Norfolk Coast Path
The Pilgrims' Way
The Ridgeway Map Booklet
The Ridgeway National Trail
The South Downs Way
The South Downs Way Map Booklet
The South West Coast Path
The Thames Path
The Thames Path Map Booklet
The Two Moors Way
Walking Hampshire's Test Way
Walking in Cornwall
Walking in Essex
Walking in Kent
Walking in London
Walking in Norfolk
Walking in Sussex
Walking in the Chilterns
Walking in the Cotswolds
Walking in the Isles of Scilly
Walking in the New Forest
Walking in the North Wessex Downs
Walking in the Thames Valley
Walking on Dartmoor
Walking on Guernsey
Walking on Jersey
Walking on the Isle of Wight
Walking the Jurassic Coast
Walks in the South Downs National Park

BRITISH ISLES CHALLENGES, COLLECTIONS AND ACTIVITIES

The Book of the Bivvy
The Book of the Bothy
The C2C Cycle Route
The End to End Cycle Route
The Mountains of England and Wales: Vol 1 Wales
The Mountains of England and Wales: Vol 2 England
The National Trails
The UK's County Tops
Three Peaks, Ten Tors

ALPS CROSS-BORDER ROUTES

100 Hut Walks in the Alps
Across the Eastern Alps: E5
Alpine Ski Mountaineering Vol 1 – Western Alps
Alpine Ski Mountaineering Vol 2 – Central and Eastern Alps
Chamonix to Zermatt
The Karnischer Höhenweg
The Tour of the Bernina
Tour of Mont Blanc
Tour of Monte Rosa
Tour of the Matterhorn
Trail Running – Chamonix and the Mont Blanc region
Trekking in the Alps
Trekking in the Silvretta and Rätikon Alps
Trekking Munich to Venice
Walking in the Alps

PYRENEES AND FRANCE/SPAIN CROSS-BORDER ROUTES

The GR10 Trail
The GR11 Trail
The Pyrenean Haute Route
The Pyrenees
The Way of St James – Spain
Walks and Climbs in the Pyrenees

AUSTRIA

The Adlerweg
Trekking in Austria's Hohe Tauern
Trekking in the Stubai Alps
Trekking in the Zillertal Alps
Walking in Austria

SWITZERLAND

Cycle Touring in Switzerland
The Swiss Alpine Pass Route – Via Alpina Route 1
The Swiss Alps
Tour of the Jungfrau Region
Walking in the Bernese Oberland
Walking in the Valais
Walks in the Engadine – Switzerland

FRANCE AND BELGIUM

Chamonix Mountain Adventures
Cycle Touring in France
Cycling London to Paris
Cycling the Canal du Midi
Écrins National Park
Mont Blanc Walks
Mountain Adventures in the Maurienne
The GR20 Corsica
The GR5 Trail
The GR5 Trail – Vosges and Jura
The Grand Traverse of the Massif Central
The Loire Cycle Route
The Moselle Cycle Route
The River Rhone Cycle Route
The Robert Louis Stevenson Trail
The Way of St James
Tour of the Oisans: The GR54
Tour of the Queyras
Tour of the Vanoise
Vanoise Ski Touring
Via Ferratas of the French Alps
Walking in Corsica
Walking in Provence – East
Walking in Provence – West
Walking in the Auvergne
Walking in the Briançonnais
Walking in the Cevennes
Walking in the Dordogne
Walking in the Haute Savoie: North
Walking in the Haute Savoie: South
Walks in the Cathar Region
Walking in the Ardennes

GERMANY

Hiking and Biking in the Black Forest
The Danube Cycleway Volume 1
The Rhine Cycle Route
The Westweg
Walking in the Bavarian Alps

ICELAND AND GREENLAND

Trekking in Greenland
Walking and Trekking in Iceland

For full information on all our
guides, books and eBooks,
visit our website:
www.cicerone.co.uk

Walking – Trekking – Mountaineering – Climbing – Cycling

Over 40 years, Cicerone have built up an outstanding collection of over 300 guides, inspiring all sorts of amazing adventures.

Every guide comes from extensive exploration and research by our expert authors, all with a passion for their subjects. They are frequently praised, endorsed and used by clubs, instructors and outdoor organisations.

All our titles can now be bought as **e-books**, **ePubs** and **Kindle** files and we also have an online magazine – **Cicerone Extra** – with features to help cyclists, climbers, walkers and trekkers choose their next adventure, at home or abroad.

Our website shows any **new information** we've had in since a book was published. Please do let us know if you find anything has changed, so that we can publish the latest details. On our **website** you'll also find great ideas and lots of detailed information about what's inside every guide and you can buy **individual routes** from many of them online.

It's easy to keep in touch with what's going on at Cicerone by getting our monthly **free e-newsletter**, which is full of offers, competitions, up-to-date information and topical articles. You can subscribe on our home page and also follow us on **Facebook** and **Twitter** or dip into our **blog**.

Cicerone – the very best guides for exploring the world.

CICERONE

Juniper House, Murley Moss, Oxenholme Road, Kendal, Cumbria LA9 7RL
Tel: 015395 62069 info@cicerone.co.uk
www.cicerone.co.uk